[英国] 埃尔米奥娜·李 著 马睿 译

牛津通识读本·

传记

Biography

A Very Short Introduction

译林出版社

图书在版编目（CIP）数据

传记 /（英）埃尔米奥娜·李（Hermione Lee）著；马睿译. —南京：译林出版社，2023.8
（牛津通识读本）
书名原文：Biography: A Very Short Introduction
ISBN 978-7-5447-9601-9

Ⅰ.①传… Ⅱ.①埃… ②马… Ⅲ.①传记-研究 Ⅳ.①K810

中国国家版本馆 CIP 数据核字（2023）第 083325 号

Biography: A Very Short Introduction by Hermione Lee
Copyright © Hermione Lee 2009
Biography: A Very Short Introduction was originally published in English in 2009. This licensed edition is published by arrangement with Oxford University Press. Yilin Press, Ltd is solely responsible for this bilingual edition from the original work and Oxford University Press shall have no liability for any errors, omissions or inaccuracies or ambiguities in such bilingual edition or for any losses caused by reliance thereon.
Chinese and English edition copyright © 2023 by Yilin Press, Ltd

著作权合同登记号　图字：10-2017-229 号

传记　[英国] 埃尔米奥娜·李　/著　马　睿　/译

责任编辑　许　丹
装帧设计　景秋萍
校　　对　梅　娟
责任印制　董　虎

原文出版　Oxford University Press, 2009
出版发行　译林出版社
地　　址　南京市湖南路 1 号 A 楼
邮　　箱　yilin@yilin.com
网　　址　www.yilin.com
市场热线　025-86633278
排　　版　南京展望文化发展有限公司
印　　刷　江苏扬中印刷有限公司
开　　本　890 毫米 × 1260 毫米　1/32
印　　张　11.25
插　　页　4
版　　次　2023 年 8 月第 1 版
印　　次　2023 年 8 月第 1 次印刷
书　　号　ISBN 978-7-5447-9601-9
定　　价　39.00 元

版权所有·侵权必究

译林版图书若有印装错误可向出版社调换　质量热线：025-83658316

序 言

赵白生

真正的自信,敢于自暴其短,甚至自我污名化。传记,一方面大红大紫、洛阳纸贵,成为纸媒时代的救命稻草。今年销量首屈一指的《备胎》,即是显例。另一方面,它官司缠身、备受诟病,里外不讨好,就连故纸堆里觅生活的文学史家也不拿它正眼相看,而是一股脑儿把它打入冷宫。这些文学史家往往是失败的传记家,在文学史里不惜笔墨大写特写文苑传,岂不怪哉!深而思之,其实不怪。存在决定本质,作家决定作品,"传记原教旨主义者"似乎一锤定音,但"解构分子"并不买账:

传记是"英国文学的病"。(75)
"弗洛伊德之所以厌恶传记,是因为它表现了一个人如何声称自己了解另一人,这主张危险且具有误导性。"(92)
"传记是一场血腥运动"。(104)
传记是一种"强奸……是对自我犯下的不可原谅的罪行"。(104)

诚哉斯言？文坛巨擘，如乔伊斯和纳博科夫，更是火上浇油，无不发挥其"毒舌"的强大本领，纷纷给传记家打棍子、戴帽子，措辞无不用其极：传记家是"传记鬼"（101）、"心理剽窃家"。流风所及，现代主义者和新小说家对传记避之唯恐不及，就不难理解。

"恐传症"弥漫西方，埃尔米奥娜·李（Hermione Lee）一不做二不休，干脆步传记大师霍尔罗伊德（Michael Holroyd）的后尘，专辟一章，清算西方历史上的文类偏见与歧视。1999年，上个世纪末，霍尔罗伊德就敲响了清算的钟声，写了一篇反"恐传症"的檄文：《反对传记案》（"The Case Against Biography"），并置于《纸上文章：传记与自传的手艺》（*Works on Paper: The Craft of Biography and Autobiography*）之首，目的不言自明：

> 但我真正想一探究竟的是，我的传记作家同行们将如何为自己辩护，如何为传记伸张正义，如何发动反击。
>
> But what I really want to find out is how my fellow biographers would defend themselves, what claims for biography they would make, and in what style they might launch their counter-attack.（19）

埃尔米奥娜·李的反击，虽然不能把诸如弗洛伊德、乔伊斯、纳博科夫等巨头一拳击倒，但她的组合拳断非花拳绣腿，而是步步为营，拳拳攻心。

组合拳的首招——史的轮廓，线条飘逸，颇有穆罕默德·阿里之风："飞如蝴蝶，叮若蜜蜂。"（Float like a butterfly, sting like a bee.）虽然埃尔米奥娜·李开头声称,她无意把这本通识书写成通史书,但贯穿始终的线头依然是史。榜样传记,是按史的脉络梳理的;国家传记,缘史而作;偶像传记,依史而书;甚至全书的整体结构,也是按照传记史的内在逻辑而分主题勾勒的。纵通,是本书的一大特点。

组合拳的重招,论的切口,洞中肯綮。通识书,即概论书的最大弊端在于,连篇累牍充斥着清单式罗列。作者的好意,用知识的火箭炮来密集轰炸,但读者并不领情,觉得吃了满口的鸡肋。埃尔米奥娜·李的《传记》,也有清单式罗列,而且还不少。但作者辅之以过渡性专题,如梦露专题、莎士比亚专题;更聚焦于里程碑研究,如普鲁塔克的《希腊罗马名人传》、博斯韦尔的《约翰逊传》、斯特雷奇的《维多利亚名流传》。这样,清单式罗列相当于群众演员,过渡性专题略等于配角,专题性研究无异于主角。如此有层次感的通识书,自然让人像看了一部传记大片,余韵悠长,回味无穷。但最关键者,无论是清单式罗列、过渡性专题,还是里程碑研究,串起这些组合拳的是作者的史识——掷地有声的论断。例如,作者一一论述了"传记的十大规则",而最后抛出的一条规则却是:

规则十:传记没有规则(19)

传无定法。横亘在面前的九条规则,似乎烟消云散。横通,令人自由附体,豁然开朗,充满着创造的冲动。

史的纵通,识的横通,有史有识,纵横交贯,让这部通识读本指向传记之本——传史之"赤裸裸",记识之"坦荡荡"。

献给珍妮·厄格洛

《传记》

是谁把书页轻翻?
昨晚我外出时
他的人生毫无遮掩地
摊在书桌的灯下,半生已过:
人到中年。
他来到了眼前。是谁把书页轻翻?

伊恩·汉密尔顿

目 录

致　谢　1

小　引　3

第一章　传记频道　1

第二章　榜样传记　20

第三章　如实描述　42

第四章　国家人物传记　58

第五章　陨落的偶像　78

第六章　反对传记　101

第七章　公众人物　110

第八章　讲述故事　133

索　引　154

英文原文　167

致　谢

感谢以下各位的诸多帮助、建议、灵感和资讯：约翰·巴顿、黛娜·伯奇、埃利克·伯默尔、迈克尔·伯登、罗伯特·费伯、罗伊·福斯特、亚历克斯·哈里斯、休·霍顿、凯瑟琳·霍兰、安·杰斐逊、本杰明·李、阿曼达·利利、斯蒂芬·马尔霍尔、露西·纽林、克里斯·佩林。

衷心感谢我挑剔又慈爱的读者朱利安·巴恩斯和珍妮·厄格洛；我深切怀念的已故代理人和友人帕特·卡瓦纳；我在牛津大学出版社的编辑安德烈娅·基根；在约克和牛津跟我讨论传记和人物写作的学生们；以及我的丈夫约翰·巴纳德，感谢他在这本书写作期间始终如一的鼓励和兴趣。

小 引

传记经历了数世纪的变化,有许多变体和呈现方式,本书仅考察其中的几个,力求理解传记的宗旨及其实现途径。鉴于"通识读本"的篇幅有限,本书集中讨论的是不列颠的文学传记——但也不尽然。在一定程度上,本书按照时间顺序论述。但它并不试图就这一文类进行全面综述,那将是非常乏味的工作。

关于传记的书籍或文章常常会遵循这样一个演化图谱:始于圣人生平或"圣徒传记",一直发展到18世纪肖像式的生动的现实主义和私密描写,到维多利亚时代保守稳健的"生平与信件",再到将生平写作当作一种艺术形式的现代主义实验,最后是长篇、专业、直白的后弗洛伊德式20世纪传记写作的"黄金时代",皆大欢喜。在某种意义上,的确可以划出这些分界线,但我觉得那种关于传记的进步主义模式会将我们引入歧途。与之相反,我看到的却是同样的关于定义、价值和宗旨的问题总在不同的背景下反复出现。

第一章

传记频道

传记的比喻

　　传记常常被比作其他各类事物，仿佛很难将它套入单个精准的定义中。用于描述它的名词包括生平、生活史、生平写作、回忆录、传略。传记被比作历史（口述史和书面史），被比作探索或旅程、侦探工作、刑事审判、戏剧中的场景或剧院的后台、讣告、颂文、八卦、心理分析、纪录片、阴魂、入室行窃、遗体防腐保存、遗迹发掘、恋母冲突、背叛、复仇、断桥、渔网、虚构作品。

　　在这么多用于描述传记的比喻中，有两个可以作为实用的出发点。一是尸检（这是个令人不安的意象），也就是当死因异常、可疑或含混不明时，对死者遗体进行的法医学检验。受过法医病理学专业培训的验尸官剖开遗体（有时要把面部皮肤从颅骨上剥下来），利用他或她的解剖学和病理学专业知识来调查、理解、说明和解释看似费解、离奇或不可思议之事。正如一位写验尸的作家所说："在死亡的那一刻，死者对自己身体的财产权

1　就终结了。"这一过程或许并非确凿无疑。虽然验尸官所学的是科学的方法和对证据的解读，但这一专业技术或许也不能"完全抹除主观性……"，"尸体不会说谎——但死亡原因或许仍然难以捉摸"。

尸检的比喻将传记视为一种死后细察的过程，实施对象是一位无能为力的传主，已经不再拥有生命——或灵魂，如果你相信灵魂存在的话。这个过程无法再伤害到已经过世的传主，却肯定会改变后世对他们的看法，取决于考察确定的结论是什么。它还会使在世的亲朋好友心如刀割。将传记比作一种法医学程序也暗示了它的局限性，因为验尸可能根本不会或不大会揭示有关传主的想法、才智、情感、气质、天赋或信念的任何讯息。它甚至可能无法就死因得出确切的结论。

这一比喻难免有些恐怖。当传记的评说者希望强调它的残忍或侵害性质时，会用到这样的比喻。亨利·詹姆斯去世前不久就曾对侄子（他的遗嘱执行人）说，他"唯一的遗愿"就是烧毁自己的大量文件，"让压榨死人者沮丧到无以复加"。他那一类人的典型特征就是认为传记是"加诸死亡之上的恐怖"，还把"压榨死人者"与盗墓贼的比喻联系起来，说自己"一直想在我的遗嘱中制定一则条款，对那些胆敢移动我的尸骨之人施以诅咒，其直白和恶毒不逊于莎士比亚"。

另一个比喻与它形成了鲜明的对比，那就是肖像。尸检暗含着临床调查乃至侵犯之意，而肖像却让人想到共情、复活、捕捉人物。肖像画家会通过刻画细节和表现技巧来模拟温情、活力、癖好和个性。然而这两则比喻的确不乏共通之处。源于生活的肖像和死后进行的尸检都是对传主的调查研究，会影响后世对他们的看法。二者都要精准地捕捉细节。二者都有揭秘性质。二者的成功都取决于从业者的专业技巧和明智决断。

1814年，黑兹利特①说"肖像绘画是用铅笔写就的传记"时，用的就是一个常见类比。对一幅肖像（或半身像，或塑像）的最高赞美，莫过于"她的唇间仿佛有了滋润的气息"，大概会有微温的触感，"看起来充满生气"。于是关于传记作家试图实现的目标，一个通常的说法就是"捕捉相像之处"。"如实描述"是另一个流行的说法，表明最忠实的传记作家理应呈现这样的作品。与肖像人物一样，传主也应该看起来充满生气，呼吸着，全身心地在场，给人以现场感及其存在的真实感。

传记作家总是用人物肖像来比喻自己的工作。普鲁塔克说他的工作方法类似于肖像画家对肖像人物的面部特别是眼神的专注。博斯韦尔对他们共同的朋友、画家乔舒亚·雷诺兹谈到约翰逊时，说后者"拥有描画人物的高超技艺，那种技艺像优秀的肖像绘画一样超群绝伦"。在撰写自己那部《约翰逊博士传》时，博斯韦尔借鉴和利用了雷诺兹为约翰逊所绘的肖像，称自己的著作是"我献给友人的佛兰芒绘画……其中……突出了最细微的特点"，一时传为佳话。这一比喻表明，传记需要捕捉到人物传主的"生命活力"，也就是济慈所说的"这东西有灵，它的双眸因之而闪亮"。托马斯·卡莱尔在1830年代写到人应该凭借同情心写出一部理想的传记时，也提到要捕捉构成人物特性的"光线"。

---

① 威廉·黑兹利特（1778—1830），英国散文家、戏剧和文学评论家、画家、社会评论家和哲学家，被认为是英语历史上最伟大的评论家和散文家之一。——译者注（全书同）

肖像的意象总算比尸检要顺眼一些,但也暗示出传记可能出现的问题——恭维、理想化、扁平化、失真、曲解。它也提醒我们,观者无论如何需要依赖艺术家的视角和技艺。另一幅肖像或许会使我们对画中人物产生全然不同的观感。对某个自我的呈现方式有着无限迥异的可能。

图1　传记的意象:源于生活的肖像

图2　传记的意象：对死者进行的尸检

这个比喻本身也有失偏颇。肖像与传记之间的区别是显而易见的："传主……很少是静止不动的。"他们会说话，会改变，会衰老，会死去。

传记的定义

有没有可能不用比喻或类比，直接为传记下一个定义呢？1971年的《牛津英语词典》给出了两个定义。第一个如今读起来相当古雅，它是这样的："人类个体生活的历史，是文学的一个分支。"（最早使用的实例出现于1683年德莱顿为普鲁塔克的《名人传》所写的序言中）第二个定义是："为某个人的一生所写的书面记录。"（首个实例出现于1791年）2001年的《新牛津英语词典》给出的定义是："由他人所写的对某人生平的记述。"还有另一种可能：传记是由他人所讲的某个人的故事。为什么是

"故事"而非"记述"？因为传记是一种叙事方式，而不仅仅是罗列事实。为什么是"所讲"而非"所写"？毕竟"传记"这个词的字面意义是"生平写作"。英语中这个词的两个词源是中古希腊语：*bios* 意为"生命"，而 *graphia* 意为"写作"。但一切传记都涉及口述层面——对记忆的讲述、证人证词、众口相传的逸闻。有些传记形式，例如纪录片，就不是写下来的。

就连这个基本定义，"由他人所讲的某个人的故事"，也并非一锤定音，总有例外出现。传记可能是由故事的主人公本人假托他人的名义所写。例如，托马斯·哈代的传记就是他本人假托妻子的名义所写的。她在他去世之后完成了书稿，最终出版的署名也是她。格特鲁德·斯泰因以同性伴侣艾丽斯·B. 托克拉斯的名义书写了自己的传记，取名为《艾丽斯·B. 托克拉斯自传》。传记也可能是由多人写成（1990年代剑桥大学出版社的《D. H. 劳伦斯传》共三卷，三位作者各写一卷）。一部传记可能是好几个人而不是一个人的故事。近年来颇为流行的传记事业"群体传记"（例如珍妮·厄格洛的《月光社员》或梅根·马歇尔的《皮博迪姐妹》）已有悠久的历史，但此前的书籍通常的形式不是把好几个故事糅进同一部叙事，而是对每个人的故事进行较短的记述，最终收入一个系列或卷目中。传记也可能讲述某个动物或物体而非个人的故事：比如关于城市、神祇和疾病的传记，关于伊丽莎白·巴雷特·勃朗宁的西班牙猎犬弗拉什的传记，巴约挂毯①的传记，以及泰晤士河的传记。

---

① 巴约为法国西北部城市，中世纪时因巴约挂毯而闻名。

传记的十项规则

如果说传记的定义需要限定,那规则呢?以下列出十种可能。

规则一:故事应该是真实的

人物传记通常关乎真人,而非虚构或神话人物。因此传记作家有责任确保真实,应该对读者讲述生活中实际发生过的事。这看似传记的一个确凿而无可辩驳的规则,但仍有许多违背它的做法。很多传记作家用情感描写、大加渲染的场景设置或悬念策略进行夸张的叙事。更有甚者,有人还会采用完全虚构的写法:捏造作者与传主的会面、臆想的片段、对传记作者身份的随想、假设的交谈。具体实例包括A. J. A.西蒙斯的《探求科尔沃:一部实验性的传记》(1934)、伊恩·汉密尔顿的《寻找J. D.塞林格》(1988)、彼得·阿克罗伊德的《狄更斯传》(1990)和埃德蒙·莫里斯的《"荷兰人":罗纳德·里根回忆录》(1999)。有些传记读起来更像小说而非历史。这倒是能吸引读者,但也有损这一文类的名声。约翰·厄普代克就曾说过,大多数传记作品不过是"附有索引的小说"而已。

即便在最为严肃和尊重事实的传记叙事中,"实际发生的事"也可能会模棱两可或令人费解。对某些人物生平而言——例如耶稣、莎士比亚或克莱奥帕特拉的生平——也许文字或语录浩如烟海,故事和传说比比皆是,但原始证据却少得可怜或根本没有。即便有更多的一手或得到确认的证据,也常常充斥着谎言、夸张或秘密。传记作家可能要花大量的时间解决其传主创造的关于自身生活的迷思或错误线索。证人、友人和敌人各有其目的，或者随着时间的流逝，他们都会记错事件或添枝加叶。传记作家必须秉持怀疑的态度，谨慎对待一切证词。谬误重复千遍会变得可信，并凝结成关于某人生平的标准版本，在一部又一部传记中重复，直到最终被拆穿。有些传记作家依赖某种单一的、或许站不住脚的假设来解释一个人的一生：例如，理查德·埃尔曼就因为凭借极其有限的证据断定奥斯卡·王尔德患有梅毒而遭到批评。有时关于一个人生平的真实情况无法确定：证据已被销毁、证人均不在场、传主无法开口。那样一来，真实的故事就不得不以无法回答的问题或记录的空白形式呈现。

规则二：故事应该涵盖传主的一生

如果一部传记值得你花钱购买（像奥登所写，"一先令传记会给你全部的事实"），你会期待它是完整的故事，或者如果传主还在世，就应该尽可能详尽。但人们关于涵盖范围的态度也发生了变化。20世纪之前，传记很少会提及传主的童年，除非所讲述的童年故事能够指向他们成年以后的行为。如今，强调公开成就还是家庭行为的相对重点发生了变化。当代传记读者期待看到的是关于传主的动机和恐惧、性习惯、金钱交易、作为伴侣或父母的行为、疾病、怪癖，乃至梦境或幻想的细节。有些——并非全部——传记作家会花时间考察传主的家世谱系，有些——并非全部——传记作家会追踪传主死后的身世和名声。

如果说涵盖"一生"暗指传记应该按时间顺序从生到死地予以记述，那么这条规则往往会被打破，仿佛根本不算数。传记可能会倒叙，可能会按照主题安排结构，可能会选择详细讲述某人生命中的某些关键时刻，也可能会在叙事中插入一些历史、文学评论、描写或自传的片段。有些传记使用一小段生平事迹来展开整个生命史。在《炎炎六月：1846年的伦敦文学生活场景》（1965）中，阿莱西娅·海特聚焦浪漫派画家本杰明·海登去世的那一个月，讲述了海登和他认识的一群作家和艺术家的生平故事。《维特根斯坦的火钳》（2001）则通过讲述"两位伟大哲学家之间的一次为时十分钟的争论"，写就了一部维特根斯坦与波普尔①两人的微型传记。詹姆斯·夏皮罗选择了"威廉·莎士比亚生命中的一年"，即1599年，试图捕捉到"日常生活的某些无法预测的偶然性，在视野更广阔的历史和传记作品中，它们往往显得太不起眼"。但这并不是现代传记写作方法所独有的。圣人生平往往会有大量篇幅描写他们的殉道而非日常生活。认识传主的传记作家往往会着重关注他们亲眼所见的那部分生活。涵盖一生并不是一成不变的规则。

规则三：不应有所省略或隐瞒

西方传记的当代读者们通常认为不该有删减和美化，认为生平写作的价值就在于它的诚实可信和彻底的调查研究。虽说有时候很难区分对虚伪的厌恶和对丑闻的热爱，但社会的公序良俗意味着人们始终秉持公开透明的信念。在一定程度上，这也是因为人们日益反对权威。我们再也不想毕恭毕敬地对待领袖、君主、神父或博士，认为他们的生活也应该供人审视。公私之间的那条界线也发生了变化。自大众媒体兴起以来，"公共

---

① 卡尔·波普尔（1902—1994），出生于奥地利的英国哲学家、学者和社会评论家，被誉为20世纪最伟大的哲学家之一。

领域"与私人生活之间那部分模棱两可的重合一直是个充满争议的问题。20世纪末和21世纪初，随着新的廉价技术和媒体趋势的出现，西方文化中将普通人（而非名人）的日常私人生活呈现出来供公众消费得到了快速而惊人的发展。真人秀、社交网站、专门描述私人生活日常的艺术作品，表明人们对于哪些内容可以公开展示的态度已不似从前。这些变化冲击着传记的写作，而后者永远是其时代的一个指标。19世纪中晚期的传记往往（某些情况除外）会删减性爱描写以及约翰逊所谓的"家务事"。我们如今认为这样的审慎（或曰虚伪）简直难以置信，除非传记所写的传主最近刚刚去世，不得不考虑在世的亲朋好友感情上能否接受，或者如果后者觉得他们遭到中伤，可能会对传记作家提起诉讼。在这种情况下，公开透明的规则可能会出现例外。

　　隐私的概念以及对审查的态度不断变化，并不是唯一可能影响传记包容性的因素。生命本身就是不断积累和重复：叙事必然会有塑造和选择。即便看似无所省略的传记——例如萨特评述福楼拜生平的存在主义巨著，或洛克哈特心怀崇敬所写的关于沃尔特·斯科特的皇皇巨制，抑或利昂·埃德尔关于亨利·詹姆斯的"权威"评论性传记——也都曾经历过一个选择的过程。

规则四：一切资料来源都应清晰标注

　　传记不是一个自由地带。它往往会引发财产权、许可和版权的法律纠纷。传记可能是应某一位遗嘱执行人，或者某出版公司或传主地产代理人的要求所写。传记作者可能需要遵守条款和条件,准许他或她使用和引用某些素材。"未经授权的"传记作家,即未曾受邀为传主作传或没有获得这类许可的人,或许无法引用关键素材,或者不得不改写转述那些素材。早在授权传记的概念问世之前很久,值得信赖的传记作家就喜欢引用素材来源或证人的话来增加其故事的可信度。因此普鲁塔克对比了他从各个权威那里获得的生平故事的不同版本;比德①在写到圣人卡斯伯特之死时,则大幅引用了一位见证人的话。从这些早期传记一直到20世纪的传记,都会列出见证人的姓名并引用他们的话,在主要叙事中插入大段证词,引用传主本人的自传式文字作为证据,并大量使用信件,以至于19世纪出现了一个名为"生平与信件"的文类。(传记作家们如今常常会被问道,信件被电子邮件和短信取代会对他们的写作有何影响。)直到20世纪,随着传记写作的职业化和对可信度及事实查验的重视,那种添加大量脚注的做法才成为传记写作的规范,以便每一处引用都有据可查。这一专业规范的历史还不到100年,却已经有些过时了。出版社不喜欢脚注,嫌它们太学究气、太占地方。有些历史传记作家的解决方案是把脚注上传到网上,有些通俗传记作家则尽量减少注释。

引用资料来源并非总能做到。如果传主仍然在世,其非授权传记可能就要用到某些不愿具名的证人的话。那些必须满足保密条件方能从某一来源获取素材的传记作家可能无法透露资料来源者的姓名。在传记中,最好能进行真实性查验,但这也不是金科玉律。

---

① 比德(约672—735)即诺森布里亚的圣比德,英国盎格鲁-撒克逊时期编年史家及神学家,著有拉丁文著作《英吉利教会史》。

规则五：传记作者应该了解传主

在传记写作的早期实例中，传主生活的年代与传记写作的年代可能相隔数个世纪。普鲁塔克在公元98—125年之间撰写了生活在公元前4世纪的希腊领袖的故事。有些中世纪圣人的传记中那些传奇传主的故事要追溯到数千年前。其他人——例如忏悔者爱德华的遗孀委托的一部他的传记，则是由差不多同时代的人撰写的。国王理查三世死于1485年，托马斯·莫尔爵士于1513年前后撰写了批判性的历史传记，相隔仅仅一代；莫尔的女婿威廉·罗珀利用自己对莫尔的熟知撰写了关于莫尔的回忆录，写作时间大概是莫尔死后20年左右。17世纪中期，艾萨克·沃尔顿在1640—1678年间撰写《崇高牧师生平》（包括多恩和赫伯特）时，声称自己有得天独厚的优势，因为他要么认识传主本人，要么与认识他们的人聊过。100年后，约翰逊博士和他的传记作家博斯韦尔两人都坚信只有熟知传主的人所写的传记才有价值、有帮助。约翰逊对博斯韦尔说，"只有与传主一起进食饮酒、有过社会交往的人，才能书写他的生平"。无论好坏，整个19世纪，人们对这种基于亲密交往的传记写作进行了大量实践和讨论，当时传记往往只在家族内部流传。如今时过境迁，熟知传主本人或与其有联系不一定被看成一项优势或要求。受传主本人或亲友之邀为其撰写生平的传记作家会觉得授权是一项沉重的负担。

规则六：传记作者应该客观

人们总是在质疑传记能够而且应该客观和权威的观念。早期那些关于圣人、殉道士、英雄、领袖和思想家的传记总是会表达对传主或好或坏的评价。16世纪到18世纪的生平写作往往充满成见和偏见，19世纪的传记倾向于过度赞美，20世纪的传记则常常专注于某个特定的视角——特别是心理分析法，这也会影响证据的准确性。有人认为，一切传记都是一种自传，在现代主义时期反对传记的权威和公开风格的背景下，这种观点尤盛。就连那些抵制这一观念，认为他们所讲的故事与自己无关，尽可能从叙事中抽离出来的传记作家也不得不承认，他们选择某一位传主是有原因的，世上不存在完全客观的叙述。人们总是站在某种立场上写作，受到历史、国籍、种族、性别、阶级、教育程度和信仰的影响。具体说来，作家和传主可能会有某种共同的经历。戏剧评论家很可能会写某位演员的传记，而音乐学者会写作曲家的传记。必须有那些行业的经历，或者至少对其有所了解，否则就很难，甚至根本不可能为登山者或园丁、化学家或建筑师书写传记。

传记作家往往会被问到他们是否喜欢或热爱自己笔下的传主。如果是为希特勒、斯大林或匈人王阿提拉写传记，这显然不大可能。但总有情感介入。那种情感也许是为那个历史时期或传主的受害者投注的。写书的动力或许源于憎恶或恐惧，希望理解某种恶毒的事业，抑或渴望修正、让一切回归正轨。无论如何，过度介入都会令事与愿违。毫无批判、一味奉承的传记，可能和出于惩罚或报复动机所写的传记一样失真。但如果没有介入，只是当作赚钱的工作或任务来完成的传记，也会以失败告终。既要投入其中，又要超然事外。柯勒律治和雪莱的"浪漫主义"传记作者理查德·霍尔姆斯曾写过一段令人难忘的话，把传记比作伸向往昔的断桥：

你站在断桥的尽头，小心地、客观地望向另一端那无法抵达的过往……在我看来，那会变成一种追寻……你永远无法抓住它们；不，你永远无法亲手抓住。但或许，如果你走运，或许能写写你如何追寻那转瞬即逝的身影，让一切在当下醒转复活。

规则七：传记是一种历史

"没有谁是一座孤岛，在大海里独踞。每个人都像一块小小的泥土，连接成整片陆地。""没有人能在生活中避免和别人推推搡搡，他不得不用尽各种办法**挤**过人群，冒犯别人，同时也忍受着别人的冒犯……描绘人生就是要呈现这些。"多恩在教导会众肩负起个人的社会责任，卡莱尔在抱怨英语传记写作过度谨慎，但两人的话都值得传记作家们深思。没有人能够孑然孤立地活在世上。在1920年代滑稽模仿19世纪传记写法的现代主义作品《奥兰多》中，弗吉尼亚·伍尔夫揶揄了传记要宣扬"时代精神"的陈词滥调。不过她虽然对这个概念大加嘲讽，却也知道，传记的任务之一就是把传主置于其自身的"时代"：问题是怎么做最合适。1930年代末，她在未完成的《往事素描》中自言自语地说写回忆录太难了，她这样描述自己的一生："我觉得自己就是溪流中的一条鱼；侧身在水中游弋，却无法描述水流。"与（写作者可以选择用多少篇幅讨论周遭世界的）自传相比，传记更有义务在描述那条鱼的同时，探讨它游弋其中的水流。

这不仅仅是视角或叙事策略的问题。个人与时代的关系也是一个政治议题。历史学家有时会抱怨传记这种撰写过往的方式很有误导性。关注某个个人的生活会歪曲历史进程，让历史事件变得琐碎或过度个人化。关于重点关注某个个人的生活有何政治意义,一直以来都有大量争论。把伟人作为焦点可能会被解读为宣传某一政治议题,或巩固某种等级化的、反平等主义的社会结构。19世纪对公共人物那种毕恭毕敬的赞美式传记被(迈克尔·霍尔罗伊德)称为"维持现状的机器部件"。女性主义的历史以及种族平等运动的历史,已经成为判断谁的生平故事值得讲述以及如何讲述的重要考虑因素。传记总会反映或提供社会政治格局的一面,无论是19世纪法国和英国集体传记百科全书背后的民族主义议程,还是后种族隔离时代的反作用导致纳尔逊·曼德拉的传记过于理想化,抑或20世纪北美黑人文化史的变化最终于2007年催生了一部拉尔夫·埃里森的完整传记,他的《隐形人》于1953年出版,他本人1994年去世。某些类型的传记在不同的国家、时代和文化中风靡一时——圣人或海军英雄、宗教领袖、足球运动员或摇滚明星的传记等等,都会让我们洞悉那个社会的某些真相。那个社会重视什么、关心什么,那里看得见的——和看不见的——男人和女人都是谁?

规则八:传记是对身份认同的研究

既然传记讲述的是一个人的故事,就要求或采取一种关于身份和自我的思维方式。传记作家和研究者们常常会讨论传记如何能够最好地呈现某个自我:应该通过逸事、有启发性的事件、描写、对话、与他人的相遇、决策时刻、单一行动、偏好、癖性、日复一日的习惯吗?任何传记作家都必须思考一下本性和教养在自我形成过程中的关系,以及内在生命与自我的外在表现之间的交涉,哪怕这些思考没有那么明确直白。

传记作家不一定要有一套关于身份认同的理论或明确准则——这事实上可能会弄巧成拙。传记作家如果屈服于某种职业诱惑，把传主用作归纳概括人类行为的由头，就可能写出沉闷乏味的作品。应用某种具体的人类行为理论——无论其源于弗洛伊德，还是边沁、马克思或萨特——来讲述生平故事的传记，事后看来都会显得局限重重或过于简化。但在生平故事的写作中，某些关于人类机能和身份内涵的观念必然会浮出水面，不过它们出现的方式往往既不够全面，也未经考察。

传记总会遭遇不同的理解和解读人类以及身份性质的方式——心理分析、哲学、小说、诗歌、社会学、民族学和历史学，它们彼此之间存在着竞争关系。那些学科的从业人员往往对传记持有一种充满敌意或怀疑的态度：有许多为反对传记而作的诗歌，特别是在19世纪和20世纪，还有许多小说家对传记不无嘲讽地怀疑或厌恶（实例可见亨利·詹姆斯的《阿斯彭文稿》或朱利安·巴恩斯的《福楼拜的鹦鹉》）。弗洛伊德害怕也不信任传记（特别是可能为他本人所写的传记），认为它有可能过度简化和过于言之凿凿。普鲁斯特反对评论家圣伯夫通过为某些作家撰写生平故事来贬低性地解读他们的作品。然而弗洛伊德却为心理分析传记的可能性深深着迷——在他的列奥纳多案例研究中即可见一斑，普鲁斯特则倾其一生撰写了一部既抵制又吸引传记式解读的虚构作品。

传记作家通常不会像柏拉图、维特根斯坦、奥斯汀或穆尔等哲学家那样，明确地阐述本我之存在，根据某一哲学体系生命可以拓展的维度，抑或行为与情感之间的关系等问题。这不是他们的任务，除非他们所写的是一位哲学家的生平。但传记必然会反映何为自我、自我是由什么构成的、它如何表达自身等问题的不断变化和彼此冲突的观念。在传记叙事中，存在一种内在的、本质的人性的观念，与自我是由各种意外、偶发事件、教育和环境塑造的观念常常会发生冲突。性格可以被归类，或者人可以被贴上笼统的、普世的身份标签的观念曾在早期的传记中占据主导地位，自18世纪中期以后开始式微，让位于对个性、独特性和特殊性的重视。19世纪末、20世纪初，随着心理分析、诸如相对论等科学发现以及艺术形式的实验产生了一种不甚明确的身份观，因而那种坚信存在一个明确的、连贯的自我，存在一种在整个生平故事的脉络中不断发展，可以给予确定性描述的身份的信念在很大程度上土崩瓦解了。从那以后，西方传记更多地讨论身份的矛盾和波动，讨论自我的不可知性。但这些相反的描述自我的方式也时有重叠和冲突，而不是遵循严格的时间顺序相互追随。

规则九：故事应该对读者有一定的价值

传记会引发道德问题。早期的古典和基督教版本的传记将其传主写成道德楷模。道德的生活或殉道成为良善行为或精神追求的榜样；邪恶的统治者和堕落则为人们提供了可怕的警示。传记的这种"榜样"性质从未消失。总有人重提这一文类的功用。如果传记可以教会我们如何过好自己的生活，或者开阔我们的视野，过上与当前全然不同的生活，它就有了一种教育目的：变成了历史和知识的一个分支。关于它如何实现这一目的，人们有着不同且不断变化的意见。传记作家们致力于坦率或"真实"的程度各不相同；他们会追问到底是小细节还是大行动更有助于雄辩地描述人物性格；关于读者究竟是应该被引导认同那些易于识别的普世特性，还是应该受到非同一般、不可重复的行为的鼓舞或激励，他们也各持己见。到底是激发认可和同情的传记更有用，还是激发敬畏和陌生感的传记更有用？

与之相反的对待传记的态度也同样重复出现，那就是攻击它缺乏道德。在极为宽泛的历史时期，诸如背叛、亵渎、可耻、好色、侵犯和曝光等词汇总是被用于描述传记。人们攻击传记辜负信任、侵犯隐私、贬低某人一生的成就、折磨受害者、简化人性的复杂、满足我们自己对八卦的胃口和哗众取宠的欲望。如果说传记是一种兜售丑闻的方式，那它无非就是传媒和娱乐业的一个低俗的分支，没有任何道德或教育意义可言。

事实上，该文类的这些相互对立的版本也并不是互斥的关系。传记总是在这两者之间徘徊，有时在同一部生平故事中亦是如此。同样，而且几乎同时，读者的动机也会在高尚远大的抱负和低俗贪婪的猎奇之间发生快速转向。但无论人们认为传记主要是道德的，还是主要是不道德的，它在我们这个时代广受欢迎都毫无疑问。讲述生平故事是我们这个时代最主要的叙事方式。西方传记的流行已经持续了两个多世纪，但在过去这四五十年里，随着社会规范日益宽松、社会更加平等、阳春白雪和下里巴人之间的界限变得模糊，以及对媒体名人的偶像崇拜，它占据了新的领域。政客、体育和媒体明星的传记，戏剧化讲述莎士比亚或伊丽莎白一世、金赛或杜鲁门·卡波特生平的"传记片"，关于各行各业的公共人物的电视或电影纪录片，以及成功的美国有线电视"传记频道"，在表明传记已经开始打破偶像、拓宽社会边界，也不再仅仅是一个文学门类。另一方面，传记已经开始得到了学术和文学理论家的严肃对待，大学的文学和历史系纷纷开设传记课程。传记如今已经跨越了大众文化和文学、大众传媒和学术，这或许要归因于以下几点：社会嫉妒或社会平等，媒体让人们对个人隐私的胃口越来越大，在一个日益世俗化的社会对当代圣人和英雄的渴望，思维简化的读者群偏爱传记的可读性而非诗歌或文学虚构作品的艰涩，抑或人们希望在一个全球困惑和毫无把握的时期，至少理解某一个人的行为。上述全部或无一适用：也许只是为了满足人类自古以来对故事的普遍热爱。

规则十：传记没有规则

 传记没有确凿的定义和规则，表明它是一个不断变形、矛盾且易变的形式。然而悖论是，它看上去却有可能是最稳固、最传统的文类，能够面对一切叙事形式的变化而岿然不动。雄心勃勃的出版社或热心的评论家往往会用"盖棺论定"这个词来形容传记。人们总觉得传记就是一个人完整的、真实的故事，是对一段生命所下的最终结论。然而，如果正相反，它是一个混乱而多变的文类，一切规则都形同虚设，那么唯一适用的规则恐怕就是，世上根本没有所谓的"正传"。

第二章

榜样传记

以下是从六位著名人物的生平故事中摘选的令人难忘的片段。

摩西带领以色列人走出埃及,并向他们转达了神的话语,多年之后,他被带到毗斯迦山顶,看到了应许之地。"现在我使你眼睛看见了,[耶和华对他说]你却不得过到那里去。"于是他在"摩押地"去世了,年"一百二十岁",众人为他"哀哭"了三十日。

苏格拉底因为宣传邪神和败坏青年被判监禁和死刑后,请人把毒芹杯拿到跟前。一位门徒跟他说时间还早,许多人在最后一晚才喝下毒药。"苏格拉底说.对那些你提到的人来说,他们那样做是很自然的——因为他们觉得那样做他们赚了。对我来说,不那样做也是自然的;因为我相信,晚一点喝毒药并不会为我赚来什么——当生命不能再给我什么的时候,如果我还黏着它,抱着它,在我看来,只是让我在自己眼里显得荒谬……过来,照我的话做,别再给我添麻烦了。"

已知世界的征服者、希腊人亚历山大大帝去见哲学家第欧根尼,希望得到他的支持,却看到他"正在享受阳光"。他问第欧根尼有没有什么希冀。"有,"第欧根尼答道,"你走开一点,别挡着我的阳光。"亚历山大与随从队伍(他们当时全都在嘲笑哲学家)一起离开时,有人听到他说:"至于我,如果我不是亚历山大,我愿做第欧根尼。"

被捕的前一刻,耶稣正在客西马尼园祈祷,请求天父:"倘若可行,求你叫这杯离开我。"他让门徒和他一起警醒,但他们都睡着了。"他来到门徒那里,见他们睡着了,就对彼得说:'怎么样?你们不能同我警醒吗?总要警醒祷告,免得入了迷惑,你们心灵固然愿意,肉体却软弱了。'"

罗马皇帝卡利古拉的施虐欲、性瘾、奢侈和变态都"非史上其他浪子可比",却宠爱他的马"飞驰"。"除了大理石马厩、乌木马槽、紫色毛毯和镶满宝石的马轭外,他还专门为它建了一座房子,配备了全套的奴隶和家具……据说,他还准备任命那匹马为执政官。"

在伯利恒,圣杰罗姆正和僧人兄弟们一起聆听圣训时,突然有一头狮子一瘸一拐地走进了僧院。其他僧侣都逃跑了,但圣杰罗姆却待狮子如上宾。"然后,狮子抬起一只受伤的爪子给圣杰罗姆看。于是他叫来了兄弟们,请他们查看狮子的爪子,快快寻找伤在何处,他们查看了之后,发现爪底被刀割伤了。"待他们用药物为它疗伤之后,"狮子摆脱了一切野性和残忍,变成了一头驯服的野兽,和他们一起生活"。

这些叙事的时间跨度足有上千年。有些故事的上述版本与故事发生的时期之间横亘着漫长的岁月,有些只不过数十年。两个圣经故事都摘自1611年钦定版《圣经》。《旧约》现存的最早版本写于公元前5世纪；《马太福音》（给出了客西马尼园内场景的数个版本之一）写于公元1世纪下半叶。《新约》的完整手稿自公元4世纪留存至今。斐多关于公元前399年苏格拉底之死的描述由柏拉图在公元前371—前367年间记录下来。亚历山大大帝生活的年代是公元前356—前323年间；普鲁塔克大约于公元100—125年间讲述了他的生平故事。卡利古拉于公元37—41年间统治罗马；罗马作家苏埃托尼乌斯在《罗马十二帝王传》中描述了他骇人的政权，该书写于公元117—138年间。圣杰罗姆生活的年代在公元3—4世纪，而圣杰罗姆崇拜直到很久以后，才在9世纪的拉丁语著述中发展起来。这个版本摘自西蒙·温特15世纪初的本国语传记。

摘录这些故事的叙事可以被归类为"初始传记"，也就是一个文类尚未形成之前的原始形式。它们全都包含关于传主的出生、年代、生平和死亡的信息。但它们并未遵循我们所谓传记的结构。它们突出了某些特征——传主提供的教义或训导，传说中他们的语录、成就或罪行——而全然忽略了其他特征。它们处理时间的方式与更为现实主义的生平故事截然相反：或时间跨度巨大，或只关注几个关键事件。它们讲述了惊人的"事实"，例如耶稣与上帝的对话、摩西死时的年纪以及杰罗姆与狮子的友谊，却没有提出任何限定或异议。当然，《旧约》对神秘事件的诗意表达，普鲁塔克对傲慢之弱点以及集暴君和哲学家这两种特质于一身的老练阐释，苏埃托尼乌斯得意地堆积关于道德败坏的细节，还有杰罗姆的历史学家对奇迹司空见惯的直白讲述，各有千秋。但这些叙事的确有一些共同点。它们在描述人类行为时没有提供动机或解释。它们希望让读者关注某一种鲜明的性格或意义重大的事件。它们都乐于讲述一个人对他人的影响,无论是门徒、受害者、某个国家还是千秋万代。它们都使用言语行为来强调自己的寓意。这里没有私人或内在生活的概念:独处的时光有上帝为证;关于信仰的话语或决定命运的行动全是公开行为。它们所表现的中心人物,无论好坏,全是超凡脱俗的风流人物。

西方传记的起源就是这类非凡人物的故事,充满教育意义。(或是远在这些实例之前很久的故事,如果把讲述传说在公元前2600年前后统治的亚述王的悲剧人生和爱情的《吉尔伽美什史诗》,或者关于历代埃及法老的纪念性讲述算作最早的传记的话。)古典时代作家的传主都是公众人物,由同代或后代人对他们的行为加以评判。有著作存世的其他古典时代的传记作家还有色诺芬,这位生活在公元前5世纪到前4世纪的雅典人为波斯国王居鲁士写了一部半虚构的传记,对苏格拉底的描述也十分生动;亚里士多德的学生泰奥弗拉斯托斯在公元前319年前后写了他的《品格论》,是一部关于懦夫、酒鬼、话痨和迷信之人等虚构类型的短小散文素描;以及拉丁作家康涅利乌斯·尼波斯,此人早在普鲁塔克之前的公元前20年代末就写了一些短篇的《名人传》,也是将罗马人和希腊人对照讨论的。还有雅典历史学家修昔底德(约公元前460—前395),以及罗马历史学家塔西佗和萨鲁斯特的鲜明的人物描述。希腊和罗马文学中也包括许多"颂文"和"赞辞"的例子,前者是歌颂死者,后者是赞美生者,这两种辞藻华丽的演讲形式都对传记产生了深远影响。

古典传记的主要事件是战争、征服、在政府和辩论中获胜、统治民众、表露智慧、重要的行为和语录。(当然,作为一位丰富多变的作家，普鲁塔克对个人细节和家庭琐事也很感兴趣。）有时，就像在普鲁塔克的故事中那样，它们被并置和比较，让一个人物与另一个人物形成鲜明的对比：于是机智迷人的希腊人阿尔西比亚德斯就和固执傲慢的罗马人科利奥兰纳斯成对出现。有时，例如在苏埃托尼乌斯的作品中，优秀和恶劣的人物特征交替出现。但这里还是有一种标准模式，开头写人物在童年的某些事件中表露的早期迹象，随后是成长的轨迹，辅之以功绩、语录或发人深省的行为实例。这些伟人到达了地位、功名、财富或权力的稳定期，然后就失败和衰落了，原因包括判断失误、不得人心、阴谋、战败、流放、背叛、失势或衰老。死亡的场景——例如柏拉图讲述的苏格拉底之死或苏埃托尼乌斯的尼禄之死——会产生强烈的效果。这些传记的撰写都有道德目的，但也是为娱乐读者。它们有一种政治意图——比方说，普鲁塔克撰写生平故事就是为了巩固希腊人与罗马人之间的联系。

普鲁塔克受到了亚里士多德的极大影响，是一位心怀道德使命的作家。在《伯里克利传》中，他说"源于美德的行为……会让人们立即进入这样一种思想状态，会在崇拜那些行为的同时，渴望模仿行为者"。他总是从个人的生平故事中汲取经验、总结教训。他证明了品格可能会受到意外、灾难和成功等事件的影响和改造。但他也相信，本质特征切实存在。他笔下机智圆滑的阿尔西比亚德斯就是个典型的例证：

阿尔西比亚德斯拥有许多技能，我们听说其中有一个尤其令人着迷，那就是他能够吸收和适应他人的习惯和生活方式……在斯巴达，他勤于锻炼，生活节俭，每日眉头紧锁；在伊奥尼亚，他讲究整洁，为人友善，过着安逸的生活；在色雷斯，他沉迷豪饮和骑乘……并非他随时能够改变个性，也不是他的性格无限多变，而是……他[无论和什么人在一起]都能呈现和接受让他们看着顺眼的外表和形象。

不是每一位普鲁塔克的传主都会让我们看到某种单一的道德，许多人是复杂的、矛盾的，有着极大的人性弱点。

普鲁塔克所写的是很久以前的人物，当然希望他们跃然纸上，但他有一个著名的段落，把自己的与历史学家的著述区分开来。

我现在所撰著的并非历史，而是传记。从那些最辉煌的事迹之中，我们并不一定能够极其清晰地看出行为者的美德或恶习；事实上，一件不太重要的事情，只言片语，或者一句笑话，经常会比成千上万人丧命的战争更能使我们了解人们的性格……就像肖像画家在作画的时候，特别用心描绘最能表现性格的面部轮廓和眼神……请读者们也容许我对于人们灵魂的迹象和征兆多加注意……而把他伟大的事功和战绩留待其他人去叙述。

这种生平写作产生了深远的影响。从15世纪到17世纪，普鲁塔克被翻译成拉丁文，后来又被译成法文和英文。莎士比亚关于罗马的剧作都是根据托马斯·诺思1579年的译文写成的。他在英国的旺盛人气一直延续到整个18世纪和19世纪。德莱顿在1683年出版的一种新译本的序言中解释说，普鲁塔克最主要的魅力并非作为道德家，而在于对人物特点的塑造，能带你到幕后去洞察细节：

> 在这里，你被带入英雄的私宅之内：看到赤身裸体的他，也逐渐熟悉他最私密的行为和对话。你会看到……奥古斯都和一群少年在界石边玩耍；儿女绕膝的阿格西莱骑在竹马上。生命中的壮观场面全都消失了；你看到的只是一个可怜的理性动物，赤条条地来，空荡荡地去；你开始了解他的激情和愚笨，会发现那个高高在上的半神，终究还是一个人。

按照德莱顿的说法，普鲁塔克的成就在于，他为笔下的伟人赋予了人性。这可不是"初始传记"的另一大分支，即圣人生平或圣徒传记的主要目的。（英文中的"圣徒传记"一词，hagiography，源于晚期拉丁语 *hagiographa*，后者又源于希腊语的 *agios*，意为"神圣的"，和 *graphia*，意为"写作"。）这些是效仿耶稣生活之人的生平故事，他们避世隐居、献身上帝，是极具神性和贞洁的典范。根据标准模式，他们早在童年的某些事件中就显示出灵性的迹象，后来还切断了与世俗（家庭、社会、政治、政府）的联系，切断的过程往往充满暴力和艰辛，或许皈依，或许致力于神圣的生活。然后，叙事便专心给出大量实例讲述这位圣人的语录、谈话、理想和奇迹，最终的高潮是一篇告别演说、神圣的死亡或殉道场景、死后证明其神圣性的奇迹，以及影响深远的证据。圣人们经历的考验——贞洁测试、与异教徒当局之间的冲突、折磨、入狱——总会被强调，而善终是整个故事的一个关键组成部分。正如古典时期的传记强调特性并提供行为类型的"典范"，圣人生平也展示了原型意义上的美德。

圣徒传记是"自古典时代晚期到中世纪末期欧洲最主要的文类之一"。它跨越的时间极其漫长,从僧侣所写并为僧侣所作的拉丁语和希腊语文本,到13世纪至15世纪期间的各国语言版本,后者很可能是为俗教徒读者所写。圣人生平从早期实例如匿名作者的卡斯伯特传(由林迪斯法恩圣岛的一位僧侣写于公元699年前后,比德在720年代撰写自己的卡斯伯特传时,又对它做了一些加工改进)和埃尔弗里克①在公元1000年前后用古英语写成的《圣徒传》,到11世纪和12世纪盎格鲁-诺曼圣人的韵文生平,再到13世纪和14世纪的合集如《南英格兰传奇》或雅各·德·佛拉金②的《黄金传说》。总的来说,随着时间的推移,这些生平故事在心理刻画上日趋复杂,日益关注圣人的皈依和自我怀疑,而非一味地罗列奇迹。15世纪以后,圣徒传记的重要地位衰落了,但它并未消失,19世纪仍有清教徒殉道者的合集,如《英格兰女伟人》,20世纪编纂的《圣人与罪人》,现代天主教英雄传如伊夫林·沃的《埃德蒙·坎皮恩传》,以及对马丁·路德·金或特蕾莎修女等当代公众人物的神圣化记述。最著名的圣人传被反复重写,其间会收集新的传闻。圣凯瑟琳是一位国王的女儿,曾在是否应该向异教徒的神祭祀的辩论中挑战并击败了皇帝马克森提乌斯和他的哲学家们,并拒绝嫁给马克森提乌斯或被铸成雕像崇拜,因此被判以碌轮的极刑,但天使们把碌轮碾成了碎片。她最终被斩首,但刀落下的那一刻,从她

---

① 埃尔弗里克(955—1010),英格兰王国的一位男修道院院长,是一位精湛而多产的古英语作家,着重于人文、圣经注释等体裁。

② 雅各·德·佛拉金(1230—1298),热那亚总教区第八任总主教,基督教圣人。

的身体中喷出的不是血而是牛奶，据说她是4世纪在亚历山大港殉道的。但将她奉为"杰出的处女殉道者"、基督耶稣的新娘以及修女、哲学家、车匠和乳母的守护神，却是10世纪以后才发展起来的，那时人们开始撰写关于她已知最早的希腊语和拉丁语版本的故事，古迹的发现和神龛的建造也是在同一时间。随着她的知名度日渐提高，后来的版本难免对她的品质添枝加叶。那些为神职人员所写的故事更突出她的哲学思辨；而俗教徒的版本则关注她击败对手的事迹和发生在她身上的奇迹。在有些叙述中，她谦恭有礼、风趣机智；而在其他叙述中，她粗鲁而凶残——如下面这一例，她拒绝被变成崇拜的对象："住嘴吧，你这蠢货！我跟你说，/你建议我去做的全是罪行！/谁会为了任何世俗的欢愉/而甘愿被打入地狱？/我的爱人是耶稣基督：/他是我的配偶，无论何时何地。"

　　圣人生平有着多重目的。它们促进了偶像崇拜、神龛的建造和纪念物的出售。它们鼓励虔诚和灵性。它们以各国语言的版本建立了普通民众和教会之间的联结。它们有着复杂的政治和社会议程，包括对当代生活的批评，以及在言谈举止、性角色和经济乃至宗教异议方面的教义。它们的传主都是"叛逆者、失败的君主、不服从的孩子、贞洁的伴侣、社会激进人士和变装者"。和凯瑟琳一样，他们也可能尖酸刻薄、挑衅专横。许多14世纪的圣人传记中都有"机智而达观的圣人嘲弄装模作样的当局，后者试图恐吓或伤害他们"。这些生平故事"往往只是榜样，却不可模仿"。传记产生的张力就始于它们：一方面希望认同和模仿，另一方面希望了解与自己有着无法想象的巨大差异的另一个生命。

图3 一位著名的圣人充满戏剧性的殉道场景

在宗教改革时期的英格兰，圣徒传记成了有争议的领域。新教创造了自己的圣人（例如约翰·福克斯始于1563年的皇皇巨制《行为与丰碑》，俗称《殉道者名录》，或弥尔顿写于1655年的关于"被屠杀的圣人"——在皮德蒙特被屠杀的新教徒——的十四行诗）。文艺复兴时期或现代早期的人文主义或怀疑主

第二章 榜样传记

义，它在艺术和科学方面的探索和实验，它对古典学问的热爱，及其对个人主义、信仰体系和政治结构的兴趣，都产生了关于传记写作的全新思考方式。圣徒传记作为一种迷信的意识形态受到了攻击。到17世纪，托马斯·富勒在他关于英格兰类型的新教传记汇编《英格兰伟人》（1662）中，对圣人传记中的"伪造"和"巨大的谎言"大加嘲讽，认为那是因为"**传记作家**缺乏对这些圣人的诚实心灵"，连带着嘲讽了它们为朝圣地赢得的大笔利润。他在讲述阿尔弗雷德大帝的故事时流露出强烈的偏爱，认为后者"热爱宗教胜于迷信；偏爱教养深厚的学人而非懒惰成性的僧侣；这或许就是为什么他没有充满奇迹的记忆传世，也没有像其他撒克逊国王那样被庄重地神圣化，尽管后者远远不配"。

圣徒传记成了一个贬义词。在20世纪初的传记历史学家看来尤其如此，他们反对自己所见的维多利亚时代圣人传记的复兴，前宗教改革时代的生平写作看起来像一个黑洞。埃德蒙·戈斯在第11版《大英百科全书》（1910—1911）的"传记"词条中宣称："传记直到亨利八世统治结束后才开始出现在英语文学中。"后来的评论家纷纷效仿此说。最近的调查称"圣徒传记的黑暗时代"在"圣人生平的一千年里"奴役着传记这一文类，是"教会控制的崇拜文化"的"黑暗时期"。现代读者不认为传记应该被程式化且充满争议。回望过去，我们更偏爱德莱顿所描述的那种古典主义"生平写作"，让我们看到赤身裸体的"可怜的理性动物"，却对圣徒传记那种"固定套路、引发论战的夸张和无耻的借用"深感失望。

榜样传记如今被视为典型叙事，人们往往会说，传记是在16和17世纪开始对个人主义感兴趣之后，才逐渐发展成为我们今天所知的文类。随着中产阶级的兴起和以民主为目标的社会运动此起彼伏,被认为适合作传的传主的范围日渐扩大。到17世纪末和18世纪,更加"私密的"生平故事开始出现,自我和个人自主性的观念得到了远胜于以往的关注。

然而如此按部就班的进步主义传记历史并非万无一失。无论古典时期的伟人生平还是中世纪的圣人传记,所呈现的都不是简单扁平的榜样典型。它们也力图通过夸张的恶行范例和失当范本对普通人进行道德教育,伴之以可怕的警示。非宗教的合集如利德盖特的《王子的沦陷》,就源于薄伽丘写于1430年代的文字,讲述了伟大人物在命运之轮转向之后日渐坠落的不祥故事。《治安官的镜子》是韵文传记的合集(1555—1587年的版本),都是"悲惨的实例",证明了"这动荡的世界,起伏如海"。命中注定的劫数被总结概括("托马斯·沃尔西如何获得高位厚禄,位极人臣,他的生活方式、排场和尊贵身份,其后又如何遭受奇耻大辱,终因叛国罪而锒铛入狱"),人物仿佛从墓中发出哀叹命运的悲悼之声,总结出惨痛的教训:"一切荣耀都是过眼烟云,尘世的幸福如白驹过隙。"

正如《治安官的镜子》所表现的那样,世俗的古典主义传记与基督教圣徒传记这两个分支并不是现代传记文学的两个界限分明的影响源头。举例来说,经过古典时代晚期和中世纪早期希腊语、拉丁语、希伯来语、阿拉伯语、西班牙语和法语等源头,亚历山大在其传记中经历了古怪的变形过程,从征服东方的希腊皇帝变成了中世纪传奇中行侠仗义的基督教英雄,异教和犹太教-基督教故事的复杂交织由此可见。古典时代领袖的演讲和基督教圣人的雄辩混杂而成的谱系,共同影响了17世纪传记写作"辞藻华丽的表现"。传记的前史留下的是一笔复杂而悠久的遗产。声称古典时代的模式被圣徒传记的黑暗时代颠覆，好在后来又为世俗的、民主的真诚和个性所取代，这样条理分明有误导之嫌。那些有着普世认可之特性的榜样生平故事并不是突然消失的；它们延续到了18世纪和19世纪。榜样传记的概念从未消亡。

伊丽莎白和詹姆斯一世时期的政治家、哲学家弗朗西斯·培根就曾把历史学分为三个非常有名的分支：编年史、生平故事以及对具体事件的叙述。他更偏爱生平故事。因为在它们讲述的单单一个人的故事中，其"行动既有伟大的又有渺小的，既有公开的又有私密的，兼而有之"，写得好的生平故事应该包含"更加真实、质朴和生动的描写"。但让他大惑不解的是，在1605年，"生平故事的写作数量竟然不多……然而有那么多值得一写的人物……零散的报道和苍白的颂文根本无法概括他们恢宏壮丽的一生"。

有几个例外或许能证明培根所言不实，但其中有些当时只有手稿流传：出版刚刚去世的君主或领袖的传记是很危险的。沃尔特·雷利爵士在伦敦塔内撰写他的《世界史》时，深知"无论谁写了距今过近的现代历史，都有可能被撬掉牙齿"。乔治·卡文迪什用极尽华丽的笔墨描述了自己的雇主枢机主教沃尔西（死于1561年[①]）的悲剧人生，手稿流传了很长时间，才最终在1641年印制成书。托马斯·莫尔爵士写于1510年代的《理查三世时代的历史》直到1557年才全书出版，书中对那位邪恶的

[①] 作者笔误。托马斯·沃尔西死于1530年，1561年是乔治·卡文迪什本人的死亡年份。

君主给予了有力的、嘲讽的、极其夸张的评论，还顺便以简练而同情的笔触刻画了爱德华四世的"情妇"简·肖尔，并在一个注释中辩解说，在"回忆那些重大事件之时"提到这样"一桩微不足道的小事"并非全无道理。故事发展到接近写作当时的时间段便戛然而止了。威廉·罗珀关于岳父托马斯·莫尔的回忆录写于1550年代，距离莫尔1535年离世已经过去了二十多年，但也只是在私下流传，直到1626年才印制成书。由于他在莫尔家里生活过多年，罗珀能够以他独特的文字功底，从知情人的视角对莫尔其人给予真实可信的描写。于是，我们听到莫尔试图向妻子艾丽斯解释她为什么不该在意他入狱一事。她显然在智力见识上远不如他，却以她一贯的"家常的"漠然回应了他的哲学："'这座房舍与天堂的距离，不是和我自己的一样近吗？'他言道，听到这里，她以一贯的家常语气……回答道，'行了行了！'"我们还看到他充满智慧和幽默地赴死："我请求您扶我一把，中尉大人，让我安全地爬上去①，下去就不用你管了，我自己来。"

到17世纪末，这类生动的个人主义传记就不再是英格兰和欧洲传记写作中的个例了，它们的深度、力度和很有说服力的细节几乎能与托马斯·莫尔的肖像画家霍尔拜因媲美。自蒙田1580年代和1590年代关于自我及其复杂性的自传性作品（最早于1603年翻译成英文）之后，就出现了一批极具个性化的17世纪法语回忆录、信件和文学逸事，它们与形式化的、古典主义传统的颂文（éloge）并驾齐驱，后者也日渐以法文而非拉丁文写成——《博学之人颂文集》就是一例。在意大利，本韦努托·切

---

① 这里指断头台。

利尼的自传虽然直到1730年才出版,却是在1558—1566年间撰写的,那是本国语版本的传记合集兴起的年代——例如佛罗伦萨人韦斯帕夏诺·达比斯蒂奇所写的领袖和作家生平,或乔尔乔·瓦萨里的《意大利艺苑名人传》(1550,1568)——它们取代

图4 深度、力度和细节:一幅伟大的17世纪人物肖像

了彼特拉克和维拉尼等14世纪作家以拉丁文写成的更早的、受到古典主义影响的短篇"杰出人物"传记合集。瓦萨里的《名人传》建立了通过描述艺术家其人，以传记的方式讨论艺术作品的强大传统。

17世纪英格兰的传记写作除了从彼特拉克或蒙田或瓦萨里那里汲取养分之外，也受到了古典主义范本的影响，主要是通过托马斯·诺思1579年翻译的普鲁塔克的《名人传》和泰奥弗拉斯托斯、塔西佗和苏埃托尼乌斯等人所著经典的新译本。但它的发展也超越了源头。它开始涉猎当代各行各业的传主——统治者、治安官、伟人、艺术家、诗人、教士、思想家——并采纳多种形式，包括个人生平、集体传记、传记辞典、讣告、"回忆录、日记、书信集、圣徒传记、人物素描和王室人物生平"。赞美颂扬与批评嘲讽兼有，普世典型与古怪个体并行，正规修辞格式与反常写法皆备。实验科学的发现和对自然世界的探索，特别是罗伯特·胡克和罗伯特·波义耳等皇家学会成员的成就，对于应该如何考察一个人的一生的观念产生了明显的影响。在那个世纪末，洛克对于人脑运作机制的探索彻底改变了下一代人关于身份形成的思考。高尚与低贱、公共与隐私的等级发生了变化。圣人生平与古典人物传记的传统开始与各种截然不同文类的传记写作发生混杂：流言小报、犯罪报道、讽刺诗歌、家族肖像。

随着生平写作日益参差多样，"传记"一词开始被人们广泛使用——先是富勒在1662年使用了"传记作家"一词，然后是德莱顿在他1683年的普鲁塔克英译本序言中将其单列为一个类型："传记，即特定人物生平的历史。"传记开始作为一个文类被讨论。两个著名的集体传记的例子表明，具体实践天差地别。

33 图5 古典主义传记：伟人的兴衰

艾萨克·沃尔顿一本正经地赞颂诗人-神父多恩和赫伯特、政治家亨利·沃顿以及神学家理查德·胡克和罗伯特·桑德森，他在1640—1678年间写作这些传记并进行了大量改写，将当时能够想到的各种考察"好人"的方式混合在一起：圣徒传记和殉道录、颂文和赞辞、葬礼布道、纪念活动，以及人物画像、泰奥弗拉斯托斯式人物素描，以及关于"死亡的艺术"(ars moriendi)也就是建议如何"死得伟大"或"死得光荣"的书籍。约翰逊和博斯韦尔两人都曾仔细阅读沃尔顿的著作。后来，他开始被过度理想化，被当作圣人一般的作家，再后来又因为所写失实而遭到贬低。一位在19世纪为赫伯特作传的作家攻击沃尔顿的传记是"坊间传说与虚假热忱的结合体"。但他充满爱意的尊重，以及在有些作品中流露的对传主的个人情感，还有他大量使用他们本人话语的做法，都给了他的榜样传记一种私密的个体意识。他没有声称自己的作品尽善尽美，只是尽可能地给出"最坦诚的描述"，且认为自己的工作是"有用的"。

　　沃尔顿在《多恩传》的结尾进行了视觉比较。临终时，多恩请人为他包上裹尸布，并请人画下他"消瘦、苍白、如死人一样的面庞"，他留着那幅画，直到生命的最后一刻。沃尔顿把这张图片与多恩年轻时的肖像以及竖在圣保罗教堂内的大理石纪念雕像进行了比对，那座雕像惟妙惟肖，"仿佛在轻微地呼吸"。传记的结尾处还有他自己对多恩的"描绘"，依据是相面术的说法："他面相快活，以一种沉默的方式证明了他的灵魂清醒机敏……他柔软的目光表明他心地温柔，充满高贵的慈悲。"沃尔顿在全书最后提出了虔诚的希望，也总结了他试图完成的使命。他所描述的那具身体"如今已经变成了基督教的一撮尘土"。"但我

图6 多恩：临终肖像

一定会见到它复活。"

　　与那些文笔优美、结构严谨、充满崇敬的回忆录有着霄壤之别的，是约翰·奥布里在1670年代和1680年代所写的不辨是非、毫无忌讳、节奏明快却结构散乱的生平故事《简传》。奥布里和留下了关于同一时代的日记的佩皮斯①一样，是那个时代典型的热爱探索之人，对一切都充满兴致：古物研究、考古学、占星学、园艺学、数学、民俗、梦境、鬼魅、星象、纹章学。传记对他而言，不过是自然科学的另一个分支。但奥布里也极端缺乏条理。他的大约400篇人物素描是逸闻趣事、八卦消息、回忆和评论的大杂烩，他称之为"skediasmata"，意为"散乱的事物"（或者用后来为他作传的小说家安东尼·鲍威尔的说法，是"一时冲动写下的篇章"）。它们的书写并没有特定的顺序，往往都是些零星碎片或尚未完成，是与古文物研究者安东尼·伍德（此人是最虚荣自负也最复仇心切的牛津学者）合作，为后者的《牛津传记辞典》所写，那是关于从1500年到1690年在牛津受教育的所有作家和主教的百科全书。奥布里在1680年对伍德说，他认为生平写作就应该坦率真实，但这样的工作是有风险的：

　　　　我在此为您所写的一切……都是真相……赤裸裸的真相，它们如此坦率，毫无隐瞒，许多段落会让闺中少女的脸颊泛起红晕。所以务必请您在阅读之后做一些删节……加上一些掩人耳目的遮挡……这些秘密事件当前不宜对外透露，应该再等三十年左右，届时作者和相关人士都（像欧楂

---

① 塞缪尔·佩皮斯（1633—1703），英国托利党政治家，历任海军部首席秘书、下议院议员和皇家学会会长，但他最为后人熟知的身份是日记作者。

果一样）已化为尘土。

伍德辜负了他的信任，给奥布里惹来了麻烦。他们发生了激烈的争吵，奥布里的作品直到20世纪之前一直只能零星出版或出删节本。即便如此，他对赤裸裸的真相的忠诚，还是在长期以来关于传记应该"真实"还是谨慎的争论中发挥了重要作用；他活泼生动的八卦微缩人物素描对后来的"短篇生平故事"产生了深远影响，例如马塞尔·施瓦布的《虚构的生活》或利顿·斯特雷奇的《维多利亚名流传》，他揭示行为和话语细节的独到眼光为18世纪人们对传闻和语录的极大兴趣开了先河。

奥布里喜欢在他的传记中插入关于人类行为的理论、迷信、普遍看法，以及关于他如何获得该信息的叙述。一篇短篇生平故事的结尾处写道："他心碎而死。"另一篇故事讲述了诗人约翰·德纳姆年轻时喝醉酒后的一次英勇行为，他用墨水抹去了"寺院"酒馆和查令十字街之间的所有路标，奥布里提到，自己"是从帮忙拿墨水瓶的R.艾斯特科特阁下那里听到[这个故事]的"。著名的美女维尼夏·迪格比（奥布里后来在纽盖特街的一家店铺门外看到了她的纪念半身像，上面的镀金已经剥落了）的生平刺激他写下了这样的评论："如果不是像我这样的闲人把它们记录下来，这些奇闻异事大概早已被人遗忘了。"他天赋异禀，能用三言两语写活笔下的人物。弗朗西斯·培根被直率地（用希腊文）描述为一位恋童癖男子，有"一双柔和而灵动的褐色眼睛；哈维医生对我说那是蝰蛇的眼睛"。生平故事篇幅最长的霍布斯其人有半夜三更大声唱歌的习惯，他"确信[那时]没有人听得到他"唱对位法乐谱（声乐）里的歌："他确信那样做对他的肺脏有益,就长期坚持,以求延年益寿。"奥布里也会因为一个特别刺激的玩笑而兴奋不已(就是他19世纪的编辑不得不删减的那一类故事):

> [沃尔特·雷利爵士]深爱着一位少妇;有一次,他在森林里的一棵树旁冒犯了一位女傧相……那女子起初当然很害怕自己的名誉和贞洁受损,哭喊道,好沃尔特爵士,您要什么?您要解开我的衣衫吗?不,好沃尔特爵士!好沃尔特爵士!沃尔特爵士!最后,当危险和欢愉同时达到高潮,她狂喜地喊道,好爵士啊好爵士。她后来怀孕了,我毫不怀疑这位主人公没有扔下母子二人不管,还有就是,她诞下的可不是一位凡人。

他也抵制不了一个好笑话的诱惑:

> 爱德华·德·维尔。生于1550年。他是伊丽莎白女王的廷臣,因为傲慢而没有朋友,又因为挥霍而身无分文……这位牛津伯爵以对伊丽莎白女王低声下气而闻名。有一次他碰巧放了一个屁,羞愧难当,就离开宫廷出走了,七年后才回来。伊丽莎白女王欢迎他回宫时说,我的伯爵,我早忘了那个屁。

从摩西的命运到爱德华·德·维尔的屁,我们走过了漫长的历史,然而传记仍在继续融合着那些互相矛盾的文风:壮丽与荒诞、传奇与八卦、哀歌与流言、庄重与愚蠢。

第三章

如实描述

1773年秋,塞缪尔·约翰逊(时年64岁)与詹姆斯·博斯韦尔(时年33岁)一起去了赫布里底群岛旅行。彼时距离二人初次在伦敦相遇已有十年。那次旅程,他们彼此为伴,住在斯凯岛上。

今晚,我们在苏格兰风笛的伴奏声中起舞,舞步十分铿锵。我觉得须尽力赢得斯凯人的善意,还是诚心诚意地和他们一起开心地玩一玩,强过只做抽象的学问。我把这趟前来赫布里底群岛的旅行看成约翰逊博士和我之间的携手合作。每个人都当尽力促成合作成功;而我有理由自夸,我的努力更令人愉快,这对我们都有好处。约翰逊博士学识渊博、风趣幽默,自是令他们钦佩尊敬;但他们只是偶尔才会如此;其间的空白需要适当地填补,甚至要对他艰深的文本加以阐释。我也足够幸运,能够经常邀请他谈话,否则他便一直沉默着。喷泉通常都上着锁,只有我能开启源头。

这段话摘自博斯韦尔的《赫布里底群岛游记》，出版于约翰逊去世一年后的1785年，距离他们的旅行已经过去了12年。约翰逊于1775年出版了他自己的游记版本：《苏格兰西部群岛游记》。这两个版本的确是一种"携手合作"——博斯韦尔后来的传记也一样，它们对同样的事件常常会有不同的叙述。博斯韦尔的《游记》也是他备受期待的《约翰逊传》的花絮。他在《游记》中提到，1773年，他询问了约翰逊"他早年生活中的具体细节"，打算"为《约翰逊博士传》收集真实可信的素材"。他"积累了大量他的谈话"，计划以"兢兢业业的研究"来弥补没有更早认识他的遗憾。那部传记最终于1791年问世，距离二人初次见面已经过去了28年，约翰逊去世也已有七年之久。

斯凯岛上博斯韦尔的舞蹈和约翰逊的谈话让两人的作传关系变得灵动而充满喜感。那些（在当时和后来）觉得博斯韦尔絮叨、闹腾又自我吹嘘，觉得约翰逊粗鲁、严苛又专横的人，总是会取笑两人的"携手合作"。博斯韦尔一直因为在自己的传主面前跳舞而备受指责。霍勒斯·沃波尔说，《游记》把约翰逊和博斯韦尔变成了堂吉诃德和桑丘·潘沙，简直就是个"江湖骗子和他的可笑随从"的故事。充满敌意的托马斯·麦考利则在《约翰逊传》出版40年后说，这是一部伟大的书，却不知为何竟由一位心智软弱、遭人嘲笑之人写成，而传主的头脑"有多聪明就有多狭隘"。这本书迄今仍然是英语世界中最著名（即便如今已经不是阅读人数最多）的传记，博斯韦尔的荒诞和约翰逊的古怪始终与它的史诗性乃至悲壮的方面混为一体，难以分割。

作为这一文类的经典实例，这本书着实古怪。一位性情乖僻、武断专横、盛气凌人的神经质的18世纪词典编纂家、传记作

图7 雷诺兹所画的约翰逊:博学之人,如实描绘

THE LIFE

OF

SAMUEL JOHNSON, LL.D.

COMPREHENDING

AN ACCOUNT OF HIS STUDIES
AND NUMEROUS WORKS,
IN CHRONOLOGICAL ORDER;

A SERIES OF HIS EPISTOLARY CORRESPONDENCE
AND CONVERSATIONS WITH MANY EMINENT PERSONS;

AND

VARIOUS ORIGINAL PIECES OF HIS COMPOSITION,
NEVER BEFORE PUBLISHED.

THE WHOLE EXHIBITING A VIEW OF LITERATURE AND LITERARY MEN
IN GREAT-BRITAIN, FOR NEAR HALF A CENTURY,
DURING WHICH HE FLOURISHED.

IN TWO VOLUMES.

BY JAMES BOSWELL, ESQ.

——— *Quò fit ut OMNIS*
Votiva pateat veluti defcripta tubella
VITA SENIS.——— HORAT.

VOLUME THE FIRST.

LONDON:
PRINTED BY HENRY BALDWIN,
FOR CHARLES DILLY, IN THE POULTRY.
M DCC XCI.

图8 博斯韦尔的《约翰逊传》：迄今仍然是不列颠最著名的传记作品　　41

家和记者,何以成为不列颠传记写作中最著名的主人公?一部连篇累牍、喋喋不休的"一把抓"叙事何以成为传记文类的最佳典范?虽说《约翰逊传》是按年代顺序叙事的,相比约翰逊生命中的前54年,这部书却将过多的篇幅用于记述博斯韦尔认识约翰逊之后的那段时间:有一半篇幅都在写约翰逊生命中最后的八年。由于博斯韦尔工作起来既慢又缺乏条理,其他好几部约翰逊传记都先于他的书出版了,所以他不断打压对手,宣扬自己的记述才是最"本真"的。由于他"兢兢业业的研究"产生了堆积如山的证词和文献,他在自己关于约翰逊行为的故事、社交事件的描述以及抄写(或模仿)约翰逊的谈话和语录的过程中,穿插了约翰逊的大量信件以及他人的信件和传闻。他自己同约翰逊的关系算是约翰逊友谊中最重要的部分,虽然他承诺书中关于自己和传主的部分都很"真实",但他也隐去了一些细节,例如关于约翰逊离奇的婚姻或关于他对女人的情感的部分。

自从1920年代发现了大量的博斯韦尔隐藏文件,加上学界关于博斯韦尔和约翰逊的皓首穷经的研究,学者们做了大量工作,来证明《约翰逊传》实际上堪称结构精妙、取舍得当。另一方面,大量传记作品追溯到"博斯韦尔化"之前的那个年轻的萨缪尔·约翰逊,或者从其他视角来考察其人——例如他的女性作家朋友海斯特·思罗尔和范妮·伯尼的传记,从而把约翰逊从博斯韦尔笔下拯救出来;或者他自己作品的不同版本,尤其是他自己重要的传记作品《英格兰诗人列传》,令他摆脱了博斯韦尔。然而博斯韦尔在不列颠传记舞台的中心位置却始终未曾动摇。

博斯韦尔所写的文人传记问世的年代,恰逢不列颠的印刷业和阅读极大膨胀的世纪。知识的民主化和世俗化、现实主义小说作为一种流行文类的日渐兴起、现有阅读材料的种类增加，都与充满活力、竞争激烈、弱肉强食、变化莫测的（主要以伦敦为中心的）图书业和文学市场有关。博斯韦尔和约翰逊都深陷在这个格拉勃街[①]专业的、以挣钱为目的的雇佣工作的世界里，博斯韦尔的《约翰逊传》之所以有趣，部分原因就在于它对这里的背景给予了如此详细的描述，却又看似从那个背景中跳脱出来。文学资助、文学竞争和文学名声是许多作家写作的动力，往往也是他们作品的主题。一个高度社会化、充满八卦和诽谤的竞争性文学世界是由俱乐部、杂志、评论和文学群体构成的。作家们在公开场合见面，一起在咖啡馆闲坐，在沙龙里聊天，一起逛街旅行，然后把那一切都写下来。在每一种艺术形式中，无论诗歌、肖像、雕塑、戏剧、杂文、小说还是新闻报道，人们对自我表达和自我分析都表现出强烈的兴趣。正如蒲柏在1733年的《人论》中所写，"人类的研究对象应该是人自己"。在那个世纪末，卢梭死后出版的《忏悔录》（1781—1788年出版）承诺以当时无人可比的坦诚向世人展示一个独一无二、无与伦比的个体。从菲尔丁和笛福到简·奥斯汀和范妮·伯尼，虚构的人格都被表现为有着生动可辨的特殊性格特质的个人，通过他们与其他人的关系来探索生命并寻求成就感。图书业的产品和过程都与这种对个性和性格的兴趣密切相关。大量文学通信被出版（始于蒲柏的信件），人们书写的自传和日记浩如烟海。

博斯韦尔对约翰逊生平的评注也并非举世无双。这个跟随

[①] 格拉勃街，又译作"寒士街"，是19世纪靠近英国伦敦旧区穆菲尔兹的街道，以其聚集了大量穷困的"寒士"、野心勃勃的诗人以及低级出版商和销售商而出名。

那位大人物游历四方、记下他说的每一句话的文学门徒，使传记在我们的心中有了一个近乎滑稽模仿的形象。（博斯韦尔被滑稽地描述成整天跟在约翰逊身后低头记笔记的形象，这是不公平的：事实上，他更多地依赖良好的记忆力，以及事后立即记下发生的事件——如果停留的时间过长，那就会像"腌渍久藏的腐败水果"——他庆幸随着对约翰逊的敬畏减弱，他"记录"约翰逊的能力日益加强了。）然而收集和出版著名智者的"语录"或"传闻"的传统可以追溯到很久以前。不妨说柏拉图的书籍就是"苏格拉底语录集"，《新约全书》就是一部"救世主语录"。17世纪的传记大量利用了"语录"。律师和东方学者约翰·塞尔登的"餐桌谈话"就由他的秘书收集，并于1689年出版。18世纪的法国文学史充斥着各种"语录"集。这类语录集突显了人们对伟人所说话语的强烈兴趣。

女人不是这类关注的对象。17世纪末、18世纪初，很多女性作家写出了不少诗歌、戏剧、小说、日记、信件、游记、杂文和赞歌，然而女人的回忆录或"语录"却无人收集。相反，纽卡斯尔公爵夫人玛格丽特·卡文迪什在1667年为（还在世的）丈夫威廉·卡文迪什撰写了一部传记，把他的美德捧上了天。（这部赞辞遭到了佩皮斯的嘲笑，后者说她是个"疯狂的、自负的、可笑的女人，而他则是让她不得不写下那一切的蠢驴"。）露西·哈钦森在1644年为丈夫、新教弑君者哈钦森[①]上校撰写了一部谦逊而充满爱意的回忆录，整本书都用第三人称指代自己，赞美他是新教的圣人："他的一生就是从一个崇高的境界进阶到另一

[①] 约翰·哈钦森（1615—1664），英国政治家，清教徒领袖之一，并在英国内战中参加了议会军队。作为1649年高级法院的成员，参与签署国王查理一世死刑令。

个境界。"19世纪的小说家和自传作家玛格丽特·奥利芬特在1882年提到这部回忆录时说:"整本书从头到尾都没有出现一个'我'。"海斯特·思罗尔1786年撰写了《已故萨缪尔·约翰逊生平逸事》,范妮·伯尼编辑了她父亲的《回忆录》。

那些有语录被崇拜者记录下来的"伟人"往往都是作家、画家或演员。人们对想象力和创造力,对精神生活怀有浓厚的兴趣。精通文艺的牛津牧师约瑟夫·斯彭斯1720年代中期遇到蒲柏,从1727年直到蒲柏1744年去世一直在记录他的语录。斯彭斯的"蒲柏语录"或《传闻》以手稿的形式流传多年。约翰逊1780年撰写他那部《蒲柏传》时读过这部手稿。斯彭斯为传记提供了素材:他从未曾撰写自己的《蒲柏传》,手稿直到1820年才出版(全书编辑出版则要等到1960年代)。"语录"的风潮持续了几个世纪:包括威廉·苏厄德的《某些杰出人物逸闻》(1795)和约翰·尼科尔斯的九卷本《18世纪文学逸事》(1812—1816)。1820年代和1830年代,斯彭斯的《传闻》出版后不久,黑兹利特出版了他的《与詹姆斯·诺思科特爵士对谈》(这位肖像画家曾是雷诺兹的学生和朋友),范妮·伯尼记录父亲伯尼博士的逸闻趣事的《回忆录》问世,德拉蒙德追溯至1618年的《与本·琼生对谈》也得以出版。言语行为受到重视。谈话是生活的重要组成部分,是一种艺术、一种娱乐形式,就约翰逊的例子而言,也是一种威吓式的竞争手段。然而博斯韦尔的非同寻常之处,在于他把"语录"变成了完整的传记叙事,同时也保留了文选的碎片特质。他开的另一个先河是,他是首批如此全面和坦诚地出版私人谈话的作者之一,也为此陷入了麻烦。无论是《游记》还是《约翰逊传》的批评者都反对他将约翰逊所有"令人不快的缺点"暴露无遗,从而"让人物蒙羞,就像一座雕塑或一幅肖像上满是囊瘤和痤子"。

《游记》中关于斯凯岛上那个场景的主要元素尽数出现在《约翰逊传》中。博斯韦尔认为他那种传记写作就是一种"携手合作"。他对自己在其中扮演的角色十分自豪。他精心编排了自己那位主要演员的台词和走位。他对传主心怀崇敬,却也不乏警觉。他坚信对话是"展示"人物性格的最佳途径。他觉得他与约翰逊的关系"开启了[那场对话的]源头",无论对他自己还是对整个世界都意义重大。他决心写出最真实的版本。"本真性是我最引以为豪的东西",他在1785年对给予他极大帮助和鼓励的莎士比亚学者埃德蒙·马龙谈到《游记》时如是说。在他(献给马龙)的《约翰逊传》"前言"和"启事"中,博斯韦尔用了一大堆对他的作品、也对这个阶段的英国传记非常关键的词语:"谈话""本真性""忠诚""准确性""亲密地"。他和约翰逊一样,认为传记写作的关键在于忠于事实和实事求是:"真实性"是他们最喜欢的词语之一。对传主的忠诚不该是死心塌地地掩盖,而当是准确塑造人物的过程。传记的有用之处,就在于它"体察入微的细节"。

在最理想的解读中,"本真性"意味着一种道德标准,是一种针对更恭敬、更虔诚的传记写作形式的反弹。这种反弹早在博斯韦尔之前很久就开始了。律师和传记作家罗杰·诺思在一部追溯至1730年代的未出版手稿中展示了自己的先见之明,逐项列出了在其后两个世纪日渐为人们所熟知的一切论调,有关"私人生活"胜于公开历史、普通人生平故事的效用,以及传记需要"诚实"等等。约翰逊(虽然从未读过诺思的著作)也在撰写

《诗人列传》的大部分篇幅之前很久就提出了他自己支持"本真性"的论点。他秉持着典型的自信，在1750年为自己的杂志《漫游者》撰写的一篇著名文章中列出了那些原则。文中宣称，传记之所以是最"宜人和有用"的写作形式，就是因为"关于某些个人的生平的叙事"使我们能与他人感同身受。几乎任何人的"公正而忠诚"的生命故事都是"有用"的，因为"人的境遇如此雷同"，我们能在他人的人生中洞察我们自己的"动机"和激情。传记作家需要选择最重要的逸闻来诠释"其主人公的习惯和行为"。传记最好凭借"对本人的熟知程度"写成，而不应该被粉饰为"赞辞"。"与其对死者大加赞美，不如对知识、对德行、对真实给予更多的尊重。"在后来发表在自己的杂志《闲散者》上的一篇文章中，约翰逊说最真实的传记写作当属由"写作者讲出他自己的故事"，因为只有他知道关于他自己的全部实情。（他没有使用"自传"一词，那个词到19世纪初才开始流传。）那些为他人撰写传记的人希望过度赞美他或者"夸大他的恶行"；那些为自己作传的人，他乐观地说，没有"欺骗的动机"，唯有"自爱"，那是人人都应该密切关注的。

　　约翰逊写作这些文章时，早已在三十多岁时出版了一部极具先驱性的传记作品《理查德·萨维奇先生传》（1744），那位性格乖僻的诗人和剧作家是他二十多岁时的密友，为了在格拉勃街苦求生存，曾经历过一次刑事审判，年纪轻轻便死在了债主的监狱里。约翰逊年轻时对这位奇怪朋友的同情启迪理查德·霍姆斯写了一部文笔优美的书，书中说《理查德·萨维奇先生传》创造了一种全新的混合式"浪漫派"非虚构的形式，集戏剧、传奇、民谣、新闻和道德说教于一体。写作这本书的过程一定让约翰逊明确了关于传记的最高目标就是"将感同身受的同情与抽身事外的说教结合起来"的观点。但约翰逊后来的《诗人列传》却全然不同。在《理查德·萨维奇先生传》写作逾30年后,《诗人列传》的写作并非出于个人的同情,而是受托为新版的"最杰出英国诗人"所写的序言,旨在分析他们的作品并确定其地位。它们的主要兴趣在于何为"天才"(尤其是在德莱顿传和蒲柏传中)。《诗人列传》在道德上遵循着普鲁塔克的现实主义传统,卖弄传闻的"有用之处",抵制"赞辞的迷雾",展示出有力的、艰辛的、有时颇有些固执的批判性关注,对另一个人的哪些信息可以大白于天下、哪些不能公之于众有着清醒的意识:"行动是可见的,而动机则是秘密。"不过,虽然他早期曾经主张传记的价值就在于它能够让人借助想象力对他人的遭遇感同身受,约翰逊的《诗人列传》却可能会充满讽刺、偏见甚或残忍的恶意,特别是当他不赞同某一位诗人的政治观点时尤其明显:

> 弥尔顿的共和主义恐怕源于他对伟大有一种充满妒忌的憎恶,他阴郁地渴望独立;对控制有着狂妄的不耐烦,又傲慢地鄙视优越感……他对自己不得不服从的一切都充满了恨意。

约翰逊铿锵有力、言之凿凿的论调背后,是一种往往十分残忍的、机会主义的文学文化。使用"本真"一词与其说是在彰显高尚的道德价值,不如说是一种廉价的广告,也可能是弱肉强食的机制在发挥作用的警报。早在1716年,散文作家约瑟夫·艾迪生就抱怨过"格拉勃街上的传记作家"都是秃鹫,"密切关注和等待着一个伟人的死亡,像许多殡葬承办人一样,准备从他身上赚取金钱"。这些掘墓人中最臭名昭著的,当属蒲柏一生的仇敌和对头、书商埃德蒙·柯尔,他盗窃文学成果、传播色情书刊、未经授权便出版作家信件,以及短期内胡拼乱凑出廉价传记的做法臭名远扬,导致他在1730年代被称为"死神最新的恐怖之一",尽人皆知。在柯尔为榨取利润而无耻出版的出版物中,前言中总会出现"保真"和"本真"等字眼,他在宿敌去世之后于1745年匆匆出版的《蒲柏传》就是一例,"由可靠的作者忠实收集,原创手稿,许多名震一时、德高望重之人的证词"。

本真性不无危险。对有些读者来说——以及在某些作者笔下,它意味着背叛而非忠诚。博斯韦尔崇拜他的传主,希望对他有利,但他也试图在一个自我推销的文学世界里扬名立万。因此,博斯韦尔的《约翰逊传》也是卑劣和高尚的动机兼有——整个传记的历史充斥着这样的例子。而且和所有令人难忘的传记一样,它也融合了许多不同的文类和视角。

它呈现了生动的视觉画面,从每一个方面、每一个角度向我们展示了现实生活中的约翰逊,往往并不怎么恭维。"我如此细致入微地记录他,"博斯韦尔在《游记》中写道,"以至于每一处细节都必须还原本真。我用佛兰芒画家的作画方式来为他创作肖像。我不会满足于画出大轮廓。我必须精确到每一根头发,或者他脸上的每一个斑点。"这幅"佛兰芒肖像"为我们提供的,是"一种持续的观看行为"(除了荷兰画家之外,这在很大程度上也受到了霍格思和雷诺兹的影响)。一旦把约翰逊巨大而古怪的身体装在他"邋遢""凌乱"而不合身的衣装里面去看,这样的形象就会在我们的脑海里挥之不去:他的痉挛抽搐,他野蛮而焦急的吃相,他走路要数步子、摇摆身体、揉搓左膝等强迫症的习惯,他"用一支削铅笔刀刮擦手指关节,把它们弄得又红肿又粗糙"的样子。

我们看到他的动作,听到他的话语;他走上舞台,像个戏中的演员那样说话,戏剧导演就是博斯韦尔。他们的朋友、演员戴维·加里克是这部传记中最重要的人物之一,而《约翰逊传》的戏剧性和绘画性一样突出,为展示约翰逊的性格精心安排了一幕幕场景。我们似乎能亲耳听到他的声音,用"矮胖子"一样的发音方式目空一切地滔滔不绝,无论是关于再婚("约翰逊说那是希望最终战胜了经验"),还是关于一条羊腿:"这真是坏得不能再坏了:没养好、没宰好、没保存好、没烹饪好。"我们听到他没在说话时发出的奇怪声响,仿佛他在"反刍",或者"像只母鸡似的咯咯叫",或者——每次在谈话中战胜对手后——"像条鲸鱼那样吐出一口气"。

这部图画剧读起来也像那个时代的一部现实主义小说。它自始至终深入探索城市社会、政治、风尚和家庭场景的内部肌理,为文学、戏剧、法律、艺术和新闻行业提供现场评述。博斯韦尔专有的惹怒约翰逊的急切努力,他要从约翰逊的生活中"收集细节"的永无穷尽的好奇心,他所促成的、产生了最好的约翰逊特质的相遇,他在约翰逊责骂他时的粗暴回击("你难道不知道弄得两个人**对骂**是很粗鲁的行为吗?"),还有他像头"熊"(他常常被比作这种动物)一样躲在自己的角落里生闷气,都很有趣。滑稽的部分原因是博斯韦尔知道他有多可笑。"我不知道为什么会蹦出这么不着边际的想法,但我问他,'先生,如果您被关在一座城堡里,身边只有一个新生儿,您会怎么办?'"(莱斯利·斯蒂芬在自己出版于1879年的《约翰逊传》中称之为"精致的滑稽":"但不管怎样,如果一个人更喜欢这样的话语而非沉默,倒是有助于让谈话不间断。")1776年,博斯韦尔安排约翰逊与激进的政治作家约翰·威尔克斯会面,希望引发火爆场面,但最终约翰逊风趣且彬彬有礼地对待威尔克斯的著名场景,就是一个很好的例子,证明了博斯韦尔的"小说"诙谐生动(且精心构思),以及他能像个变色龙一样,随时呼应和模仿约翰逊:"如果我直接向他提议说,'先生,您愿意与杰克·威尔克斯共进晚餐吗?'他一定会暴怒,很可能会回答说,'与杰克·威尔克斯共进晚餐,先生!我宁愿与刽子手杰克共进晚餐。'"

但两人的关系不止是滑稽喜剧,它的部分有趣之处就在于,我们希望看到传记作家和他的传主之间如何发展出了那种无关性别却充满温情的依恋。博斯韦尔本人的抑郁和焦虑,由于他自己的父亲处处责备而把约翰逊当成父亲一样的崇拜之情,以及约翰逊对他的教育和建议,都构成了一个动人的故事:正如每当博斯韦尔为一点家庭琐事大惊小怪时,约翰逊就会"笑起来,说,'先生,想想看,十二个月后,这事看起来该有多微不足道啊'"。虽然博斯韦尔固执地说自己以约翰逊为榜样,不会呈现给读者一部"赞辞",但他也希望"为[他]这杯传记的美酒中注入每一滴发自内心的甜蜜回忆",引用他人的话证明"很少有人在和他见面之后,没有变得比以前更加智慧和良善",并说约翰逊固然十分"暴烈","手拿一根手杖,无论谁接近他都会挨他一棒",但他也同样"文雅、热情,还很礼貌"。"'嗯,(他说),我们聊得不错。'博斯韦尔:'没错,先生;您挥动手杖,戳伤了好几个人哪。'"他精心使用了对比的写法,与在谈话中挥动手杖戳伤别人相对照的,是约翰逊展示出自己伤感、温柔、充满爱意的一面:有一次,提到一个"满城追着猫开枪"的小伙子时,约翰逊"陷入了温柔的幻想……想到他自己的爱猫,说'但霍奇可不能被打死;不,不,霍奇可不能死'"。

博斯韦尔笔下的文人约翰逊是一个史诗英雄(也是个充满喜感的滑稽人物),这部18世纪末传记的新特点之一,就是将世俗的、资产阶级的日常生活作为突显英雄品质的手段。其英雄主义就在于约翰逊对真理的追求,他的忍耐,他阴郁、孤独、困扰而多情的头脑与他哲学上的坚毅之间的搏斗,还有他竭力克服对死亡的恐惧:"真是受够了,先生,整个生命都在驱除这样的想法。"博斯韦尔把约翰逊的头脑比作古罗马斗兽场,说他的看法就在角斗场的中心与"恐惧"搏斗,像一个"非凡的角斗士"对待袭击他的"野兽"一样,这样的文字把他的理性主义世俗英雄变成了一位基督教殉道士。这不是圣人传记,但博斯韦尔给了约翰逊精神上的胜利、门徒、智识影响力,以及伟大的死亡。

这部传记混用了各种文类,也混用了各种思考自我的方式。约翰逊和博斯韦尔都认为传记是展示道德价值观的有用工具。在那个意义上,他们延续了源于普鲁塔克和基督教圣徒传记的榜样传统。但在传记中呈现个体身份是复杂的、微妙的,也是全新的尝试。至少要展示两种自我、两条行为线索。笼统地说,一条线索来自约翰逊笔下的主人公蒲柏,另一条来自卢梭,博斯韦尔年轻时非常喜欢卢梭的小说,而约翰逊却很厌恶此人。书中所展示的与卢梭相联系的行为是感伤的、温柔的、泪水涟涟又坦诚相告的——例如,"这就是他的情感",约翰逊在读诗时暗自饮泣。与蒲柏有关的行为线索是有力的、嘲讽的、细心敏锐又坚忍克己的:"他建议我……在旅途中认真阅读人类这一部大书。""让我们努力看清事物的本质吧,"约翰逊在1758年写给一位朋友的信中说,"然后再询问我们是否应该抱怨。"

那种对性格多面性的复杂感受对传记写作产生了深远的影响。约翰逊并非固定不变的存在,他的传记作家也不是。虽然他们都已经变成了那么久远的历史,但在两人谈话与合作的舞蹈中,人物似乎始终都在我们面前移动、聊天和思考,不光是在象征意义上,也是呈现在我们眼前的生动画面——例如这一处,当博斯韦尔即将离开英格兰前往乌德勒支时,他来跟留在哈里奇的约翰逊告别:

> 我尊敬的朋友送我来到海边,我们在那里拥抱,温柔地告别,承诺写信联系。我说:"先生,希望我离开之后,您不会忘记我。"约翰逊:"不会的,先生,更有可能的是您忘记我,而不是我忘记您。"船离岸启程后,我的目光很长时间都没有从他身上移开,他以惯常的方式晃动着巨大的身躯;最后,我看见他转身往城里走去,从我的视线中消失了。

第四章

国家人物传记

谈话、友谊、合作、争吵;讲述个人感情和遭遇、尚未完成的作品以及政治观点的信件;关于成瘾、情爱和弱点的忏悔叙事;关于家庭生活的日记;在小范围内流传的手稿:19世纪初期的文学中穿插着一个传记写作的大网。"自我塑造"有多种形式。在欧洲,卢梭的忏悔式个人主义以及他与天然情感和德行的联系、歌德的超越社会法则的"亲和力"、赫尔德[①]关于自我定义的主观性的哲学,全都对生平故事的讲述产生了深远影响。在美国,爱默生和梭罗等超验主义思想家的智识独立宣言坚称,真正的自我身份必须依赖"自立"并与自然建立联系。自我表达贯穿于每一种文学门类。传记、人物素描、自传、回忆录、日记、游记和通信彼此重叠。对英国浪漫主义作家而言,出版的作品(往往是充斥着丑闻的自传性作品,即便它们被写作时加了不少粉饰)与朋友间传阅的私人写作之间的边界是松散的。内在生命

[①] 约翰·戈特弗里德·赫尔德(1744—1803),德国哲学家、路德派神学家、诗人。其作品《论语言的起源》成为浪漫主义狂飙运动的基础。

与群体关系紧密地联系在一起。作家们描写彼此，共同工作和生活（有时会造成灾难性后果），出版并评论彼此的作品，为私人文件的存留和出版苦恼不已，并焦虑地等待着适当的传记作家横空出世，为逝者恢复名誉。

传记写作的重点在于同理心。威廉·黑兹利特说他1820年代与老迈的肖像画家詹姆斯·诺思科特的《对谈》是"博斯韦尔再现"，但他比博斯韦尔更偏印象派："我的目标是捕捉到语调和风格，而不是逐字逐句地重复话语甚或观点。"柯勒律治认为传记或回忆录中如有过多的"细节"，可能会"让真实的人物变得几乎不可见，如肖像画的表面蒙上了灰尘"。詹姆斯·斯坦斯菲尔德在写于1813年的不列颠第一部关于传记的书中，主张传记要同时拥有"充满同情的情感"、"公正客观"和"道德示范"，并主张删减那些"不能为逝者带来极大荣誉"的"细节"。

然而传记写作也涉及八卦、趣味、嘲讽和幽默。浪漫主义传记具有杀伤力。例如，对柯勒律治非同一般的谈话方式的描写就能证明这类写作会有多恶毒。黑兹利特（他在1798年初见柯勒律治，1820年代初以钦佩和失望交加的复杂心情为后者写了传记）描写了一个在谈话时自我分裂的"离题万里"的头脑："如果柯勒律治先生不是他那个时代最令人赞叹的谈话者，他就很可能是最棒的作家……可以说他就是靠自己讲话的声音谋生的。"曾在柯勒律治晚年见过他的托马斯·卡莱尔在1850年代有过一段很有杀伤力的描述，说柯勒律治"说出一连串稀里糊涂、不清不楚的话，它们即将埋没一切已知的思想的地标"，他歪歪斜斜地从花园小径的一边走到另一边（"他永远搞不清楚应该走哪一边"），他那悲伤的、鼻音很重的、抑扬起伏的声音："'啊，您的茶都凉了，柯勒律治先生！'好心的吉尔曼夫人有一次……递给他一杯泡得有点久但绝对没问题的茶如此感叹道。'很不错喽！'他抽着鼻子，用一种低沉喑哑的声音嘟囔着说，半是客气，但主要是虔诚，我至今仍然记着他的语调：'很不错喽！'"

那种为记录他人所用的尖酸刻薄是传记的主要特质之一，原因是作者不喜欢柯勒律治那种不清不楚的理想主义。19世纪初期的传记经历着不少观念之战，反映出那个时代的政治图景——各个时代的传记都是如此。传记写作也可能非常大胆和激进。黑兹利特主张民权，这使他充满热情地在《时代精神》（1825）中为政治家和诗人写了不少人物素描，并编辑了工人阶级雅各宾派作家托马斯·霍尔克罗夫特的回忆录。威廉·戈德温为妻子玛丽·沃斯通克拉夫特撰写的短篇传记《〈女权辩护〉作者回忆录》出版于妻子难产死后不久的1798年，因为诚实地记述了她的女权主义、无神论和反体制观点而引起了公愤。这类传记十分危险，也会引发图书审查的反弹。

然而戈德温认为同情才是关键，50年后，卡莱尔在他出版于1851年的关于"人类世界的一位天才"的晚期浪漫主义传记中，也是这样认为的，那位天才就是名不见经传的诗人约翰·斯特林，1844年便英年早逝了。不同于卡莱尔后来为腓特烈大帝所写的史诗性历史传记，这是一部忏悔式传记，充满了悲伤的哀歌，悲悼"这个最友好、聪慧和美丽之人的灵魂；他曾在人世间与我一同漫步走过一个季节，我此后的征途上会一直保存着他的记忆"。当博斯韦尔的《约翰逊传》在1830年代再版时，卡莱尔撰文写道，传记是一种神圣的事业。

在博斯韦尔的《约翰逊传》中，许多微小的现实细节竟不可磨灭地留在我们的记忆中，像魔法一样闪着奇异的光芒！……有些微不足道的，或许不怎么高尚甚至有些丑陋的事件，只要真实而生动地呈现，就会在易感的记忆中留存，在那里变得高尚起来……带着独属于逝者的感染力。因为过往的一切对我们而言都是神圣的；逝者都是神圣的，哪怕他们在世的时候曾经卑劣和邪恶……

他举的例子是一天夜里博斯韦尔与约翰逊手挽手沿着河岸街散步的一幕，一位"娼妓"上前搭讪：

现实的神秘力量啊！这不仅不是最糟糕的事件，反而在如今，七十年时光匆匆流过之后，对我们产生了一种意义。请务必想想看，这是真实的，是的的确确发生过的！……约翰逊说，"不，不，姑娘，这可不好"；然后"我们聊了起来"；……与此同时，那个不体面的人，只留下匆匆一瞥，便消失在了无尽的黑暗里。

他问道，传记为何能做到这一点，为何能激活现实的"一丝微光"呢？

一个重大而极有价值的秘密就是……：有一颗包容的爱心，随后便能拥有这样的……这才能使整个胸怀变得宽广，激发每一种心智感官发挥适当的作用，也就是了解的作用；如此，便一定会生动地呈现出来。

这是为传记这门人文学科所作的最伟大的辩护之一,也非常符合那个时代的精神。如果如今被问到传记成功的秘诀是什么,我们大概不会回答说:"有一颗包容的爱心"。而"一颗爱心"对传记写作来说是很危险的基石。在大部分19世纪传记中起极大作用的同情与尊敬的冲动往往会产生偶像化传记。虽说从1830年代到1890年代,人们写作了许多种不同的传记,但这个时期的特点后来被追溯性地概括为洗白历史和图书审查。与前一代人那种冒险的叙事全然不同,维多利亚时期传记的标志性特征是合乎道德与含蓄矜持。卡莱尔预见到了这一点,他在评论批评家约翰·吉布森·洛克哈特1837年关于岳父沃尔特·斯科特的《回忆录》时写了如下文字,当时那本书因为曝光了"私人生活的圣洁性"而引发众怒。

英国传记多么精致体面啊,上帝保佑它紧闭的双唇!一把体面的达摩克利斯之剑永远地悬在这位可怜的英国传记作家头上(正如它永远悬在可怜的英国生活之上),把他推向了面瘫失语的边缘。

然而谨慎日益成为规范,要知道那可是阶级意识、宗教信仰、社会宏愿、严肃的福音派道德标准、工作伦理、对欧式革命的惧怕和为国效忠的观念成为小说和诗歌中的核心主题,也成为中产阶级日常生活的主旋律的时代。文学遗产和名声正面临清理,正如洛克哈特在1828年的彭斯传记中那种愧疚的语气(他为诗人的"放荡"寻找借口,指出那是"他的天才的道德影响"),或者拜伦充满丑闻的日记于1824年在他的出版商的办公室被销毁，又或者雪莱的家人力图在他死后把他神圣化。当已故诗人们充满强烈情感的真实故事冲破这层层屏障，我们总能听到一声撕心裂肺的呐喊——如雪莱惊人的"不寻常关系"灼烧着爱德华·道登那部谨慎的、有所保留的1888年传记的书页，或者1878年济慈写给范妮·布劳恩[①]的情书得见天日。

19世纪中晚期的传记往往是由某一位后代或门生所写的。基本素材——信件、日记、秘密——往往归家人所有。如果传记作家受家人委托，他（在罕见得多的情形下，也可能是她）只能阅读到家人给出的东西，而且不得不小心避免冒犯他们。由亲友所写的保护性传记的例子有很多，包括阿瑟·彭林·斯坦利1844年的《托马斯·阿诺德博士传》，后者曾任拉格比公学校长，也曾是他的老师；约翰·福斯特关于他敬仰的朋友查尔斯·狄更斯的传记（1872—1874）；G. O. 特里维廉为他的舅舅麦考利[②]所写的传记（1876）；哈勒姆·丁尼生关于他的父亲桂冠诗人的传记（1897），在他的母亲艾米丽·丁尼生严格的审查目光下写成。查尔斯·金斯利等名人的遗孀虔诚地纪念已故的丈夫。写传记的亲属非常清楚他们妥协的立场：莱斯利·斯蒂芬一贯觉得自己的哥哥、立法者詹姆斯·菲茨詹姆斯·斯蒂芬缺乏同情心，但还是受托为他写一部毕恭毕敬的传记，当他郁郁寡欢地准备动笔时，他问自己："如果博斯韦尔是约翰逊的弟弟，会怎样？"他的女儿弗吉尼亚·伍尔夫在1919年的小说《夜与日》中嘲讽这类家族传记的写作，加入了她那整整一代文学家对

[①] 范妮·布劳恩（1800—1865），浪漫主义诗人济慈的未婚妻和灵感源泉。

[②] 托马斯·巴宾顿·麦考利（1800—1859），英国诗人，历史学家，辉格党政治家，曾担任军务大臣和财政部主计长。

维多利亚时代传记的严厉批评。

  但关于这种充满敬爱和崇拜的传记,可以说的还有很多。福斯特的《狄更斯传》经过了审查,也不够准确,但同样给了它非凡的传主一个充满同情、热情洋溢的特写。伊丽莎白·盖斯凯尔为同是小说家的夏洛蒂·勃朗特所写的传记则是一个温柔而动人的故事。1857年,盖斯凯尔作为女人为另一个女人撰写传记,几乎没有先例可循。她比自己的传主大六岁,很喜欢后者的作品。两人初次见面是在1850年,盖斯凯尔当时40岁;她刚刚出版了《玛丽·巴顿》,勃朗特也刚刚出版了《简·爱》。勃朗特1855年去世(年仅38岁)后,盖斯凯尔受到帕特里克·勃朗特牧师(他比自己所有的孩子活得都长)的请求,为他女儿写一部传记。她开始带着同情和尊敬研究传主的人生,此时她的身份既是名气与之相当的小说家,也是深受丧亲之痛的女人。勃朗特的母亲和兄弟姐妹都去世了;盖斯凯尔也在年幼时经历过双亲去世,还曾有两个孩子夭折。她的写法是保护性的:她希望为勃朗特辩护,否认《简·爱》出版后面临的道德沦丧和文笔粗糙的指控,方法则是没有公开自己所知的勃朗特写给远在布鲁塞尔的已婚男子赫格尔先生的狂热的情书,并刻意强调她的女性气质和宗教上的坚忍态度,而非职业成就。

  盖斯凯尔记下了三个引发联想的语录作为导引。第一条是:"如果你爱自己的读者并希望被他们阅读,就要收集传闻!"第二条提到了传记作者与传主之间的"温柔联系"。还有一条来自勃朗特的一个朋友,说她"沉默的人生中充满了无边无际的情感和智识"。盖斯凯尔着手写就了一部关于丧亲之痛、孤独、痛苦、基督教的刚毅以及"高贵的忍耐"的叙事作品,用小说式的生动描写向我们讲述了暗沉阴郁的约克郡霍沃斯荒野上发生的一切。故事的大部分篇幅都用于描写勃朗特作为女儿和姐姐,在生活中的那些微小的家常细节。一个很能说明问题的例子是夏洛蒂在写《简·爱》的日子里,中断写作去削土豆表皮的芽眼,因为管家泰比年纪太大,视力退化得厉害。

> 勃朗特小姐是个讲究的当家人,当然忍受不了这个;但她也不忍心伤害忠诚的老仆……于是她会悄悄溜进厨房,无声无息地拿走盛蔬菜的碗……中断写作的浓厚兴趣和充沛灵感,仔细削掉土豆上的斑点,再不声不响地把它们放回原处。这个不起眼的过程大概能够证明她在履行自己的职责时是多么整齐有序和全情投入,哪怕是在"文学的精灵"附身之时。

紧接着下一段一开头,就写到勃朗特在写作中的措辞是多么"得体贴切",仿佛在写作和持家中,精益求精和一丝不苟是相辅相成的,即便这两件事或许会发生冲突。

盖斯凯尔写到她作为一个作家而不是家庭主妇的传主时,特别突出了女性作家的身份:

> 如果一个男人成了作家,他很可能仅仅是换了一个职业而已。他把迄今为止专注于其他某项研究或追求的那部分时间投入写作中;他放弃某种法律或医学职业……或者放弃他迄今一直试图谋生的某一部分实业或生意;由另一

图9 夏洛蒂·勃朗特与伊丽莎白·盖斯凯尔——两个女人、两个朋友、两个小说家：传记是同情的艺术

位商人或律师,或医生,顶替他的职位……但没有其他人可以顶替女儿、妻子或母亲,以及上帝特意安排去填补那个空缺之人的那份安静沉默而旷日经年的职责:一个女人人生中的主要工作很难由她自己选择……但她又不能逃避自己拥有[天赋的最特别的才能]这一事实所意味的那份职责。她不能把天赋藏在一张餐巾纸里:它就是要使用,要为他人服务的。

夏洛蒂·勃朗特后来的传记作者们指责盖斯凯尔(用卡罗琳·埃尔布兰的话说)为她恢复了"女性角色的安全感",宣传了"她始终不渝的信仰的虚构说法"。但盖斯凯尔的崇拜者们很喜欢这部传记那种小说家的感同身受和慷慨宽容。玛格丽特·奥利芬特称之为一种新型传记,是"为每一个从世人的视线中消失的女人"所作的辩解。克里斯托弗·里克斯认为它是"一个女人为另一个女人所写的最伟大的传记"。盖斯凯尔的传记作者珍妮·厄格洛说"《夏洛蒂·勃朗特传》看似充斥着大大小小的沉默,但它却是那么意味深长地诉说着一切"。

维多利亚时期的人物传记或许非常雄辩和生动。虽说为尊重和矜持所笼罩,我们却总能从字里行间读到性情的发作、奇异和乖僻的个性。的确,"怪人传记"是整个19世纪都蓬勃发展、颇受欢迎的文类。各种回忆录、集体传记、小册子和"非凡杂志"讲述着各种怪人未经审查的生平故事。亨利·威尔逊的《非凡人物》故事集首版于1821年,直到1870年代还广为流传。弗雷德里克·费尔霍尔特的《不寻常人物》(1849)、约翰·廷布斯的《英格兰怪人怪事集》(1866)、威廉·拉塞尔的两卷本《怪人传》

(1864)以及罗伯特·马尔科姆的《传记猎奇》(1865)也一样大受追捧。当时有许多怪人、财迷、宗教和医学怪人、非凡女性和地区奇人(《三个非同寻常的约克郡人物》)的故事集。廷布斯为他的英格兰怪人分类如下:"富裕时髦之人、幻想家、骗子和疯狂的传教士、隐士、胖子、巨人、侏儒和壮汉……奇怪的旅人、艺术家、戏剧人和文人。"不符合以上任何一类的怪人则被归入"其他"。

尽管如此,就主流传记而言,这一时期的"生平与信件"却充斥着一种古板的气息。它们遵循长篇编年体叙事的格式,和那个时期的小说一样,往往都有数卷之长,从信件和日记中大量节选摘录(但都经过谙于世故的审查)。讲述的故事多半是公共成就、职业挑战、友谊、旅行、战斗、政治困境或信仰危机。童年时期的问题、个人隐私、绯闻和丑闻都只是轻描淡写地一笔带过。主要人物都是政治家或领导人、陆军或海军英雄、牧师、作家和教师。发展轨迹逐渐向上向前,语调基本上是严肃的、不加批判的。乔治·艾略特的鳏夫约翰·克罗斯在1885年出版的传记就极为得体,以至于格莱斯顿抱怨说:"那根本就不是什么传记……那是长达三卷的矜庄。"格莱斯顿也在他的朋友约翰·莫利所写的传记(1903)中得到了同样的礼遇,像通常的维多利亚时期传记一样,它的高潮也是他在家人的怀抱中安然死去,(应他女儿的要求)略去了格莱斯顿罹患口腔癌的可怕细节,最后一页仿若摘自某一部维多利亚时代小说:

[1898年5月]19日一大清早,他的家人都跪在床前,他躺在那里,已进入弥留之际,然后没有一丝痛苦,便停止了

呼吸。窗外的自然——森林、宽阔的草坪和澄澈如洗的碧空——全都闪耀着最美的光彩。

那一种偶像化传记，无论是它宣扬的观念还是它的散文风格，都遭到了下一代人的嘲讽。但这种传记英雄崇拜的出现自有其充分的理由。传记从来就不仅仅是一个人的生平故事，它向来不乏政治和社会意义。19世纪传记的政治与强化一种国家叙事有关。在北美，在独立战争与内战之间，一种独特的国家文化被铸造出来；在欧洲，通过一个剧烈动荡的时期，各个国族都在重塑自己的独特身份。在那个世纪之初的不列颠，巨大的社会变革、对动乱的恐惧、拿破仑战争之后的政治镇压，都导致人们将英雄人物的生平故事作为一种安全保障。后来，它们变成了帝国自信和坚定信心的表达方式。众所周知的一部传记为爱国主义的生平写作奠定了基调，那就是罗伯特·骚塞的《纳尔逊传》（1813），书中为传主所有的性格弱点寻找借口，为的是让"一个名字和一种典范"永垂不朽，"在这一刻，他和他的故事激励着英格兰成千上万的年轻人；那是一个让我们自豪的名字，是仍将继续为我们提供力量和保护的典范"。

但不需要成为纳尔逊才能为这种国家叙事添砖加瓦，也不需要成为一部三卷本传记的传主才能名垂青史。在整个19世纪的欧洲和美国，人们都热衷于为所有被认为值得纪念的人编纂传记辞典。贝尔纳普的《美国人物传记》合集于1790年代问世。在欧洲，从1830年代以后，就不断有多卷本的杰出意大利人、瑞典人、荷兰人、比利时人、奥地利人和德国人传记辞典出版。1811年到1828年，路易-加布里埃尔·米肖的52卷《世界古今名人传》在法国出版,涵盖各种各样的公众人物,并在法国引发无数人效仿,全都旨在通过个人生平故事打造一种普遍通用的国家叙事。

在不列颠,国家肖像画廊于1856年建立,维多利亚时代的伟大肖像画家之一G. F. 沃茨这样总结它的历史的、爱国的目的:"一个建立起伟大功勋的民族,它的国家人物就是……永远不该从我们的视线中消失的人。"不列颠名人的肖像——以及后来的照片——构成了这个国家的一种视觉人物传记合集,也是为这个国家打造的。同类画廊的印刷品版本则花费了更长的时间建立。自从托马斯·富勒1662年的《英格兰名人传》以及诸如《不列颠人物传记》(1747—1766)这种多卷本的大型传记辞典出版以来,关于名垂青史——或遗臭万年——的名人的短篇传记合集有过很多,根据县郡、地区、类型或职业分门别类。19世纪中期,有"著名和卓越的英国人"、"著名英国法官"、"著名印第安酋长"、"恶名昭彰的嚣张劫匪"、"著名犹太拉比"、"各类恶人"、"好仆人生平故事"、海军将官、使徒、单身汉国王、重婚者、主教、殉道者、医生、预言家、花花公子和弑君者的生平故事集。例如,《杰出鞋匠生平》(1883)讲述了"形而上学的鞋匠萨缪尔·德鲁"的故事,"这个自学成才的康沃尔郡人娴熟地运用自己孤独的手艺,同时为未来成为神学家打下了基础"。在这些合集中,女性人物多半是圣人、诗人、仆人、罪人和王后,篇名类似"贵妇生平故事"或"大不列颠几位因写作而出名的夫人的回忆录"等。一个名为《英国女性名人传》的合集作者是约翰·桑福德夫人,出版于1883年,其中包括简·格雷夫人等新教圣人的圣徒传记,列出了书写"女性传记"所必需的条件:

通常认为,女人的生平故事不应展示任何特别惊人的事件或收集构成非常生动叙事的素材。在很大程度上,因为受性别限制而只有私人生活,她们往往不是所在时代的标志性轰动场景的参与者……因此,女人传记的主要志趣不在于它所记录的事件……一个女人安静的日常生活通常只能呈现出一系列家务,或家庭生活中的日常琐事……然而她们并非因此就变得不值得关注。追溯人物性格的发展才是一切传记的主要目的。

在这些以教育为目的的国家主义出版物中,最著名也最畅销的,当属萨缪尔·斯迈尔斯主要以男性人物为主的《自助》(1859)和《工程师们》(1861—1862),赞美那些英勇地推动和增加"我们作为一个国家的动力"的"默默无闻者"的工作和能量。在其所记述的数百位人物中,有一个例子为它建立了基调:伯肯黑德①的威廉·杰克逊("如今是北德比郡的议员")的故事,他在家中十一个孩子中排行第七,父亲在他年幼时就去世了,因此他前往码头工作,后来又到了账房,"偶然得到了一套《不列颠百科全书》后,他从头到尾仔细阅读那些卷册,有时白天也读,但主要都在夜晚。后来他有了自己的生意,勤勤恳恳,获得了成功。如今……他与地球上几乎每一个国家都保持着商业关系"。

斯迈尔斯是诸如"实用知识传播协会"这类教育运动的推动者之一,这些运动的宗旨是鼓励工人们通过教育而非革命实

---

① 英格兰默西赛德郡一城市。

现自助。他的故事，以及类似的具有启发性的世俗故事，"在机械时代早期的意义如同圣人传说在中世纪的意义"。然而在19世纪末的文化人物和国家领袖系列传记，例如约翰·莫利的《英格兰文人》（自1877年开始出版）、《十二位英格兰政治家》（自1888年开始出版）以及乔治·格罗夫的《音乐与音乐家辞典》（从1879年开始出版）的背后，也存在着一个引发争论的议题。

1885年，在就有无必要编纂一部《世界古今名人传》的英国版问题讨论了多年之后，由乔治·史密斯出版、莱斯利·斯蒂芬编辑（后来，斯蒂芬因压力过大和劳累过度退出之后，编辑工作由西德尼·李承担）的《国家人物传记辞典》开始了漫长的出版历史。初版于1900年编纂完成，共63卷，包括近29 000位已故英国人的生平，1901年又出版了三卷补遗卷。各类增补和修订在整个20世纪一直持续，直到1992年开始在一个全新的、大大扩充和全面修订的《国家人物传记辞典》基础上开展工作，于2004年出版了《牛津国家人物传记大辞典》。

莱斯利·斯蒂芬在他（模仿18世纪的原型）称之为"大不列颠传记"的文本中着手提供"尽可能最全面的信息，将其整理为全面的条理化格式"。词条必须是"严格的传记体"，实事求是，不"过度堆积"细节，公正客观而不失友善，"由同情传主的人士撰写"。被收入这部集体性国家历史的理由是民主的、世俗的。众所周知的大名当然在列，但也收入了莱斯利·斯蒂芬所谓的次要英雄：海军舰长、乡村牧师、教师、商人、运动员。这些生平故事都是根据讣告、回忆录、序言、信件重建的，"真的可以只通过阅读辞典便能大致了解他们"。另外还有些更加可疑的人物："妓院老板、柔体杂技演员、赌徒、异装癖者和百岁人瑞。"

女性只占全部词条的4%,盖因她们出现在公共生活中的频率较低,妻子和母亲一般只是男性的附属。

关于谁的人生故事值得记录,谁的传记值得撰写,我们的观念已经随着时间的流逝而发生了变化。1993年,在《国家人物传记辞典》于1900年完成出版近100年后,一卷《未录入人士》出版了(增加了所有时期的总共1 074个名字)。编辑克莉丝汀·尼科尔斯在序言中就前任们将其排除在外的情况有一段经过深思熟虑的评述。她指出从17世纪末到维多利亚时代中期的不列颠:

> 常常有许多人是初版编辑们没有注意到的,或许也不无道理,因为他们的成就并非总是显而易见的英勇事迹或发明……却也为一个不断迅速变化、人口和财富都在扩张的社会提供了稳定的基础。这些人包括探险家、化学家、热气球驾驶员、水文学家、托运人、廷臣、建筑师、水手、发明家、医生,以及务实的男女而非空想家或诗人,投机者而非思索者、实干者而非空谈者——如若没有他们,国家结构翻天覆地的变化可能就无法顺利进行。必须经由时间的流逝,才能认识到他们的贡献。

从1850年代到20世纪中期,"出现了大量商人、工程师、科学家和女人——所有这些类别或多或少都被忽略了"。

但尽管有那么多历史盲点,19世纪的《国家人物传记辞典》还是提供了一种全然不同于伟人"生平和信件"的传记。莱斯利·斯蒂芬的妻子于1895年去世之后,他写了一篇题为《被遗忘的捐助人》的感伤文章，赞美"那些被遗忘的千万人"的深远影响。这一维多利亚时代的主题往往被用作把女人留在家里的借口，也为英雄主义提供了一个替代观念，为撰写"默默无闻"之人的传记提供了一个理由。从乔治·艾略特的《米德尔马契》（1871）中也能看到这样的主题，在该书最后一页，作者说多萝西娅默默无闻却又惊心动魄的一生是很多人的缩影，他们"微不足道的行为"产生了"不绝如缕的"影响："你我的遭遇之所以不致如此悲惨，一半也得力于那些不求闻达，忠诚地度过一生，然后安息在无人凭吊的坟墓中的人们。"[①]

伟大的国家主义产物《国家人物传记辞典》出版的背景，是19世纪高产而日益专业化的传记产业。其出版的时机也恰逢人们就关于传记写作的伦理进行激烈而广泛的辩论之时。在法国，这样的辩论尤其热闹，那里的人们往往鄙视传记，认为它是下里巴人的文化生活，对传记和历史的相对优缺点也争论不休。哲学家维克托·库赞认为个人生平故事会让历史沦为"乏味无聊的琐事"。在他著名的《人之子》（1863）中，欧内斯特·勒南没有把传主写成上帝之子，而写成了一个出色的人，他认为有必要为传记辩护，认为它是理解基督教发展的最佳方式。大众传媒的兴起，关于在世之人的新闻式、往往是丑闻式"传记"的大行其道，被某些人看成一种民主病，将文学文化降格为"人物展"和"个人黑料"。

在美国和不列颠，人们也感受到了同样的焦虑，由于新闻业无孔不入、名人文化开始兴起，以及私人和公共领域之间的界限

---

① 译文引自项星耀译：《米德尔马契》，第980—981页，人民文学出版社1987年版。

前所未有地动摇,导致了关于私人生活是否应该公开展示以供大众消费这个问题的辩论——居然和100年后我们面临的问题惊人地相似。公众人物(如帕内尔①)会因为私下的丑闻而被迫下台,著名作家也因其他作家的生活被曝光而大惊失色。勃朗宁想象房屋的门面被拆掉,以便人们窥见屋里的一切。丁尼生公开诅咒那些等着"当众"撕扯诗人心脏的"食腐秃鹫",并在私下里说,"伟人的生活"正在"像猪一样被剖开"。乔治·艾略特说传记是"英国文学的病"。萨克雷警告女儿说:"**记住**,我死后不可有任何关于我的传记。"

亨利·詹姆斯在《阿斯彭文稿》(1888)和其他文本中以惊人的天才笔触写到作家的私密生活被"出版界的恶棍"侵犯。他激越地坚信"一个人的抽屉和口袋不可被翻个底朝天",还烧掉了许多私人文件,(徒劳地)希望让写传记的侵犯者"失望",并对罗伯特·路易斯·史蒂文森等好友在死后"被展出亮相"怒不可遏。奥斯卡·王尔德在1895年受到审判并名誉扫地,这令他感到十分激动和惊恐(他写信给埃德蒙·戈斯说):"是的,此事的确有着可怕而残暴的戏剧性,也实在有趣——不过我们得说,就这样一件事而言,趣味是建立在如此令人作呕的恐怖之上的。"他一方面因为作家的私生活被曝光而惊恐,另一方面也为之着迷。例如,1907年,和伊迪丝·沃顿一起乘坐机动车环法旅行时,他就迫不及待地想去拜访乔治·桑位于诺昂的故居,看看她和情人们——用他的话说——"那么兴奋地厮混"过的房间。他也满怀激动地阅读传记、回忆录和信件。

---

① 查尔斯·斯图尔特·帕内尔(1846—1891),19世纪爱尔兰自治运动领导者、英国下议院议员。

"洗劫""侵犯""背叛""含蓄",这些都是关于传记式侵犯的辩论中的关键词汇。"传记伦理"成为严肃讨论的主题,玛格丽特·奥利芬特写于1883年的一篇文章就讨论了这个主题,她认为,"品德高尚的"传记作者有义务对"死者的无助"负责,毕竟后者的"私人抽屉"很容易被"寻找不利于他们的证据的人洗劫一空"。她的结论是,传记式背叛"违反了社会道德"。

奥利芬特提到了那个时代最为臭名昭著的"传记式背叛",即对备受尊崇的维多利亚时代先哲卡莱尔的背叛。1870年代,卡莱尔把自己的大部分文件交给了他的朋友、历史学家约翰·安东尼·弗劳德,包括他关于已故妻子简·韦尔什·卡莱尔的充满懊悔的"回忆录",以及两人之间的信件,指示弗劳德在他认为合适的时候出版那些文字,并在他死后为他作传。弗劳德看到那些材料诉说了一个失败婚姻的惊人故事,觉得既然卡莱尔如此开诚布公,他应该将导师最真实的故事公之于众。卡莱尔1881年去世之后,弗劳德立即出版了《回忆录》,然后又出版了一部两卷本的充满敬意和活力的《卡莱尔传》(1882年和1884年),以及充满伤痛的《简·韦尔什·卡莱尔的信件与回忆》(1883)。他为这些出版活动辩解,理由是卡莱尔本人坚信"一个人是否伟大,要看他有多少行为被细察"。全国各地的咒骂声呼啸而来。关于传记的争议总是需要有人挨骂,而弗劳德挨骂,是因为他揭示这些残忍的家事"玷污"了伟人的名声,滥用了自己所知的事实,并未经授权使用了私人文件。"弗劳德式恶行"("froudacity")成为表示背叛、缺德和失真的俗语。他死后,他的后人出版了《我与卡莱尔的关系》(1903),解释说他隐瞒了卡莱尔"很难同居一室"以及简如此不满的真正原因:卡莱尔性无能,"是那种根本不该结婚的人"。新一轮的愤怒接踵而至,扩展到了关于男子气概、婚姻和离婚的医学及法律讨论。"坦率的传记也有其局限性,"一位评论家在《英国医学期刊》中怒斥道,"而且迄今为止也从未被认为可以包括一个男人的性经验史。弗劳德公开了一个一生致力于写作的男人的生殖器缺陷,而他居然还假装敬佩和爱戴那个男人,算是树立了一个最糟糕的榜样,这是英国文学的一个污点……"

弗劳德的《卡莱尔传》是一个很好的例子,说明传记总是与它的时代最关心的社会问题有着紧密的联系,以及传记作者与传主私交甚密有多危险。"写传记的永远是犹大",奥斯卡·王尔德在1891年如是说。弗劳德从未有意或希望成为犹大,却几乎不由自主地在传记变得公开和直接的过程中扮演了一个重要角色。一种自觉意识正在发展成形:关于如何实践这种技艺,关于传记的美学而非伦理意义的兴趣,关于它应该在怎样的程度上忠于传主的私密内在的自我的疑问。这一章的主人公卡莱尔曾经思考过那一切。1843年,他在自己的日记中写道:

> 这个世界与我的生活无关。世人永远不会了解我的生活,哪怕他们书写和阅读一百部关于我的传记。在所有上帝创造的人中,只有我自己知道,或者有可能知道,关于我的生活的主要事实。

第五章

陨落的偶像

1881年，萧伯纳开玩笑说传记这个文类最需要的，就是一本名为《维多利亚女王：出自一位讨厌她的熟人之手》的书。利顿·斯特雷奇在1900年代领会了他的意思。他和其他年轻的英国作家生活的年代经历了灾难性的历史动荡和惊人的社会变革，喜欢萧伯纳、H. G. 威尔斯和萨缪尔·巴特勒胜过卡莱尔或丁尼生，秉持反战主义而非爱国主义，偏爱坦率而非得体，大笑而非庄重，世俗而非宗教。他们全面否定了维多利亚时期的传记，说它们是"笨重而费力的"庞然大物，"尽是些美德的观念"。例如，伊夫林·沃在1928年写道，两卷本的颂文就是为了"帮助我们的父辈在瞻仰伟人的遗体时保持端庄得体"，"伟人的面部恬静安详，一切生而为人的污点都被清理干净了"。那些父辈的孩子们着手改变传记故事的写作方式（而书写父辈就是他们做出这一改变的实践）。"传记的艺术"利用微缩主义、技艺与狡黠、充满想象力的虚构技巧、讽刺、戏仿和漫画手法。"遗体，"沃写道，"已经变成了牵线木偶。"传记作家可以与传主平起平坐，而不必是对后者肃然起敬、顶礼膜拜的门徒。传记作家充满自觉意识；传记甚至可以被看成一种自传。最重要的是，传记的目的是要借助心理分析这种新型工具的帮助，揭示知名人士隐秘的内在自我。

文化转型被过度简化了。19世纪的传记并不像它的批评者们声称的那样乏味而冷漠；20世纪初期的传记也并不全是坦率真诚的、心理分析的、大胆实验的。许多保护性的、得体的传记继续被写作出版，例如爱德华·马什1918年理想化金童诗人鲁珀特·布鲁克的回忆录，或鲁珀特·哈特-戴维斯的《休·沃波尔传》，时至1952年，这部传记仍然只字未提沃波尔是同性恋一事。然而各种大大小小、地方性和全球性因素的涌现都在这一重大变化中起到了作用：卡莱尔-弗劳德与王尔德的丑闻、维多利亚女王之死、争取参政权运动、弗洛伊德、世界大战。弗吉尼亚·伍尔夫所谓的"新传记"有着明确的特征。那些特征在大约40年里以多种方式出现在传记作品中，包括：沃尔特·佩特的《伊壁鸠鲁的马吕斯》（1885）和他的《虚构的肖像画》（1887）；马塞尔·施瓦布1895年的短篇生平故事集《虚构的生活》；埃德蒙·戈斯的回忆录《父与子》（1907）和他关于传记的杂文；利顿·斯特雷奇的《维多利亚名流传》（1918）中的四个短篇人物故事，还有他不那么出名的《维多利亚女王》（1921）和《伊丽莎白和埃塞克斯》（1928）；杰弗里·斯科特的《泽利德的画像》（1925）；弗尼吉亚·伍尔夫关于传记艺术的杂文、虚构传记《奥兰多》（1928）和《弗勒希》（1933），以及她未完成的回忆录《往事素描》（1939—1941）；哈罗德·尼科尔森的《英语传记发展史》（1928）和他怪诞的人物肖像《有些人》（1927）；安德烈·莫洛亚的《爱丽儿：雪莱传》(1923年,1924年译成英文)和他的《传记面面观》(1928年,1929年译成英文)；阿瑟·西蒙斯的传记实验《探求科尔沃》(1934)；以及埃米尔·路德维希的《传记的艺术》(1936)。

这里的"传记"一词面临着压力。正如在18世纪,"语录"和讽刺兼有,日记和谈话并蓄,"生平写作"成为一个更有用的词汇,用于描述这种自传/传记式回忆录、讽刺素描、虚构或心理分析探索,以及关于如何写作生平故事的研究的混合物。弗吉尼亚·伍尔夫在《往事素描》中使用了这个词汇,讨论了有必要把个人的生命史放在家庭、遗传、环境和"隐形的因素"的背景中,把"鱼放回水流中"。她指出,为达到这一目的,必须发展出新的写作手法。模糊或打破各种文类之间的界限是反思传记的必行之事。

（通常并不因冒险而闻名的）埃德蒙·戈斯写出了一本无法归类的非凡之书《父与子》,这是一本深刻而有趣的回忆录,书写了他离奇古怪的童年时光。那是一个开拓性的文类,既不是父母的传记,也不是自传,而是"对两种性情的研究"。戈斯讲述了自己在一群激进的加尔文派"教友"之间长大,由鳏居的父亲菲利普·戈斯抚养成人,父亲是一位博物学家,在对科学的好奇心和宗教信仰之间矛盾挣扎。这本书曝光私人家庭生活的直率坦白超出了当时的读者习惯的程度。戈斯写父亲一丝不苟地根据严格的原则艰难地把一个男孩抚养长大,既可敬,又堪怜。书中有些滑稽又悲伤的场景是儿子开始怀疑父亲是否真的绝对正确,例如他拿一种"偶像崇拜的行为"做实验,对着起居室的椅子祈祷("哦,椅子！"),以此来充满恐惧地测试上帝是否降

图10 伍尔夫和斯特雷奇。讽刺、游戏与风格：现代主义者的传记观

怒于他("但没有什么后果……上帝根本不在乎"),或者他在圣诞节偷吃了一口不准吃的李子布丁,"精神上极为痛苦":"哦!爸爸,爸爸,我吃掉了献给偶像的肉!"《父与子》因真情实感而得到赞誉,也因"走向极端"而受到指责。但它作为一部生动的、人性化的父子关系叙事作品有着很长的艺术生命,为许多后来的小说化回忆录确立了一个典范,如菲利普·罗斯的《遗产》或布雷克·莫里森的《永失慈父》。

"处死父亲"是利顿·斯特雷奇的部分目标。《维多利亚名流传》被恰当地描述为"俄狄浦斯式传记"。斯特雷奇作为帝国统治阶级家庭的孩子,聪明、有教养、瘦高个儿、理性到病态,对友谊充满激情,热爱法国和18世纪文学,对弗洛伊德的心理分析痴迷不已,在他剑桥和布卢姆斯伯里派的圈子里都是个诙谐幽默的同性恋"人物"。虽说他在相当短暂的一生中(他死时年仅52岁)写过不少历史、"人物肖像"和批评,但他的成名之作,也是他主要为后世所记住的作品,却只有一本。《维多利亚名流传》产生了极大的影响,如今已经很难重新想象了。那是一本战争年代的书,写于1912—1918年间。它选择了四位公众人物,没有一位是作家:一个伟大公学的校长,这个国家最受人敬爱的战时护士-女英雄,一个从英格兰圣公会前往罗马的有权势、有野心的牧师,以及不列颠最著名也最悲惨的军事领袖之一。这四个人——阿诺德博士、弗洛伦斯·南丁格尔、枢机主教曼宁和戈登将军——此前已经有人为其写过充满敬意的传记了(斯特雷奇抄袭和歪曲了那些素材)。是时候揭穿四人的假象了,他们令人敬畏的公共活动可以被重新解读为对个体创伤和压迫的升华,他们是一个历史时期的代表人物,而在其怀疑主义的后代看来,他们也在一定程度上参与和促成了第一次世界大战的杀戮和混乱。

斯特雷奇在一篇充满王尔德风格的序言中列示了自己的技巧,那篇序言提出要用轻松的、讽刺的、离题的方法,否定和"揭露""维多利亚时代的"沉重、庄严和敬意。一个"小桶"被沉入维多利亚时代的大海深处,即将"从那幽深的海底捞上来一些典型的样本,使之大白于天下,让人们带着仔细的好奇心去审视"。科学的精确方法会揭示一些此前模糊和隐藏的东西。传记将使用非常规的解读角度,攻"其两肋,或其后背"。这些军事隐喻带着一种心照不宣的性挑逗意味。这将是为维多利亚时代的人们解除圣职的尝试,将他们所有的神经衰弱和隐秘欲望公之于众。

事实上,那些文章显示出很多这篇序言中未曾暗示的情感和慈悲。尤其是,在斯特雷奇笔下,南丁格尔和戈登都是孤军奋战、奋发图强的强迫症患者,是无能的英国官僚制度的对立面。他赋予那些失败的小人物一些动人的感染力,像曼宁那篇文章中的枢机主教纽曼和《弗洛伦斯·南丁格尔》中的阿瑟·休·克拉夫。当然,他的语气往往是嘲讽轻慢的,特别是在写到男女分校公学体系的中流砥柱阿诺德博士时,斯特雷奇那一代人厌恶那种教育体系的庸俗市侩、爱国主义的装模作样、鼓吹阳刚的基督教思想和未经审视的性影响:

> 阿诺德博士从未有过无法感知道德沦丧的危险。如果说连意大利的风景都能让他想起那种邪恶,在拉格比公学的男孩子中间,他又如何能忘记?每天看到这么多孩子落

入魔鬼之手,让他极度地焦虑不安。

但书中也不乏其他语气。南丁格尔遭遇家人反对的情景被描绘得仿佛小说里的一个情节,我们仿佛听到一个维多利亚时代的母亲大惊小怪的声音:

> 太奇怪了;亲爱的弗洛到底是怎么了?……真让人难以捉摸,她好像对丈夫没兴趣……就好像家里没有那么多日常琐事要处理……

他以约翰逊式的明晰总结了把戈登派往苏丹的行政失误:

> 他整个一生的历史,他整个人的性情,似乎让他无力完成他被选派的职责。他首先是一个战士、一个狂热的人、一个大胆的冒险家,而现在,他居然被委派去执行一场可耻的撤退。

《维多利亚名流传》的政治议题通过语气和行文结构诡秘地表达出来,那就是,和所有传记实验一样,反对从前的一切。如今我们已经不那么熟悉斯坦利教长1844年那部充满敬畏的《阿诺德博士传》,或者在克里米亚战争之后将弗洛伦斯·南丁格尔神圣化地称为"提灯女神"了,也就很难看出斯特雷奇的书为何在当时看来那般大胆、有趣和惊人。后来的读者因该书的不实叙述、纨绔气质和(用明智的艾里斯·奥里戈的话说)源于"高高在上"的"单薄"而十分恼怒。斯特雷奇后来的传记实验,对维多利亚女王［因悼念而变得无力（他写了一个与主题无关且被大量模仿的临终场景，对女王的一生只是用倒叙一笔带过）］和对性"反常"的伊丽莎白女王的弗洛伊德式解读，如今读来已经非常过时了。但《维多利亚名流传》是一部极具先驱性的作品，为传记理论建立的过程提供了蓝图。

戈斯在1910年《不列颠百科全书》的"传记"词条中定义了"真实"或"纯粹"的传记，即"对一个灵魂的生命历程的忠实描述"，其讲述不带有任何道德目的，他认为这是一种"非常现代"的概念。戈斯在1925年为其17世纪的传主塔勒芒·德雷奥作传时，赞扬他像斯特雷奇一样，"从未受到惊吓，从未感到愤怒"。"他希望记录实情，并不害怕事实。"塔勒芒·德雷奥堪称法国的约翰·奥布里，写过一些邪恶的"微缩"人物传记（充满了诸如"这位骑士是个疯子，而且是法国最大的渎神者"这类句子）。

这些"现代的"传记理想得到了多位作者的回应。早在戈斯和斯特雷奇之前，法国作家马塞尔·施瓦布就曾指出，短篇传记，最好是关于没什么名气或性情乖僻人物的传记，最能引发读者的联想。怪癖、奇人，以及明显的身体特征，诸如克莱奥帕特拉的鼻子、亚历山大的饮酒、路易十四的瘘管，要比宏大的历史事件更能说明问题。施瓦布将传记和历史对立起来，认为特殊性和偶然性要比"总体性和延续性"的意义更为重大。

维塔·萨克维尔-韦斯特的丈夫、外交官、日记作者哈罗德·尼科尔森也赞成并实践了短小、巧妙而有趣的传记写作。和戈斯一样，尼科尔森将"不纯粹的"（圣徒传记、维多利亚时代传记）和"纯粹的"（真实的、精巧建构的、现代的）传记对立起来。这种正确与错误、旧与新的二元对立，是传记理论建立过程中的一种频繁且不断延续的策略。但传记总会从这类条理清晰的规律中跳脱出来。尼科尔森预见到了"科学的"（社会学的、心理分析的）和"文学的"（想象的、编造的）传记之间的分裂，但那样的僵局从未真正出现过。

法国评论家和传记作家安德烈·莫洛亚在他1928年的克拉克讲座中力图为传记争取与其他艺术形式平等的艺术地位，还故意借用了E. M. 福斯特的《小说面面观》中的"面面观"一词。莫洛亚的《爱丽儿》，即他的《雪莱传》，突显出强烈的浪漫主义风格。他认为传记应该像诗歌一样通过反复出现的主题（水的意象在《爱丽儿》中处处可见），像小说一样通过感同身受的内在性（它能直观地打开通往传主内在自我的钥匙）来打动读者。埃米尔·路德维希写过歌德、俾斯麦和威廉二世等德国伟人的心理学传记，他的写作动力也是凭直觉寻找人物的本质。在美国，加梅利尔·布拉德福德是《圣人与罪人》（1931）和《人妻》（1925）等通俗传记和主题人物合集的作者，他造出了"心理描述"一词，意为"简洁的、本质的、艺术的人物刻画"，亦即以一种"科学的精神"抓住"人的灵魂"的复杂"差异"。

人们对那种"差异"，对人心内部的鸿沟和矛盾有着十分清楚的意识。1913—1927年，普鲁斯特相继出版了《追忆似水年华》（1922—1932年间首次被译成英文），那是他为社会中的自我书写的现代史诗，以相当的深度和长度探索了记忆与身份的中断和间隙。"相对论"还是一个新的物理学概念。关于在那个公开发挥或拒绝发挥职能的自我之下埋藏和隐藏着什么的观念，通过弗洛伊德的精神分析进入了文学领域。

弗吉尼亚·伍尔夫关于传记的著述虽然在当时不能与莱

斯利·斯蒂芬、卡莱尔、佩特、戈斯、斯特雷奇、尼科尔森和普鲁斯特相提并论，却很有创意，也很有影响。和许多当代评论家一样，她对传记这一文类也持一种演进观念，认为它需要甩掉过去，采纳一种当前尚未实现的形式。正如她关于"现代小说"的著述和在该领域的实验一样，她认为传记写作必须改变，才能适应20世纪的新形势。她自幼读莱斯利·斯蒂芬和《国家人物传记辞典》长大，希望能创造一种不同于微缩版维多利亚时代生平写作的"新型"传记。但她也对博斯韦尔、卡莱尔、黑兹利特和英国传记历史上的其他创造性人物很感兴趣，而她对"没什么名气"或"性情乖僻"的人物生平十分痴迷，则与她父亲选择收入《国家人物传记辞典》词条的标准有关。

伍尔夫对传记写作和对小说一样感兴趣。她的小说总是在尝试用激进的实验方式讲述生平故事，但她也读过大量传记，写过许多以生动的笔触唤起人们记忆的其他作家的人物素描（她用杂文书写已故的作家，在日记和信件中写在世的作家——往往充满了无情的讽刺），尝试写虚构化的传记，也就此话题写过不少雄辩的文章。在《新型传记》（1927）一文中，她主张无所畏惧、勇敢和生动才是"现代的"、反维多利亚时代传记的特质。事实需要巧妙地操控，真正的生活是内在生活，可以有艺术技巧、选择和笑声。人物可以通过"一个语调、一次转头、一些瞬间抓住的细碎表达或趣闻逸事"加以展示。但她那个时代的传记尚不够"微妙和大胆"，无法实现那种传记所必需的"花岗岩与彩虹"——事实与想象、真相与艺术——的"古怪融合"。

在《传记的艺术》（1939）一文中，她仍然认为传记作者绝不可能是"自由的"，在这一点上他们与小说家不同。在撰写这篇文章时,恰逢她接受委托为好友、画家和艺术评论家罗杰·弗赖伊作传,那次经历让她深感挫败。她把自己举步维艰的原因写入了这篇文章。任何在传记中发挥"想象"的尝试都会遭遇"事实"的阻碍。但她又说,事实是不稳定的存在。"过去被认为是罪恶的事,如今借助心理学家为我们赢得的事实看来,或许只是不幸;或许是好奇心……对性爱的兴趣在生者的记忆中就已有所改变……许多旧的章节标题——大学经历、婚姻生活、职业生涯——事实上都是非常武断的人为区分。"因此传记作者的任务应该是成为先驱者,"走在其他人的前面,像矿工的金丝雀[①]"(选择这个意象本身就表明,事实会随着时间的流逝发生变化),"测试氛围,发现错误、失真,以及过时的传统是否存在"。在有着"上千台相机"的年代,传记作家的任务是"承认同一张脸会呈现出彼此矛盾的面向"。观看角度发生了变化,我们关于"伟大"和"渺小"的观念也应随之改变。

  伍尔夫关于这一文类的批评的核心,是她意识到我们每个人的内在生活从未曾在传记中得到足够充分的反映。这是她这一观点的最为雄辩的论述:

    过往,乃至它的每一位居民都神奇地被封存在一个魔法箱里;我们所能做的只是观看、倾听、倾听、观看,过不了多久,那些小小的人物——因为他们的确比真人小得多——将开始行动和说话,在他们行动的过程中我们会用各种他们全然无知的方式对他们进行排列组合,因为他们

[①] "矿工的金丝雀"是指旧时矿工会带一只关在笼子里的鸟进入矿井,将鸟的死亡作为警示,说明井内毒气的水平达到了危险的程度。

活着的时候以为自己可以自由行动；而在他们说话的时候，我们会在他们的语录中发现那些他们从未意识到的意义，因为他们活着的时候坚信自己只是直抒胸怀。而一旦你阅读一部传记，一切都不同了。

解决这一棘手难题的一个方案是将传记改写为诙谐的、戏仿的小说，这多少是在回避问题，却十分有趣。《弗勒希》(1933)通过伊丽莎白·巴雷特·勃朗宁的西班牙猎犬的眼睛——和鼻子——讲述了那位女诗人的故事。《奥兰多》(1928)的副标题也是"一部传记"，成书出版时五脏俱全：有致谢、有插图、有索引。作传者看上去是个没有名字也没有性别的人物，在书中开启了徒劳地寻找传主的旅程。奥兰多抵制传记的规则，从男人变成了女人，生活了三个世纪，拒绝任何关于身份、性别和顺时进程的决定要素。("因为她有各种各样的自我要拜访，远比我们能够容纳的多得多，因为只有当一部传记能够解释六七个自我时，才被认为是完整的，而一个人很可能会有成千上万个自我。")

伍尔夫通过虚构戏仿的方式颠覆了传记规则，总算为自己的好友和双性恋情人维塔·萨克维尔-韦斯特撰写了一部揶揄的私人回忆录，它可以既隐秘又袒露，充满色情又能通过审查。这种新型传记写作也是一项女性主义事业（虽然她本人并不明说），表明女人的生平需要新的写作形式，这正是伍尔夫一直主张的。

这种游戏的、风格化的虚构方法能否作为严肃的传记工具？如今读来，当时的其他实例也都和《奥兰多》一样，更像是突破文类的有趣实验而非专业传记写作的先例。格特鲁德·斯泰因在《三个女人》(1908)中发明了一种讲述美国普通妇女生平故事的新语言,在私密的、唠叨的、吹牛的、八卦的《艾丽斯·B.托克拉斯自传》(1933)中彻底颠倒了自传和传记。(毕加索1906年创作的那幅壮硕的斯泰因肖像是另一个例子,表明艺术领域的现代主义实验可以创造出强烈鲜明的人物个性。)艺术史学家和博斯韦尔的编辑杰弗里·斯科特在《泽利德的画像》中为18世纪荷兰作家伊莎贝尔·范·图耶写了一部精致的戏剧化生平故事,后者与伏尔泰有染,博斯韦尔曾向她求婚,她还为邦雅曼·贡斯当[①]所爱。佩特式美学家和王尔德的崇拜者A. J. A.西蒙斯为《哈德良七世》的作者弗雷德里克·罗尔夫(笔名巴伦·科尔沃)写了一部传记,采纳的形式是探求它难以琢磨的传主,一位失败的神父、流亡者、不幸的同性恋者和恶毒的信件写作者。《探求科尔沃》既是侦探故事,又是精神旅程,也是关于传记的沉思录。这里处处是神秘的学问、古怪的遭遇、别出心裁的象征主义文风,的确是一部十分奇妙的作品,读完此书,读者甚至无法确信世上是否真的有过弗雷德里克·罗尔夫其人,又或许连他的传记作者的存在也是谜团。

唯美主义——朦胧形象、印象派、艺术性——为传记的发展指明了一个方向。不过,大多数历史、政治或文学人物的传记最感兴趣的并不是形式实验。自20世纪初期以来,唯美主义者和历史学家、职业传记作者和实验性传记写作者真正有了相似之处,还是通过弗洛伊德精神分析的强大信条。西格蒙德·弗洛伊德自1890年代开始发表他关于癔症与心理学的研究结果,从

[①] 邦雅曼·贡斯当(1767—1830),出生于瑞士洛桑的法国小说家、思想家、政治家,以心理主义小说《阿道尔夫》而闻名。

图11 毕加索的斯泰因：强烈鲜明的人物个性

第五章 陨落的偶像

1920年代开始，它们由斯特雷奇的弟弟及弟媳詹姆斯和阿里克斯·斯特雷奇翻译成英文，由霍格斯出版社出版。弗洛伊德称赞《伊丽莎白和埃塞克斯》，认为它表明斯特雷奇"深得精神分析的精髓"，才能够"触及［伊丽莎白］最隐秘的动机"。精神分析的做法由弗洛伊德定义,并在《朵拉》、《小汉斯》、《鼠人》或《狼人》等病例中予以陈述,与某些传记的过程十分相似(也影响了后者):追寻线索,建立行为模式,通过关注重要细节解读整体性格,确定哪些是相关的,在童年经历中寻找成年行为的隐秘原因。弗洛伊德把这个过程比作考古发掘,这个隐喻对分析和传记都适用。但弗洛伊德却极其强烈地反对这一文类。

> 任何写传记的人都投身于谎言、隐瞒、虚伪、恭维,甚至藏起自己缺乏理解的事实,因为传记的真相根本不存在,即便存在,也无法利用。

亚当·菲利普斯[①]在一篇文章中引用了这封写于1936年的信,该文指出,弗洛伊德认为"这个文类……算是他自己的学科的竞争对手"。菲利普斯指出,弗洛伊德关于传记的"疑虑""或许也错位表现出他本人对精神分析本身的疑虑"。如果说"真实"的自我难以追溯,哪怕在分析中也是如此,传记又如何有望发现它?"弗洛伊德之所以厌恶传记,是因为它表现了一个人如何声称自己了解另一个人,这主张危险且具有误导性。"而正如菲利普斯挖苦地指出的那样,这恰恰为弗洛伊德本人的传记作者厄内斯特·琼斯和彼得·盖伊制造了难题。

在"心理传记"的第一例《达·芬奇的童年回忆》(1910)中,弗洛伊德把达·芬奇的生平和作品解读为一个精神病和同性恋的故事,病因是他童年时对母亲的爱受到了压抑。那种

---

① 亚当·菲利普斯(1954—),英国心理治疗师、随笔作家。他自2003年起担任企鹅现代经典作品西格蒙德·弗洛伊德翻译项目的总编。

图12 西格蒙德·弗洛伊德与列奥纳多·达·芬奇。精神分析与艺术家；一场传记革命

性压抑的一部分被升华为"对知识的渴望"——如此既能解释达·芬奇的古怪,又能解释他的天才。这种"令人兴奋的推断式"分析(众所周知,它的根据是对一个单词的关键性的错误翻译)所展示的,是"经验观察与伟大理论"之间的一个经典的传记紧张关系。然而,虽然它看似为不可靠的猜想,却为传记式审查提出了一个强有力的挑战。弗洛伊德指出:

> 如果传记研究真的力图理解其主人公的精神生活,它就绝不该像大多数传记那样,出于审慎或拘谨,对他的性活动或性特征保持沉默。

为什么对一个伟人之病态的探索会令人厌恶?因为——他很奇怪地指出——大多数传记作家对其主人公/传主都有一种婴儿般的依恋,希望把他们理想化,把他们变成自己的父亲。(为女性作传的女性传记作者根本没有被弗洛伊德放在眼里。)虽说他们所用的术语不同,但弗洛伊德的心理学研究主张与现代主义者在同一时期期待书写更大胆、更坦率、更有想象力的传记的渴望十分相似。

弗洛伊德对传记的影响是巨大的。在后弗洛伊德时代,就连不相信精神分析的人,也深感有必要陈述其传主的性爱、疾病、梦境和婴儿期。安东尼·斯托尔指出:

> 在心理分析成为常规做法之后,传记作家开始觉得,除非他们能够设法揭示其传主在童年初期所受的情感影响,否则他们的描述就是不完整的。

心理传记如今已经过时了,但在那些不能说绝非弗洛伊德式的当代传记中,仍然能够看到它的语言留下的一些残余痕迹(我们的日常对话也一样),如一场细雪,润物无声。所以克莱尔·托马林才会谈及简·奥斯汀的"童年创伤"和"抑郁",维多利亚·格伦迪宁才会写到特罗洛普①的"疏离"。

精神分析传记——有时与马克思主义的政治分析或社会学数据相结合——把传主放在诊察台上,把他们的行为一一套入某种模式。萨特那些理论先行的文学传记无疑受到了弗洛伊德和马克思两人的影响,把"存在主义精神分析"和社会学背景研究套在传主身上,为的是建构出"自由与制约"的"整体化"陈述,这样的解读——举例而言——使福楼拜(《家庭中的白痴》)成为"一个既神经质又很伟大的作家"。萨特利用自己的传主来证明"一具尸体是人尽可剖的";或者换句话说,"只要使用适当的方法,并获得必要的文件,每个人都是完全可知的"。他使用了一种"全面的综合法,从生到死"。"全面的"传记可以"仿佛从生命的内部"解释人物的生平,与此同时,也把传主变成了"他们的历史时代、阶级形势及其童年制约因素的产物"。但在萨特所写的巨细靡遗的、全然掌控式的热内传和福楼拜传中,没有疾病是不自觉的,没有事件是偶然发生的,没有行为是不可解释的,反而让他的许多读者更向往"不确定和无秩序"。朱利安·巴恩斯的《福楼拜的鹦鹉》的叙述者评论道:

---

① 安东尼·特罗洛普(1815—1882),英国维多利亚时代的小说家和公务员。在他最著名的作品中,有一系列被统称为《巴塞特郡编年史》的小说,围绕着想象中的巴塞特郡展开。

> 看看发生在福楼拜身上的事：在他去世一个世纪后，萨特像一个肌肉发达、不顾一切的救生员，花了十年时间拍打着他的胸脯，往他的嘴里吹气；十年时间里他尽力想把他唤醒，为了使他能安坐在沙滩上，听他实实在在地告诉他，他对他的看法。①

埃里克·埃里克森先驱性的弗洛伊德精神分析法传记《青年路德》(1958)中所呈现的传主经历了源于某种俄狄浦斯情结的"漫长的身份危机"。路德"受困于一种冲突综合征，我们早已经学会辨认那些冲突的轮廓，也学会了分析其组分"。因此路德对粪便的痴迷可以追溯到"他孩童时期被打屁股"的经历。他的"身份危机"始于传说中他二十几岁时有过的一次昏厥。就算那次昏厥并未实际发生，它也可以被接受为"半历史"，只要它有一点点事实基础，能够产生"一种符合心理学理论的意义"就行。

从1920年代到1960年代（甚至更晚），心理传记一直是一个繁荣发展的文类。各种作家、政治家、世界领袖、作曲家、艺术家、科学家和心理学家都被放上了诊察台。这当然引起了反对的声音。美国作家伯纳德·德·沃托曾在1933年说精神分析"被用于确认事实，是一种荒唐的工具"。"精神分析传记……无法让我们获知实际发生的事实。相反，它告诉我们当时一定发生了什么。"然而利昂·埃德尔在1950年代指出，心理学的价值，特别是对文学传记而言，在于展示"消极的东西也可以转变

---

① 译文引自但汉松译：《福楼拜的鹦鹉》，第106页，译林出版社2016年版。

为积极的"，传主可以克服某种"创伤"并把它变成艺术。他的论点让心理传记听起来像是歌颂传主克服逆境的中世纪圣徒传记。理查德·埃尔曼提出，只要"是传记作者在运用心理学理论，而不要让心理学理论操控他"，心理传记就还是有价值的。近年来的心理传记评论家往往同意它那种理论先行的临床方法会产生扭曲的效果，而且精神分析和传记这两种过程的目标截然不同。

20世纪中期的某些最为精湛的文学传记——利昂·埃德尔的《亨利·詹姆斯传》（1953—1977）或乔治·佩因特的《马塞尔·普鲁斯特传》（1959）——如今看来都因为作者的精神分析偏见而有所扭曲。埃德尔解读的詹姆斯的性格成因包括父亲奉承母亲、与哥哥的竞争关系以及一次受伤的重创，将他的小说分析为对这些经历的无意识表达。因此我们看到，詹姆斯青年时代观察到的家中女性占主导地位作为小说的"吸血鬼主题""浮现"出来："害怕女人和崇拜女人：这一爱情主题以惊人的方式出现在亨利·詹姆斯所有的作品中。而通常爱情……对生命本身构成了一种威胁。"有一次，埃德尔根据詹姆斯的一本笔记本中的一连串姓名"莱德沃德""贝德沃德""戴德沃德"，提出："走向婚床就是走向死亡。亨利·詹姆斯因而选择了安全的路径。他一直单身。"埃德尔的詹姆斯有时看上去并不知道自己作为作家究竟在写些什么，"他所服从的是比写作的技艺更深层的指令……是心理学层面的指令"。"他提到父亲……以及提到哥哥时所用的词语，讲述了一个作者从来不打算让我们知道、他自己也不完全知道的故事。"不管埃德尔关于詹姆斯的社会、个人和文学背景的叙述有多丰富和深入，他的传记的这一类时刻都显得太过刻意和幼稚化了。

佩因特的《马塞尔·普鲁斯特传》也同样理论先行，用"母亲"和"疾病"作为钥匙，解锁了普鲁斯特的整个人生和作品。佩因特主张，普鲁斯特"没有发明任何东西"：他伟大的文学成就不是小说而是"充满创意的自传"。他利用自己的经历，对其进行合成并转化，创作了"对普世真理的隐喻式表达"。佩因特从内在证据出发，以事无巨细和"权威性的"精确度，把普鲁斯特人生的每一处细节与他的作品匹配起来。（奇怪的是，他选择不采访普鲁斯特的任何友人，他写这部传记时，他们中有许多人都还在世。）目的是"在艺术家日常的、客观存在的生活的面具之下，发现他从中提取精华、创作出作品的隐秘生活"。

理查德·埃尔曼的《乔伊斯传》是另一部20世纪中期书写文学"天才"的传奇传记，它抵制这一类刻意安排，兴致勃勃地写到乔伊斯对精神分析的矛盾感情。乔伊斯称荣格和弗洛伊德为"瑞士丁丁"和"维也纳当当"，无暇顾及荣格对《尤利西斯》或他的女儿露西亚的分析，但他一直在写一本梦境日记，而且对无意识的运作很感兴趣。埃尔曼的方法是不对乔伊斯进行精神分析，但也很乐意使用诸如"恋母情结"或"矛盾情绪"等术语。他的目的是把他生活中的一切（他也以同情的、幽默的、雄辩的细节讲述了他所知的一切）指向他的作品。他要表达的主题是，天才是如何从平庸和混乱中找到秩序和意义的。因此和更为传统的榜样性传记一样，书中反复出现胜利和超越的语调。在《尤利西斯》的结尾，"精神从束缚中解放出来"。这样的时刻"以最精华的纯粹发生在斑驳的日常生活中"。埃尔曼在自己的恢宏巨著的结尾写道，乔伊斯的生活从表面看来似乎是"不上正轨，好像总是在临时对付似的",但他用作品的"华丽铺张"来应对那一切,使他的生命"达到尊严和崇高的境界"。

这三种复杂的、私密的、最为权威的、备受赞誉的传记在如今看来——事实上一切传记到最后都会被这么看——更像是解读那些伟大作家生平的历史时刻而非绝对权威的纪念碑。

现代主义实验和弗洛伊德病例为传记提供了意义深远的方法。二者都在20世纪中后期为繁荣的、丰富的、流行的英美职业传记传统注入了养料。长篇的、现实的、彻底历史化的传记因为强有力的人物塑造和描述、幽默、坦率和私密而获得了新的活力。其中许多,例如《维多利亚名流传》,都是从前一代人中选取传主的。利顿·斯特雷奇这位打趣的简约主义者居然是这类传记的第一位也是最大的传主,这真是传记历史上的讽刺,不过倒也恰如其分。

迈克尔·霍尔罗伊德的作品(还有他为奥古斯塔斯·约翰和萧伯纳所写的传记)遵循了斯特雷奇的坦率、讽刺、客观和生动的准则。他的斯特雷奇传记呼应了1960年代的性爱自由和政治上的激进风潮,开启了备受欢迎和尊崇的不列颠和爱尔兰传记的一个特别强大的时期。理查德·霍尔姆斯所写的雪莱和柯勒律治传,克莱尔·托马林所写的简·奥斯汀和佩皮斯传,彼得·阿克罗伊德的狄更斯传,维多利亚·格伦迪宁的丽贝卡·韦斯特、伊迪丝·西特韦尔和特罗洛普传,希拉里·斯珀林的艾维·康普顿–伯内特和马蒂斯传,珍妮·厄格洛的盖斯凯尔和霍格思传,约翰·理查森的毕加索传,罗伊·福斯特的叶芝传,菲奥娜·麦卡锡的威廉·莫里斯和埃里克·吉尔传是其中一些出色的例子。

与此同时，大量经过扎实、全面研究的关于作家、艺术家、思想家、政治家、科学家和国家领袖的专业和学术传记（主要）从北美和欧洲的出版机构涌现出来。[某些权威的样本包括：欧文·埃伦普赖斯的斯威夫特传（1962—1983），马克·肖勒的辛克莱尔·刘易斯传（1961），沃尔特·杰克森·贝特的济慈传（1963），贾斯廷·卡普兰的马克·吐温传（1966），威妮弗雷德·热兰的夏洛蒂·勃朗特传（1967）和盖斯凯尔传（1976），卡洛斯·贝克的海明威传（1969），罗纳德·保尔森的霍格思传（1971, 1991—1993），阿瑟·迈兹纳的福特传（1972），R. W. B. 刘易斯的伊迪丝·沃顿传（1975），马修·布鲁科利的斯科特·菲茨杰拉德传（1981）和梅纳德·麦克的蒲柏传（1985）。]没有任何一个领域的主要人物如今还没有被作传，就连次要人物的传记也越来越多。在这些艰苦写作和仔细研究的纪念碑中，有许多都不是自觉地精心写就的，但它们都尽可能全面和准确地为一个意义重大的生命记录了一部编年史。

虽然当代传记并非总是巧妙和严格筛选的，它却受到了关于这一文类的现代主义讨论和实践的影响，因此它坚信要实事求是、幽默和现实主义，强调童年和性经验，在记录公开成就的同时探索内在生活，也不愿（只有几个臭名昭著的例外）进行道德说教、有所偏袒或求全责备。然而传记仍然是虔诚的行为。虽说它希望真实和坦率，它仍然会受到审查压力的束缚，还有可能不得不应对只能部分讲述的素材、日渐消失的证据、不情不愿或不容染指的传主。同样的挑战和矛盾总是反复出现。

第六章

反对传记

文学界反对传记的部分源头是唯美主义,主张艺术作品的独立性和纯粹性,或无道德性。福楼拜和法国象征主义诗人的例子激起的一种观点认为,艺术是不容侵犯的实体,它独立于生活,不该受到传记式解读的侮辱。比方说,波德莱尔认为,"诗歌既有别于、又高于它所在的世界"。作为个人的艺术家,也就是众所周知的叶芝所谓的"那个坐下来吃早餐的充满偶然性和不连贯性之人",本该与作为创作者的艺术家截然不同。"艺术家越是完美,其体内遭受苦难的凡人与善于创作的头脑之间的分离就越是巨大。"T. S. 艾略特高调宣称的艺术独立性得到了詹姆斯、叶芝、福特和其他致力于建构自己原创、自由、权威的审美体系、面具和模式的现代主义作家的支持,无论他们本人对其他作家的传记有多感兴趣。在《芬尼根的守灵夜》中生造出"传记鬼"或"传记恐吓"等词语的乔伊斯在《一个青年艺术家的画像》中发出了艺术非人格化和不可见性的终极诉求:"艺术家,正如造物的上帝一样,存在于他创造的作品之中、之后、之外或之上，隐而不现，修炼得成为乌有，对一切持冷漠的态度，兀自在那儿修剪自己的指甲而已。"这类现代主义宣言对英美学术界的"新批评"派产生了持久的影响，后者贬低传记是"对作品源头的荒谬探求：荒谬，是因为与一部自成一体的作品有关的一切，顾名思义，都只能存在于作品的内部"。现代主义对传记的厌恶也影响了法国新小说派，该派的作者们，例如阿兰·罗布-格里耶，主张"一种纯粹以形式自觉来定义的作者身份"，以及20世纪末（尤其由罗兰·巴特提出）的"作者死了"的批评理论。

那种在理论上将文本与人生分离的主张造成了一种旷日持久的僵局：一边是作为通俗的、不纯粹的、保守的、未经审视的一般读者消费产品的传记，另一边是文学和历史的学术研究。从20世纪中期到20世纪末，人们往往（或遗憾或开心地）指出传记"在很大程度上仍然没有被理论化"，说它"在当代批评理论[和]社会历史撰写领域缺乏合法性"，"看似重要性或科学性不足，不值得研究或教授"。直到近些年，传记才成为各种书籍和文章的常见课题，也才成为固定的学术科目。例如，夏威夷大学自1978年起建立了传记研究中心；不列颠的好几所大学也都开设了传记写作课程和院系；位于堪培拉的澳大利亚国立大学有传记学院，纽约城市大学有传记研究中心，维也纳也有一个学院是专门进行传记历史和理论的"系统"研究的。

另一方面，写给一般读者阅读的传记，特别是关于非文学人物的传记，则基本上全然无视这些批评争论和学术辩论。通俗传记，从低端小报风格的媒体人物大揭秘，到经过扎实研究、附有大量插图的政治人物和历史领袖生平，是一个繁荣发展的行业（虽然每隔几年就会有出版行业的人预言"传记之死"，就像过去总有人预言"小说之死"）。但是风靡全球又无所不在的传记也引发了很多恐惧和憎恶。对传记表达敌意的方式可能不是美学批评，而是与当年反对埃德蒙·柯尔或者和丁尼生或亨利·詹姆斯的立场一样，从道德伦理上反对它的侵入性。通常在"火种保存者"与"出版恶棍"之间发生冲突时，就会出现这种反对之声。1990年代，美国作家珍妮特·马尔科姆强有力地发出了反对传记的主张，就是因为她卷入了西尔维娅·普拉斯的传记作者与特德·休斯的痛苦战斗中，后者一生致力于捍卫自己和孩子们的隐私、掌控普拉斯档案的出版权、监控普拉斯的和关于普拉斯的资料的出版情况，引发了大量来自普拉斯支持者的诽谤中伤：

> 通过传记这种介质，著名死者残存的秘密从他们身上被拿走，倾倒在全世界面前以供观看。的确，写书的传记作家就像职业盗贼，破门而入，在他有足够的理由认为收藏珠宝和现金的某些抽屉里翻查一番，得意地带着战利品扬长而去。驱策着传记作家和读者写作与阅读的窥阴癖和八卦心理被一套学术机制包装起来，那套机制的发明就是为了赋予这种事业以银行业一般温文有礼和踏实可靠的假象。传记作家简直被描述为一种施恩者。他的形象是牺牲数年时间在工作中，不知疲倦地坐在档案馆和图书馆，耐心地与证人面谈。他任劳任怨，他写的书越能反映他付出的努力，读者就越相信他经历了发人深思的文学体验，而不是暗地里倾听闲言碎语和阅读他人的信件。很少有人承认传记的

越界性质,但传记之所以成为一种大受欢迎的文类,这是唯一的解释。读者对这种文类给予的惊人的宽容(无论什么小说,写得哪怕有大部分传记一半糟糕,都不会得到他这般谅解)只有一种原因,那就是他与传记作者在某种令人兴奋的被禁之事上结成同谋:共同悄无声息地沿着走廊前行,站在卧室的门前,试图通过锁眼朝里窥探。

马尔科姆的修辞(翻查、盗贼、窥阴癖、侵犯)呼应了19世纪人们提到私人生活被曝光之恐惧的表达方式。然而传记如今得到的纵容要比那时大得多,且往往都能避开被彻底封杀的命运。新闻报道称"传记是一场血腥运动",或将"传记行业"描述为"挖掘那些受到创伤的、无力辩解的、无地自容的东西,把它们统统付印出版",常常提醒我们,这一文类自古以来便会让人想起丑闻和诋毁,着实可耻。

几乎完全用曝光、快感和惊愕等词汇来讨论传记也是可能的,正如贾斯廷·卡普兰在1990年代的一篇文章中所指出的,"以如今的标准看来,没有窥阴癖、色情的兴奋感的传记就像棒球场上出售的没加芥末的热狗一样索然无味"。他举了几个哗众取宠或报复心切的传记的例子,例如凯蒂·凯利关于南希·里根的传记,说那本书基本上是"开枪扫射",还有受害者们愤怒地攻击传记的例子。例如,杰梅茵·格里尔因为被威胁要为她写一部不受欢迎的传记,便称传记是一种"强奸……是对自我犯下的不可原谅的罪行",还把为在世作家作传之人描述为"知识界的噬肉菌"。娜塔莎·斯彭德愤怒地抗议关于她丈夫斯蒂芬·斯彭德的一部非授权传记"趣味下作"并有"重大错误",抗议某些传记作者的"侵犯技巧"和可能引发的"严重得无法估量的伤害"。

在世传主或其亲戚和遗嘱执行人控制传记作家的努力可能会适得其反。塞林格诉伊恩·汉密尔顿的诉讼案导致汉密尔顿撤回了想出版的传记,但随后又出版了一本书,事无巨细地描述了塞林格阻碍出版过程之事。娜丁·戈迪默起初赞同并鼓励一位传记作家,但后来撤销了授权,因为他违反了他们达成的协议,即对她提出的一切反对意见均予以回应,此外他还拒绝删除她不赞同的段落,这一切让她不得不面对她本想避免的那种八卦宣传。罗纳德·苏雷什·罗伯茨霸道的、指手画脚的趣闻式叙事充满了他本人对个人和政治事务的意见,以及对戈迪默作品及大量有趣的原始素材的细读,遭到了戈迪默在纽约和伦敦的出版商的拒绝,后者原本同意出版他的传记,但拒绝的原因是它不再"有授权"。于是罗伯茨把它交给了一家(可以出口图书的)南非出版社,醒目地在书中收入了戈迪默及其出版商早期对他所说的热情洋溢的话语,并以数不清的访谈交代了她不希望他收入的一切素材的细节,还冷嘲热讽地说戈迪默本人对种族隔离的压抑时代的反抗与她对他著作的"审查"之间显示出矛盾的反差:"她本该代表言论自由的,却希望全面掌控一切。"戈迪默退而对此事保持高贵的沉默,无疑是希望跟他的书相比,自己的作品能名垂青史。

诗人和小说家们反对传记时,往往不是出于伦理道德或保护理由,而是因为在他们看来,传记是一种极度简化,是对他们所做之事的古怪歪曲,也妨碍了一位作家最主要的雄心,那就是凭借自己的作品得到评判、载入史册。有时他们会确保自己

图 13 作为媒体产品的通俗传记：侵犯隐私与哗众取宠

先介入此事。多丽丝·莱辛在她的自传《刻骨铭心》(1994)的第一卷中带着她特有的刻薄说："坐下来写自己时，你难免会有那种最乏味的设问句需要回答。"其中之一是"究竟为什么要写自传？"。答案是："自卫；传记总是要被写的。"当作家们把虚构的传记作家写入作品时，后者通常被描述为愤世嫉俗、机会主义、迟钝粗鲁的魔鬼或装聋作哑的蠢货。因此在拉金的《后辈》中，杰克·博洛托夫斯基是个无趣而粗鲁的美国青年，利用自己的传主菲利普·拉金（"那种老派的天生有本事把事情搞糟的人"）作为学术进阶的必要跳板，而卡罗尔·安·达菲笔下那位虚荣、浅薄、自私的传记作家冷酷地剽窃他的《最好的朋友》："我的脸/出现在你所有的镜中；/它小小的、诧异的双眼，/它的颧骨、性感的下巴，/它一无天赋的、书封上的微笑。"

虚构的传记作家通常被描述为寄生虫、强迫症或跟踪狂。他们出现在（大量）当代小说中，例如佩内洛普·莱夫利的《据马克说》、艾莉森·鲁里的《关于洛林·琼斯的真相》、A. S. 拜厄特的《占有》和《传记作家的传记》、金斯利·埃米斯的《传记作家的胡子》、伯纳德·马拉默德的《杜宾的生平故事》、威廉·戈尔丁的《纸人》和菲利普·罗斯的《退场的幽灵》。例如，在《退场的幽灵》(2007)中，年迈的小说家纳森·朱克曼试图保护去世很久的英雄和他青年时代的导师、隐居作家E. I. 罗诺夫免受"横冲直撞的未来传记作家"虎视眈眈的攻击。朱克曼和怀念着罗诺夫的女人都表达了他们害怕传记这种简化一切和曝光一切的形式，称其是一个才智"低劣"之人对一段重要人生的肆意侵犯，动机无非就是想"让作家受到责难"。朱克曼问自己他是否会成为那位传记作家继罗诺夫之后的下一个目标，继而对自己叹道:"也真是令人震惊啊!一个人无论取得了怎样的造诣和成就,最终也难逃传记审判的惩罚。"

当它不被诅咒时,小说中的传记便是怀疑主义的小说探讨的主题,其中最著名的是以下这个频繁被引用的形象,来自朱利安·巴恩斯的《福楼拜的鹦鹉》:

> 网,可以下两种定义。根据不同的视角,你可以选择其中的一种。通常情况下,你会说,它是一种有网眼的器具,用于捕鱼。但是你可以在不破坏逻辑的情况下,反过来下定义,像一位诙谐的词典编纂者曾经做过的那样。他称网是一种用绳子编织起来的有很多洞眼的东西。
>
> 对于一部传记,你也同样可以这么做。当拖网装满的时候,传记作家就把它拉上来,进行分类,该扔回大海的就扔回大海,该储存的就储存,把鱼切成块进行出售。但是想想那些没有捕获上来的东西:没有捕获到的东西往往多得多。一本传记,站立在书架上,胖乎乎的,十分小资的样子,自负,端庄:一先令的传记故事将给你所有的事实,十英镑的传记故事还将给你提供所有假设。但是请想一下,那些没有被捕获的一切,那些随着传记主人公在临终时呼吸了人生最后一口气后而消逝的一切。①

"反对"传记,无论是出于道德原因还是美学原因,个人原因还是职业原因,几乎总是与有关财产、所有权和控制的争论有

---

① 译文引自但汉松译:《福楼拜的鹦鹉》,第40页,译林出版社2016年版。

关。这类争论往往是焦虑而痛苦的,充满了敌意和妒忌、竞争和疑惑。传记不是什么中立地带:它会引发强烈而狂热的感情。在特德·休斯的呼喊中,有绝望、愤怒甚至无望:"希望我们每个人都能拥有他或她自己人生事实的所有权。"

第六章 反对传记

第七章

公众人物

对于本人就代表社会性世界的传记作者而言，社会性自我才是真实的自我；只有和他人并存时，自我才会存在。独体自我是对社会性自我的压力，也可能是后者的反响，但它没有独立的生命。

一个伟大的人……是被他不得不行使的职能塑造出来的；他不自觉地设立的人生目标是把自己的人生变为一件艺术品……如此他便获得了……那种雕塑一般的特质，使他变成了艺术家的绝佳模特。

防卫性和保护性做法包括用于保护某一个体在他人在场期间有意培养的那种印象的技巧……表演中所需的表达连贯性指出了我们的人性自我与社会化自我之间的重要差异。作为人，我们想必是每时每刻都会有不同的情绪和能量差异的生物。而作为在观众面前表演的人物，我们绝不能受到任何波动的影响。

由理查德·埃尔曼、安德烈·莫洛亚和欧文·戈夫曼提出的上述观点，全都把个体生命描述为在公共剧场演出的、被建构出来的表演，是由选择和职能塑造的，有赖于他人的接受和认可。这样的描述不仅适用于"伟大的人"：人人都在建构"呈现出来的自我"。社会人类学家欧文·戈夫曼还提到了"印象管理"和"整套自我生产的方法"。如他所说，有时，表演会失败，或作为一种愤世嫉俗的策略得到曝光，或整个建构付出的代价过大。他引用萨特所举的风趣的例子："一个希望**表现得**专注的小学生，眼睛紧盯着老师，认真地倾听每一个字"，这位小学生会"因为表演专注的角色而筋疲力尽，到最后一个字也没再听进去"。

传记与身份的表演面向，也就是个体的公共角色的关系如何？一部传记的传主越是抛头露面，这个问题就越紧迫。显而易见的答案是普鲁塔克提出的，并得到了培根和德莱顿等评论家的赞同，那就是传记的任务是绕到公共表演的背后，向我们展示在家中"赤身裸体"的真实的人。然而上述引文表明，真实的自我可能很难与表演的、公共的、社会性的自我区分开来。理查德·埃尔曼认为传记是"社会性自我"的记录，言外之意就是，传记作家可能对任何一种其他的自我无话可说。

亨利·詹姆斯在1877年初遇罗伯特·勃朗宁时，十分惊异自己看到的那个毫无诗意的、粗鲁的、喋喋不休的公共自我。他半开玩笑地觉得一定有"两个勃朗宁——一个深不可测，一个俗不可耐。前者从不在社交场合露头，后者不会有一丝一毫让人联想起《男人与女人》"。后来，这一想法启发了一部题为《私人生活》的短篇小说，叙述者面对要表演一个备受赞赏的作家的难题,意识到有**两个**他存在:"一个走出去,另一个待在家里。一个是天才,另一个通身俗气。"

文学传记作者通常并不试图把那个表演的、公共的、日常的自我从私下里写作的自我中剥离,而是寻找它们之间的联系。那正是文学传记的意义所在,不过有些成功、有些失败就是了。对哲学家的传记作者而言,生活和工作这两种表演之间的关系是一个更有争议性的领域。人们往往认为关于这一点只有两派观点,具体如下:"一派认为传记掌握着理解哲学家作品的秘诀,另一派认为理解哲学家的生活与理解他的[原文如此]作品无关。"可以说,哲学家的著述或许和他或她的私人生活没有多大关系,正如一套数学命题或化学公式与数学家离婚或化学家的早餐没什么关系一样。但更可行的做法似乎是持中间立场。对某些类型的哲学家而言,例如奥古斯丁、维特根斯坦、苏格拉底,他们的生活**就是**作品,或者说他们的生活与作品有关,哪怕是对立的关系。因此可以说(没有任何著作的)苏格拉底的"生活就是作品,作品就是生活"。维特根斯坦关于语言和伦理的著作《逻辑哲学论》的哲学评论家们常常会指出同样的联系:"无论谁在阅读或试图阅读《逻辑哲学论》时,都难免会想,它的作者究竟是个怎样的人……我们对他那个人了解得越多,他与他的哲学作品的联系和分离就越有趣。""他把自己献给了哲学研究。""真的很难创造一个生命,其内心的煎熬和自愿承担的逆境能够更好地诠释源于维特根斯坦的生命哲学的困惑了。"维特根斯坦的话,诸如"如果你不愿意知道你是谁,你的写作就是一种欺骗",或"你所写的关于自己的一切,都不如你本人更加真实",可能会使他的评论者们希望把对个人的评价与对哲学的评价联系起来。雷·蒙克所写的维特根斯坦传记表明,他"既不希望,也不认为自己可以,把成为自己想成为的那种人的任务,与成为那种他想成为的哲学家的任务截然分开"。

哲学和传记也不无关联,因为某些哲学家(如笛卡尔或海德格尔)所思考的关于自我的现实与我们如何理解自己的问题,也是传记关注的问题。可以说,传记的目标也很像哲学的目标。正如维特根斯坦所说,也正如雷·蒙克主张的那样,那个目标就是达成"那种能够看得见联系的理解"。传记关于叙事建构如何能够代表"真实的"人生或自我的焦虑,或许类似于或接近于哲学上关于人类行为如何呈现和理解的论述。的确,就此而言,哲学可以让传记作家心安。如果像哲学家阿拉斯代尔·麦金泰尔系统阐述的那样,"人类行为"是"表演出来的叙事",如果"我们都在活出我们自己人生的叙事并……用我们活出的那种叙事来理解自己的人生",那么"叙事的形式就适用于理解他人的行为"。正如在哲学中一样,这类叙事的有效性或许有赖于故事是如何建构出来的,"带有何种程度的特殊性"。然而无论讲故事的人的具体特质如何,传记作家都无须害怕(至少像某些哲学家论述的那样)"对一个人的人生进行叙事性论述一定会歪曲那段人生"。

当人生是由行为和叙事而非语词或观念组成的,传记作家就会面对不同类型的挑战。传记与那些一生的全部成就都是公共行为(政治家、银行家、医生)、一生的工作不涉及语言(作曲家、画家、数学家、运动员)或通过表演他人的语词或音乐(演员、歌唱家、钢琴家)的传主又有何关系呢?传记该如何讲述这类公共角色的故事,或者面对像亨利·詹姆斯评价西奥多·罗斯福时所说,是"纯粹的行为"的人物时,传记该如何渗透到他们私密的自我中去?

领导人或活动家的传记必须把传主的主要表演置于其背景中去,也就是造就他们的政治条件、他们所在的或对其加以改造的社会,以及他们的种族、阶级、民族和性别,当然还有他们身边的许多其他人物。传记作家必须意识到,人们对于他们传主的职业的观点——也包括他们自己的观点——是不断变化的。比方说,如今人们对一个19世纪到非洲的基督教传教士的生平的看法可能与150年前不同。体育人物、摇滚明星或电影演员的传记不但要考察个体的个性和生平故事,还要写到环绕在他们身边且往往创作了主要表演的整个班底,包括星探、演出承办人、经理、经纪人、制片人、资助人、公关人员、摄影师、导演、作家和观众。"猫王"的传记根本无法忽略汤姆·帕克上校;披头士乐队的集体传记也无法略过布赖恩·爱泼斯坦不提。任何人,如果是通过职业为人所知的,无论是法官还是园艺师,乐队指挥还是厨子,都要求传记作家掌握当时当地围绕着该职业的势力网络和社会假设,考察一下对传主及其职业的态度是否随时间发生了变化,并厘清公共表演与个人身份之间的关系。

任何公共生活也都有其秘密,有其古怪离奇和矛盾之处,传记作家的任务就是先要发现、继而理解它们。关于这一点,最幽默也最动人的评论当属W. H. 奥登写于1930年代的十四行诗《名人志》,诗中所写的正是一个英雄的公共人物无法为外人道的私人生活:

> 一先令传记会给你全部的事实：
> 他父亲怎样揍他，他怎样出走，
> 少年作什么奋斗，是什么事迹
> 使得他在一代人物里最出风头：
> 他怎样打仗，钓鱼，打猎，熬通宵，
> 头晕着攀新峰，命名了新海一个：
> 最晚的研究家有的甚至于写到
> 爱情害得他哭鼻子，就像你和我。
>
> 他名满天下，却朝思暮想着一个人，
> 惊讶的评论家说那位就住在家中，
> 就在屋子里灵巧地做一点细活，
> 不干别的；能打打唿哨，会静坐
> 会在园子里转转悠悠，回几封
> 他大堆出色的长信，一封也不保存。①

这首诗既是爱情故事，也是关于传记局限性的讽刺诗，还是关于人生选择的沉思——就最后这种情况而言，第二个人物是第一个人物的平行人生，是"未曾选择的路"。而这表明，有必要为第二个人物，那个籍籍无名的被爱之人，写出另一种类型的生平故事——与标准老套的"一先令传记"大为不同，此人悄无声息地过着日常的生活，不渴求声名，也不关心不朽。

关于一个公众人物的传记作者会面对怎样的挑战，一个雄

---

① 此处所选为卞之琳先生译本。

辩的例子就是美国金融家和艺术收藏家J. P. 摩根,"世界上最有权势的银行家",他的野心、势力和控制总会让人们把他与他的童年偶像拿破仑相提并论。摩根的传记作者、在摩根去世大约70年后才开始为他作传的琼·施特劳斯不但要掌握皮尔庞特·摩根图书馆的(绝大部分是未经开发的)海量档案,还要为这个本质上的美国故事研究和掌握19世纪末的大企业、银行业、股市、新闻界和政界、美国铁路、钢铁工业、国际船运业、博物馆、收藏、房屋装修和镀金时代社会的情况。与此同时,她要写的人物是出了名的充满戒备和古怪之人,"寡言无礼、低调、既不好内省也不善表达",有魅力、有说服力、抑郁、有臆想病、保守、风流成性又对妻子不忠、贪婪索取又慷慨慈善。有时很难猜测他那标志性的大蒜头鼻子后面的脑袋里究竟在想些什么。

还有一个问题。在一个世纪的时间里,人们对摩根的态度没有多少变化:他"被右派赞美为推动经济进步的英雄,被左派诋毁为代表资本主义贪婪的标志性人物"。随着她年复一年的研究进展,施特劳斯发现她太过执着于"愤世嫉俗的大亨"这个先入为主的成见了。她揭示的证据改变了整个图景。她与自己的假设背道而驰,努力改写自己的叙事,力图使笔下的人物更加真实和复杂。

这类对迷思的修正性工作或重新思考可能会构成关于公众人物的任何严肃传记写作的一部分。世俗的圣徒传记的确仍在被诉诸笔端。理想化的榜样传记至今仍然常常被当作苦难少数群体的代表、革命领袖、政治囚犯或被压迫者的代言人的哀歌。某些群体投入了巨大的政治和文化资源来维护某些人物不可侵犯的传记形象,例如甘地、史蒂夫·比科、特蕾莎修女、马丁·路德·金、罗莎·卢森堡、切·格瓦拉，当然还有最重要的，纳尔逊·曼德拉。埃利克·伯默尔最近对曼德拉进行了分析，即那个被"英雄符号化"为"世俗的圣人和民主的架构师"，一位"被过于赞誉，以至于已经变得平庸乏味，由于被挖掘出意义而使得公共面孔背后的那个人的意义全然消失了"的全球和国家"偶像"。她指出，南非或其他任何地方的传记作家都不可能以除"国家的象征意义"之外的其他方式来书写这个人物。在这里，传记呈现总是与口头证词、新闻报道、传记片、纪录片和"标志性"照片联系在一起的，例如切·格瓦拉头戴贝雷帽（1960年代，它出现在每一位西方马克思主义门徒的墙壁或套头衫上），或像曼特尼亚①所画的死去的耶稣一样，弹痕累累地躺在玻利维亚的医院里的标志性照片。在许多情况下，神圣化之后便会产生反弹，转向另一个极端，即中伤诋毁。因此各种各样的揭秘中会写到特蕾莎修女自私的右翼政治观点、路德·金的性活动，或格瓦拉在哈瓦那监狱里的暗杀行动以及他对同性恋的虐待。当然，这些揭秘也各有其政治和文化目的。

和19世纪对"国家传记"的重视一样，一旦传主代表或启迪了某种关于国家神话或特性的辩论，传记的政治就会作为焦点凸显出来。这会让我们想到丘吉尔、撒切尔、戴高乐，尤其是英国最伟大的海军英雄霍雷肖·纳尔逊。《新版国家人物传记辞典》的"纳尔逊"词条说他在死后被"神化"，其过程就始于绘画作品突出了"他倒下的时刻，其构图完全是在模仿基督被从十字架上抬下来的样子"。一部由海军历史学家约翰·萨格登所写

---

① 安德烈亚·曼特尼亚（约1431—1506），意大利画家，也是北意大利第一位文艺复兴画家。

图14 切·格瓦拉：一个传奇的制造和摧毁

的2004年的纳尔逊传记花了很长篇幅应对一个被大大神化的公众人物的挑战。萨格登写了900页，才写到纳尔逊生涯的一半。他的故事始于1805年的纳尔逊之死，以及逾"30个纪念他的纪念碑"的竖立。"纳尔逊的传记也是纪念碑，"他指出，"也同样反映出观念的变化。"早期由詹姆斯·克拉克和约翰·麦克阿瑟所写的两卷本传记出版于1809年，在很大程度上参照了萨格登所谓的纳尔逊自传的"沾沾自喜的碎片"，后者把自己的人生写成了一个充满毅力、英雄事迹和公共职责的模范故事。纳尔逊与艾玛·汉密尔顿夫人长期的情色关系为人所尽知，因此作者们无法宣称自己不知道这些，而"只是宣布不讨论这一主题"，只关注他"辉煌的公共性"。骚塞写于1813年的英雄传记"巩固了这位海军上将作为真正的不列颠英雄的地位"。（虽然骚塞，如他自己所说，不是什么海军专家："我面对那些海洋名词就像一只猫走进了瓷器店，战战兢兢，生怕犯错和露馅。"）1849年由托马斯·佩蒂格鲁所写的一部全面而坦率的传记被"轰出了市场"，因为它证明了纳尔逊的孩子是他通奸所生。19世纪末，纳尔逊的传记把他呈现为"海军成就的终极典范"。《国家人物传记辞典》指出，在第一次世界大战爆发前的那些年，海军联盟正在推广"特拉法加日崇拜"，将纳尔逊视作"不列颠帝国及其庞大海军力量的象征，对抗焦虑的护身符……纳尔逊其人……已经基本上被忘记了，只剩下了英雄纳尔逊"。他的热忱、天真、傲慢、活力、缺乏外交技巧、易感和自我中心都在一座纪念碑里被抹平消失了。

第二次世界大战期间，纳尔逊的英雄形象再度变得有用。萨格登指出，"极度呆板的劳伦斯·奥利弗……在一部英国电影中塑造了这位海军上将,为的是赢得美国人的支持,共同对抗欧洲的独裁者"。一部由卡萝拉·欧曼所著的1946年的经过扎实研究的传记和1958年对纳尔逊信件的编辑让这个人物变得有了深度。但到了1960年代,萨格登指出,海军历史就不合潮流了,纳尔逊的爱国品质也看似"过时"了。关注点越来越集中在他的性爱征服而非海军征服上,最终的高潮是特里·科尔曼出版于2001年的"勇敢地离题万里"但难免"复仇心切"的传记。萨格登对读者许诺说自己会抛开"偶像崇拜"和"诋毁责难"而倾向于"公正客观的评判"。然而,虽然他写出了纳尔逊的复杂特质,遣词造句却并没有完全摆脱英雄主义的语调:"纳尔逊总是把自己的事业当成国家的事业。无论对错,他的斗争为的是王国的利益。他的荣誉就是国家的荣誉,他的胜利就是国家的胜利。"古老的传记传统死而不僵。

纳尔逊总算是受到敬爱和尊敬的人,而暴君和大屠杀的凶手们又为传记作者提出了不同的问题。如果传主是希特勒、斯大林、尼禄、伊迪·阿明、波尔布特或罗伯特·穆加贝,某些政治传记作家倒是不会再出现谄媚倾向(导致迈克尔·霍尔罗伊德称他们是"历史的男仆")。威吓的、大肆毁灭的公众人物要求传记论述足够稳定和清晰,特别是当神话的传播已经远超现实,或者如拿破仑或亚历山大大帝那样,传主既曾被理想化,也曾被贬损丑化,两阵营旗鼓相当。

对那些遗臭万年的公众人物进行精神分析,诸如将希特勒写成童年创伤的产物等等,一直十分流行。有趣的例子是丽贝卡·韦斯特1947年所写的爱尔兰纳粹鼓吹者、"哈哈勋爵"威廉·乔伊斯的传记,它就是一部关于自卑情结的研究,或者尼古

图15 纳尔逊：国家英雄及其纪念品

拉斯·莫斯利为他的父亲奥斯瓦尔德·莫斯利①所写的痛心的回忆录，一切事关控制："他觉得自己能像决定语词那样决定世

---

① 奥斯瓦尔德·莫斯利（1896—1980），英国20世纪政治人物，不列颠法西斯联盟的创始人和领导者。

界。"关于那些可怕的公众人物,还有些不那么理论先行的论述,像艾伦·布洛克写希特勒和斯大林的双人传记,将主要焦点放在事实和背景上,但就连这种思考缜密的写法也会在不经意间透露出愤慨之情:

> [《我的奋斗》的]700页给人留下的持久印象,是希特勒的思想如此粗野庸俗,精明算计又冷酷残暴……毫不容忍,没有人性……然而同样惊人的,是无论他的观点多么粗鄙,它们居然那么连贯和自成一体。为生存而斗争是一项自然法则;铁石心肠是最大的美德……权力是精英种族的特权;大众只能执行命令……武力是获得巨大成就的唯一途径……斯大林想必心服首肯。他们两人是20世纪"**糟糕的简化者**"最难对付的代表人物,19世纪的历史学家雅各·布克哈特曾经预言,这一类人将是接下来那个世纪的典型特征。

这种克制的语气与近期的一部更偏民粹主义的斯大林传记形成了鲜明对比。西蒙·塞巴格·蒙蒂菲奥里有着21世纪得天独厚的优势,能够看到此前无法接触到的俄罗斯档案和资料。他的《斯大林:红色沙皇的宫廷》(2004)和《青年斯大林》(2007)用冒险故事或惊悚故事的喧嚣劲头追溯斯大林职业生涯的惊人事实,避开了精神分析解读或历史教化,但也常常会停下来提醒我们,这个热闹的故事是一个心理不健康的屠杀者的故事。这是对悲惨的世界史的过山车式解读,这部传记不是冷静的思考,而呈现了一连串动作与事件。

斯大林的统治毁掉了数百万人的人生，产生了数百万部未曾写出的传记。这样的历史时期抹去了那么多人类故事，让那么多故事只能通过口头证词、沉默的照片或令人惊悚的猜想重新建构，在颠覆的同时，也强化了传记写作的意义。我们希望找出，比方说，安妮·弗兰克生平的一切细节；另一方面，我们也很清楚，世上有那么多被消灭的人生故事，它们的细节已经沉入史海，无处搜寻了。

从这样的历史荒原中浮现出来，在公众心中产生强烈共鸣的非凡人生故事，可能尤其会引发争议。能挺过斯大林主义、有着最强大生命力的人物之一，是作曲家肖斯塔科维奇，这是个极端复杂的传主人选。肖斯塔科维奇极为多产的音乐人生（1906—1975）跨越了俄国革命、战争年代、斯大林统治下的"大清洗"和强制艺术家噤声、"社会主义现实主义"的约束、共产主义、冷战和文化解冻。他得到了每一种荣誉，受到了每一种攻击，从早期的声名鹊起到党内威胁，从对他"妥协的"音乐宣言的批判，到他去世后、后苏联时代对他的讽刺和隐性颠覆的修正主义认同。除了"笼统的陈词滥调"和被迫道歉外，肖斯塔科维奇拒绝对自己的作品发表任何言论，这当然无可厚非，他还把某些作品压在箱底多年，他在音乐中复杂的、密码式的对自我指涉和典故的运用，以及常常被附加在他的作品之上的官方标题，这一切都让传记作家感到障碍重重。

在他生前和死后俄罗斯的巨大变化，使人们对他的态度也产生了天翻地覆的变化。苏联讣告和早期传记赞美他坚持"苏联人道主义和国际主义理想"。而在他晚年忠实的助手所罗门·伏尔科夫1979年的《见证》一书出版之后，他的名声又急转直下,伏尔科夫声称该书誊抄了肖斯塔科维奇充满悔恨、讽刺、自责而反动的私人谈话,并称肖氏为"圣愚"("yurodiry")。然而伏尔科夫的可靠性被许多人质疑。随着大量一手描述和信件开始浮出水面,随着肖斯塔科维奇伟大作曲家的名声开始为全世界所知,传记作家不得不清除"猜测和意识形态的倾向性"。劳雷尔·费伊2000年的那部一丝不苟、严谨仔细的传记在传主的各个差异极大的版本中做出了谨慎的选择。她说:

> 为肖斯塔科维奇作传仍然随时会碰到政治和道德的弦外之音。最极端的情况是,它不过是用一种正统观念取代了另一种……真正信仰共产主义的公民作曲家被另一个同样无法令人信服的滑稽形象所颠覆,自始至终都是秘密异见人士……我们迫切地需要把那个真实的人与这些迷思剥离开来。

试图用作曲家的生平解读音乐总会遇到难题,加上肖斯塔科维奇的动机和意图中所隐藏的漫长的生存之战,让一切变得更为复杂难解。举例而言,他最著名的四重奏,即(写于1960年的)第八弦乐四重奏,是一部充满强有力情感的作品,写于他访问德累斯顿之后,被某些评论家说成是"用作品为德累斯顿大轰炸的幽灵招魂"。然而,在写作这部作品之前不久,他因为被迫成为一名共产党员,刚刚经历了劳雷尔·费伊所谓的"情绪崩溃"——他曾经明确拒绝入党。伏尔科夫引用他的话说这部四重奏虽然是"作曲系布置的'揭露独裁主义'的命题作品",事实上是一部"自传"作品。这部四重奏中用了先前作品的典故,

图16 自我隐藏的作曲家：作品中的人生

还用他的名字的首字母作为反复出现的动机,因而只要不是"盲人",都能看出来这一点。一封写于1960年的信证实了伏尔科夫的说法:"我写了这部观念落后的四重奏,估计谁也不会感兴趣……扉页上完全可以写'献给这部四重奏的作曲家'。"2002年,肖斯塔科维奇的女儿加林娜回忆父亲当时曾说:"我刚刚写了一部为纪念自己而作的作品。"然而这部四重奏大获成功之后,他接受劝说,把献词改成了"献给独裁主义的受难者们"。他或许是被迫写出这句献词的,但(正如他的儿子马克西姆·肖斯塔科维奇所说)它也的确可以被作为自传解读。"如果你觉得'独裁'的意思就是'极权主义'的话,就没有什么矛盾了。肖斯塔科维奇正是可怕的极权主义政权的无数受难者之一。"劳雷尔·费伊跨越这些模棱两可的方式,描述了这部四重奏对首次倾听之人的强大震撼,虽然他们"在理解……这部四重奏的内容时得到了错误的引导……但他们还是被它悲剧的深度震撼了"。他们意识到它"在本质上"是自传性的,尽管这部四重奏中有许多对他自己的早期曲谱的引用,并坚持运用他的"铭词",这被认为是暗指他"与黑暗的反动势力的斗争"。

从1936年到1937年这段时期,那些势力对肖斯塔科维奇的压迫尤其难以承受。在他的歌剧作品《姆钦斯克县的麦克白夫人》演出大受欢迎之后,《真理报》上的一篇著名的文章对他进行了很有威胁的批评,题为《是混乱,不是音乐》。据说肖斯塔科维奇曾想过自杀。他当时写了自己的《第四交响曲》,带有两个冗长而低沉的外部乐章,一个葬礼进行曲,最终缓慢地逐渐进入弱音(*pianissimo*)和沉默。这部交响曲是1936年完成的,但一直没有公开演奏,也许是因为外部压力,也许是他害怕报复。

它在他的抽屉里压了25年，直到1961年才演奏。相反，他在1937年写的《第五交响曲》是一部更为传统的作品，在定音鼓声中迎来了欢欣鼓舞的结尾，大众好评如潮。这部作品被给予的副标题是"一个苏联艺术家对于公正的批评给出的现实、创造性的回答"，这很可能是一位新闻记者给出的副标题，而肖斯塔科维奇默认了，或许"是为了获得平反而使用的一个小花招"。《第五交响曲》大获成功后，他对指挥家鲍里斯·海金（后者当时还不知道有《第四交响曲》）说："我用强音（*fortissimo*）和大调结束了整部交响曲。大家都说它是一部乐观主义的、积极向上的交响曲。我很好奇，如果我用弱音和小调结束整部作品，他们又会说什么呢？"1970年代，他对伏尔科夫说：

> 我觉得大家都很清楚《第五交响曲》中所要表达的东西。那种欢快是被迫的，受到威胁创作出来的……就好像有人一边用棍子打你一边说，"你得欢快，你得欢快"，你颤抖着起身，大步走开，嘴里嘟囔着，"我们得欢快，我们得欢快"。那是一种什么样的美化和颂扬？

肖斯塔科维奇的人生是传记作家们面对的巨大难题，是因为他们要通过作品解读他的人生，要信任证人的话，要了解当时的历史背景，要确定应该相信什么，还要试图寻找公共生活的隐秘目标，当然还有最重要的：解释天才。

全然通过表演度过的人生也为传记作者提出了不少其他难题，那些名人似乎把自己全然呈现在了公共领域。对这类人物，特别是女性人物的评论数不胜数，不留情面，其中大多没经过思考、没价值、没根据、没教养。她们人生的丑闻和悲剧似乎只是她们表演的一部分,是她们声名鹊起的条件。她们的视觉形象贡献了巨额的媒体销售,对某些人而言,在她们去世多年之后仍然如此。然而——或者说因此——她们的生平仍然是个谜团或无法深入研究,被她们自身的神话吞噬了。这类名人足够有名,一听名字就知道是谁:嘉宝、卡拉丝、戴安娜、"猫王"、皮雅芙、麦当娜、迪伦——要求传记作家区分"偶像"形象和现实、神话和事实、表面和内心。而且总有可能,根本没有什么内心,只有表象和表演。

在所有这类现代传主中,最诱人也最难以捉摸的,或许仍然是"玛丽莲"。如果不那么严谨地使用"传记"一词,把照片书、图片集、剪报和引语、"她的传奇的遗产"展览、关于她神秘死亡的耸人听闻的惊悚故事("证据指向有预谋的杀害")、女性主义解读、她的故事的虚构版本,以及关于"明星"的建构和女性身体通过好莱坞体系被商品化的社会学分析全都包括进来的话,关于玛丽莲·梦露的传记堆积成山。

所有的版本都承诺呈现一个更深入、更真实、更逼真的玛丽莲。像大部分"明星传记"一样,所有版本都承诺"深入到公共形象之下,去探寻背后的真实生活",并把她"呈现为一个人,而不是电影界的发明",但它们全都在循环利用八卦,再现那些最著名的形象。许多人提到与传主特殊的亲近感:"我立刻被她吸引了。"几乎所有人都直呼其名——要么是她的真名诺玛·珍妮/琼,要么是她在好莱坞的艺名。每一个版本都在讲她童年所受的虐待和忽略、疯狂、强奸、性、美、"金发傻妞"的形象、吸引力、人格魅力、色情、好莱坞和电影业、宣传、名气、权力、婚姻、离婚、流产、堕胎、嗑药、酗酒、自毁和死亡。只要为"玛丽莲"写传记，就无法不应对这些热门话题，也无法避开乔·迪马乔、阿瑟·米勒或肯尼迪兄弟不提。那正是这一任务吸引人的地方：这是一个轰动的、充满象征意义的美国故事。

那些传记全都在写她的矛盾：浑然天成与人工雕琢，既好表现又内心脆弱，有趣又悲惨，既是金发傻妞又是天才演员，妩媚又拘谨，性爱经验丰富又看似天真无邪，童贞又成熟，速朽又不朽。一部对这类描述的综述《玛丽莲·梦露的多面人生》（2004）写到了50多年来的变化，从"性象征到悲悼的象征，从一个承诺性解放的希望故事到一个关于孤独有多危险的警示故事"。作者萨拉·切奇威尔指出，我们永远看不到那个"隐秘的"玛丽莲。一部又一部传记中反复提到的二元对立——"公开/私密、虚假/现实、幻想/真实"——无法揭示一个"真正的"自我：它们只是在重复"她深陷入其中的那个终极的非此即彼"。

最深入解读的版本由三位著名美国作家所著（分别是乔伊丝·卡罗尔·欧茨、诺曼·梅勒和格罗丽亚·斯泰纳姆），全都选择了双重身份作为传记的主题。诺曼·梅勒在他1973年的题为《玛丽莲》的小说中对"玛丽莲"的解读是，她既突显了女人最终极的妩媚本质（描述的笔调充满情欲，"一个丰满的……性爱天使……就像一个水蜜桃在眼前爆开，汁水四溅"），又是一位女性拿破仑，是人类挣扎的原型故事的史诗级代表。乔伊丝·卡罗尔·欧茨在她虚构的爱神与死神的寓言中，让金发美女"玛丽莲"一生都受到黑暗王子的追求，她半是微笑的面具（"金发碧眼的女演员……住在她丰满的身体里，像一个被填入到人体模型中的孩子"），半是被抛弃的"不幸的小女孩"，总是在寻找自己失踪的父亲。

女性主义作家格罗丽亚·斯泰纳姆对梦露的悲剧命运发出了愤怒的哀叹，她在1987年把她描述为两个人格的分裂，一面是可怜的、缺爱的诺玛·珍妮，玛丽莲一生都在试图逃离那个身份，另一面是公开的、人工建构出来的玛丽莲，她"把自己的身体当作天赐，用来获得爱与认可"。"一旦公开的策略失败，那个私密的诺玛·珍妮似乎就再次变成了她唯一的命运……于是抑郁和无望席卷而来……身体变成了她逃不出的囹圄。"这部把梦露作为"典型的女性牺牲品"的保护性挽歌如今看来或许过于宽容了，但它的基调与许多男性笔下的"性感女神"的更衣室讥笑和影射形成了强烈对比。安东尼·萨默斯1985年的版本尤其尽是挖苦："对父亲形象的需要似乎变成了玛丽莲幻想绣帷的一部分"；"一天，玛丽莲总算打破了自己不守时的记录"；"玛丽莲如今在纵容自己对权谋的热爱以及她性情中丑陋的一面"。观察视角的鲜明对比所展示的，不仅是对一个女性超级明星的不同解读，它还让我们看到了传记一直以来的传统，即对非凡的著名女性的写法与出色的著名男性的写法截然不同：那些女人可不是"行为榜样"或令人钦佩的楷模，而是怪咖，是警示，是恐惧、欲望或嘲弄的对象，是危险的事故，是制造麻烦的地带。

两个最著名也最广为复制的"玛丽莲"形象是她穿的白裙在地铁通风口被风吹起来的宣传照（大大的诱人的微笑、漂亮的双腿、滑稽的性感、自然的生命力与都市矫揉造作的结合、展示给满脸崇拜的旁观者的形象），以及经由另一位迷人的、短命的媒体人物安迪·沃霍尔处理的那张脸。沃霍尔为玛丽莲作画始

图 17 极度曝光：人生被压扁为神话

于她1962年去世后不久，部分原因是他自己一直痴迷于名声和暴烈的早逝，与之并列的还有持枪的"猫王"和肯尼迪死时的杰基。在《玛丽莲双联画》（1962）中，他利用一幅经过剪裁的宣传照，把它放大并转而用丝网印刷出来，成为玛丽莲50幅一模一样的形象的基础，最终呈现为每组5张的10组图片。在双联画的左半边，头像是彩色的，用的是绚丽的金色、粉色和蓝色。右半边是黑白的；有些头像被黑色墨水涂抹得很严重，有些则逐渐消隐几近虚无。"一排又一排重复的头像让我们想到了邮票、广告牌海报，但或许首先想到的……是电影胶片……这是对生的赞美，对死的哀悼。"沃霍尔的玛丽莲形象与我们希望传记达到的所有目标背道而驰。它们是扁平的、重复的、平庸的、合成的、新闻式的、不做揭露的。然而它们也为她的人生故事提供了一个非常合适的版本：极度曝光，一下子就能辨认出来，除了已经建构出来为大众消费的东西之外，没有传达任何内容。在那个意义上，它们是现代世界公众人物传记的视觉对应物，不可挽回地被压扁为神话。

第八章

讲述故事

"天哪，传记到底该怎么写？"1938年，弗吉尼亚·伍尔夫受托为好友罗杰·弗赖伊作传时自问道，我在1996年为伍尔夫作传时，也在开头引用了这句话。这看似一个提示性的开篇，因为她的生平故事已经为人所熟知（所以我无须以"阿德琳·弗吉尼亚·斯蒂芬生于1882年1月25日"来开头），而她本人也对传记及其惯例很感兴趣，发表过很多论点，也表示过不少疑虑。我并没有完全按照时间顺序书写她的生平，而是在部分程度上按照主题组织，灵感来自她本人在评价她笔下人物的内在生活以及写及时间、记忆和视角时所用的实验性小说策略。任何传记叙事都是一种人为建构，因为它不可避免地涉及选择和规划。没有一位传记作家会写下传主从生到死的一生中每天所做、所说、所想的每一件事，那样一本书写下来所花的时间，会比传主的生命还要长。鉴于我的传主本人就对生平故事该如何讲述很感兴趣，我决定强调传记叙事的人为性质，关注她一生中的特定方面，关注不同的"自我"。其他当代传记作家也同样进行过形式方面的实验,嵌入关于其与传主关系的明确的评价,利用小说策略,或在时间和视角选择上动用巧思。

这里要提出一个与这些不同类型的实验不同的观点。历史学家-传记作家罗伊·福斯特面对叶芝把自己的人生变成神话及其对为叶芝作传之人的强烈影响时,希望"还原一个人参与生活、参与历史的感觉:特别是在他的国家的历史中,在一个有着剧烈波动和斐然成就的时代"。"[叶芝的]自传规定了一种安排他的生平的方式,即按主题安排的方式……然而说到底,谁也不是按照主题来过一生的,而是一天一天地过下去;无论W. B.叶芝有多伟大,在这一点上也不例外。"福斯特使用稳定的时间顺序和大量调查研究所得的细节,让我们看到了叶芝关于自己的权威叙述背后的东西。然而詹姆斯·奥尔尼在一篇对这部传记赞赏有加的评论中问道,是否真有可能始终如一地遵循时间安排,"不按主题前行而是逐日记述"。他引用保罗·瓦莱里的话,想知道"是否有任何人试图写一部传记,并在撰写的每时每刻都装作丝毫不了解传主人生的下一刻会发生什么,就像传主自己对此一无所知一样"。此外他还指出,福斯特的传记"开始是按时间顺序记述,但逐渐退化成了完全阐释性和主题性的叙事,在顺序上既有回溯又有前瞻"。

伍尔夫和叶芝的例子表明,不同类型的叙事或许适用于不同类型的传主。如果我为之作传的是,比方说,马丁·路德·金、伊恩·佩斯利或贝娜齐尔·布托,在传记中实验新的形式大概就没什么好处。对那些传主来说,更有用的做法是从美国奴隶制和民权运动的历史写起,或者从新教统一主义在北爱尔兰的复杂根源,或者从印巴战争和布托王朝的兴起开始写起。

就政治或历史传记而言，叙事形式必须稳妥可靠，才能为大块的事实提供扎实的支撑。

如本书开头所说，讲述生平故事没有什么确定的规则。但的确**有**一些无法回避的惯例。无论是怎样的故事，涉及哪一个种族、民族、性别、阶级、语言或历史，始终都要有时间、地点、人物和事件。大多数传记都是向前继续发展的，将主要人物置于当时的背景中，在情节中插入关于传主作品的论述、历史复杂性的论述或次要人物的记录，并使用描写和观察、文件资料、证人证词、外围资料和第一手知识来建构整个故事。传记作家或许会选择关注传主一生中的某一个特定部分。他们或许会从死亡开始写起，或者讲一个能说明问题的传闻，或者开篇先写传主死后名声日隆，而不是从出生第一天开始写起。他们或许会在叙事中留下空白和谜题，也可能试图消除这些。他们或许会引入道德判断或个人观点。但他们都希望给读者一个尽可能全面、清晰和准确的关于传主生平的版本。他们也都希望特定的事实和细节加起来能给出关于该传主的总体认识，从而使他们的传记能够暂时性地就一个问题给出最真实的答案：她，或者他，是个怎样的人？

然而就连那个基本清单也会引发很多其他的可能性。我在上文中假设的金、佩斯利或布托的传记也可能会有不同的开头：描写1968年在孟菲斯的洛林汽车旅馆阳台上听到一声枪响，一个人随之倒下；讲讲1930年代安特里姆郡的巴利米纳[①]；描写一

[①] 英国北爱尔兰安特里姆郡的一个镇，被认为是北爱尔兰圣经地带的中心城市，拥有很大的新教社群。

下位于信德省①布托家族陵墓内的布托的坟墓,如今已经变成了一处圣地。开头当然希望引起读者的兴趣,但它们也确定了传记作者的基调。以下是几个例子:

"世上热爱雪莱的人比比皆是,但这本书不是写给他们的。"理查德·霍尔姆斯在全书的第一句话告诉我们,他不打算搞偶像崇拜或浪漫化,他要质疑那些标准版本,他十分大胆,也很清楚自己这么做的原因,此外他也知道**他的**《雪莱传》会是另一个版本,但绝不是最终的版本。

"丽贝卡·韦斯特(生活于1892—1983年间)的故事是20世纪所有女人的故事。"维多利亚·格伦迪宁开宗明义,掷地有声,读者一眼便知她的传主为何重要、她有何感想,以及她可能选择了怎样的叙事视角。

"这是最好的时代,也是最坏的时代。在亚历山大和伊迪丝·蒲柏位于伦敦的家中,伊迪丝正期待着她第一个孩子的到来。"蒲柏学者梅纳德·麦克在他1985年那部权威的诗人传记的开头呼应了狄更斯,暗示这将是一部宏大的历史故事,有着19世纪小说丰富厚重的质感。

"1984年2月1日,一个背着帆布背包、脚穿步行靴的英国人大步迈进比勒陀利亚艾琳区的一座平房。他有六英尺高,金发盖住了宽大的前额和那双专注的碧眼。他只比最终杀死他的疾病早了一步。他45岁,却像个少年一样生机勃发。"尼古拉斯·莎士比亚的《布鲁斯·查特温传》一开始所用的现在时态就让我们看到了一个惊心动魄的冒险故事和关于一个非凡之人

---

① 巴基斯坦东南部一省,首府卡拉奇是巴基斯坦的旧都。

的一部鲜活生动的报告文学。

"1933年6月的一个炙热的下午,拉尔夫·埃里森以游民身份第一次也是最后一次出行,充满恐惧却又极为渴望地登上了一列从俄克拉何马城出发的烟熏火燎的货车,那是一趟危险的旅程,他希望能把他带到位于亚拉巴马州塔斯基吉的大学;几十年后,他在俄克拉何马成长的记忆仍然萦绕在他的脑际,同时也成为他的灵感源泉。他曾在很长时间里压抑那些记忆,然后终于有一天,他开始迫切地需要它们。"阿诺德·兰佩萨德的《拉尔夫·埃里森传》的这段冗长的开头展示了过去与现在、灵感与回忆之间复杂的相互作用。它告诉我们,我们将开启一段全面详尽的传记之旅,这位传记作家对传主的内在和外在生活无所不知。

在上述的每一个例子中,或者你希望选取的任何例子也都一样,开头几句话便确定了整部传记的视角。传主不同,这种视角的差异也极大。要为一个从未被写过的不知名的人物作传,虽说不得不证明该传记存在的价值,但也无须声明自己的特殊性并贬低此前的版本,反复被写的人物的传记则必须如此。基调和视角通常都会表明这是一个不为人所知的传主、一次复苏、一个打破偶像的举动、一个关于某一位在世之人的中期报告,还是一次修正主义的回归,因为有了新材料或者揭开长期保守的秘密的诀窍,旨在彻底改变我们对某个众所周知的故事的既有观念。

一部记述弗吉尼亚·伍尔夫所谓"无名之人"的传记,和一部重述莎士比亚或拿破仑生平的传记,其目标大相径庭。由于传记总会涉及当时当地的社会和文化政治,因此关于何为主要何为次要、何为获准何为惊人、何为主流何为另类的假设,也会随着时间的流逝而发生变化。关于传记不断变化的标准的一个惊人的例子,是近年来"群体"传记流行起来(这是一个古老的文类,又焕发出新的生命力),起因就是人们有志于将传记这种形式民主化,此前它往往都关注单个的主要人物,另一个起因则是,用珍妮·厄格洛的话说,希望"发现我们原本可能遗漏的过往"。

这类传记可能是关于王室家族或政治王朝的,但它们也可能会挑战一种"主流话语"。在1990年代为一个移民澳大利亚的工人阶级、共产主义妇女作传的一位女性主义传记作家,就给选择"另类"传主的传记作家提出了权威性的问题:

> 如果一位传记作家更希望建构的历史版本不是,比方说,库克船长仅凭一人之力以大英帝国主义之名霸占了澳大利亚,而是他手下一位水手的版本,或者一位抵抗侵略的土著人的版本,该作者就会遭遇一连串的问题。其中一个核心问题就是:谁来开口说话?

为另类或隐蔽的人生,特别是女性生平所写的传记——琼·施特劳斯为亨利·詹姆斯的妹妹艾丽丝所著(1980)、布兰达·马多克斯为乔伊斯的妻子诺拉·巴纳克所著(1988)、克莱尔·托马林为狄更斯的情妇艾伦·特南所著(1990)、埃里森·莱特为弗吉尼亚·伍尔夫的众仆人所著(2007)的传记——都源于女性主义对"鲜为人知的历史"的兴趣。在《一间自己的房间》(1929)中,伍尔夫想象女人的生命有许多未曾被讲述的故事,

"这些永远无人知晓的生命仍然不会被记录"。伍尔夫关于一段未被记录的人生可能是什么样子,或者它会如何被讲述的观点在100年后或许看似不同了。正如非裔美籍传主、原住民、生活在后殖民和发展中国家的人、男女同性恋的生平故事或工人阶级的历史一样,女性主义传记(它当然会和其他那些类别中的任何一个重合)也是一个不断变化的文类,而非固定不变的存在。

这一文类经历了一个反对"单独的领域"、国内优先事项、温和的隐形或反常的例外等历史假设的时期。然而女性传记已经不需要再像1980年代的卡罗琳·埃尔布兰那样,询问一个女人的生平故事"应该是什么样的",或者指出"如果历史上曾经有过女人的传记的话,它们全都是在标准化讨论的约束下写成的"。掘出无名之人或为女人的生平故事争取新的地位和意义(这一提高认识的过程被称为"对改变公共领域的女性主义计划至关重要")的阶段,如今已经可以用过去时态谈及,历史学家卡罗琳·斯蒂德曼在《过去时态》中就是这么做的:"关于已经失去、永远不可能完全还原的一切的感知,已经成为现代女性历史最强有力的修辞工具之一。"(当然,她补充道,还有工人阶级历史也是一样。)

讲述女人的故事往往是从差异谈起的。任何关于女人传记的讨论都会指出:"事实上,书写男人和女人生平的过程**是**不同的……什么是可以接受的、什么是可能的、什么是想象和尝试的,往往都存在差异。""如果男人的传记故事主要都是外部事件,那么大部分写女人的传记都是外部和内部事件的混合物。""或许的确如此,大多数女人在很大程度上都是根据她们的私人生活被评判的,而男人的评判标准几乎清一色是他们的公共生活。"如果为作家作传,"那么如果作家是女人的话,能够获取作者的隐私的愿望似乎更为强烈"。女性作家的生活如果有被虐史、心理疾病、自我伤害、自杀,则往往会在传记中首先被当作受害者或心理学病例,然后才会被当作职业作家。在伍尔夫或普拉斯的传记中,围绕着这类故事所要达成的目标显而易见,或者举例而言,戴安娜·伍德·米德尔布鲁克关于自杀了的忏悔型美国诗人安妮·塞克斯顿的传记,就利用了传主与心理分析师谈话的录音带。即便为女人作传的各式各样的陷阱——个人化、过于保护、魔鬼化、惩罚式、居高临下式——如今已经不那么普遍了,但如何为越来越多地出现在公共领域的女性作传仍然是一大难题。"如今仍然很难解释女人在公共领域的影响力和声誉",一位女性主义批评家谈及斯蒂德曼为20世纪初期的社会主义政治家玛格丽特·麦克米伦所写的传记时如是说,后者试图设法移除"挂在女人传记的脖颈上的内在性的重负",讲述一个只涉及"公共生活"的故事。

男性和女性传记的一个迄今仍然存在的差异,体现在以何种姓名称呼的问题。如今的传记早已不再称传主为"奥斯汀小姐""伍尔夫夫人"或"盖斯凯尔夫人"了。但由于在漫长的历史时期,相对于男性伟人的传记,关于女性的传记更为关切和私密,一部关于著名英国女性小说家的传记大概仍然会从头到尾称传主为"简"或"夏洛蒂",而著名的男性英国小说家通常不会被称为查尔斯或安东尼。有些为女性作传的作者解决这个问题的做法是把名换成姓,或者把童年昵称换成婚后姓名,取决于讨论的是早期还是晚期生涯,是私事还是职业。《新版牛津国家

图18 "井口"女孩：群体传记、女人生平、劳工生活

第八章 讲述故事

人物传记辞典》也对此有过缜密思考：

> 玛丽安·埃文斯[笔名乔治·艾略特]（1819—1880），小说家，一生中用过好几个名字：玛丽·安妮·埃文斯（出

生姓名)，玛丽·安·埃文斯(1837年起)，玛丽安·埃文斯(1851年起)，玛丽安·埃文斯·刘易斯(1854年起)，以及玛丽·安·克罗斯(1880年)。

在《国家人物传记辞典》的网络版中，使用这些名字中的任何一个，都可以查到乔治·艾略特。

姓名称呼只是传记书写传主的视角的一个标志。该视角的建构从该书的封面、书名和目录页就已经开始了。这些类文本元素或许在一定程度上是出版商而非作者所为，但它们设定了人们对某一类叙事的期待值。

简·奥斯汀的生平故事通常都有类似的封面，因为当前只有一幅她的存世肖像，由她的姐姐卡桑德拉所画。但所选的肖像是原版的、看上去很不高兴、一点也不浪漫的形象，还是经过下一代人修饰过的、温文尔雅的版本，也是对当前传记视角的一处暗示。

书名也能说明问题。一部名为《莎士比亚：传记》的传记与《尘世间的莎士比亚：莎士比亚如何成为伟大的剧作家》或《1599年：威廉·莎士比亚生命中的一年》所提的主张截然不同。目录页也是叙事的组成部分。一部关于济慈的传记如果只是由有编号的章节组成（因此在目录页中没有各章题目），就比目录页中含有诸如"济慈先生的出身"、"神性的火花"或"致命打击"等章标题的传记少了一些规范性或小说气质，但后一种的导览作用也降低了不少。有些传记作家（多数是欧洲人）在各章标题下又有节标题，像索引那样。因此让-伊夫·塔迪耶1996年的《马塞尔·普鲁斯特传》就会有诸如"驳圣伯夫：仿作

图19 奥斯汀小姐；简·奥斯汀；简……

504、为写作而生 507、金融投机与善习 509"等标题,给人的印象是这部传记的组织结构有着极高的精确性。有些传记作家在给各章确定标题时模仿传主的做派,仿佛假装自己是小说家。因此阿德里安·弗雷泽为兴致昂扬、装腔作势的爱尔兰小说家乔治·穆尔所写的传记就有诸如"国家警察协会时代的小唐璜"或"拿撒勒的耶稣与伊伯里街的圣贤"之类的章标题。

各式各样的选择——是完整的脚注还是缺少脚注,索引中是否包括标题、概念、名字以及插图的尺幅和编号等等——都与讲述故事的方式,以及目标读者群体有关:是一般读者还是专业读者,是普及读物还是学术专著。篇幅也暗示了视角的选择。为什么这位传主被认为值得写 900 页?或者为什么一位大名鼎鼎的传主的传记只有 150 页?作者省略了什么未写?

传记的叙事技巧确定了基调并创造了一个观察角度,随着事实的披露和故事的进展,这些叙事技巧却往往很少被注意到。偏爱激烈的高潮("这是她一生的转折点"),或者戏剧化总结("亨利·詹姆斯选择了安全的路径。他一生未婚"),或悬疑期待的叙事("他后来会对这个决定懊悔不及,从她再也未曾回望过的这一刻起,旧日的生活就一去不返了"),用利昂·埃德尔的话说,试图"借用某些虚构的技巧,却又不至于变成虚构的传记"。有些传记作家相对更为随意地使用"一定曾"、"也许曾"、"或许"和"大概"。有些人使用某种预先确定的理论来讨论传主生活中的重大事件——疾病、某种家庭关系、某种伤害或虐待——把那种理论套入生平故事中。有些传记作家使用大量的描写和场景设置,有些则为笔下的人物创造共情的而非仅仅基于事实的描写。这是一种冒险的策略,但如果传记作家本人

也是小说作家,会产生不错的效果,例如V. S. 普里切特为屠格涅夫所写的文笔优美的短篇生平故事:

[屠格涅夫的母亲]瓦尔瓦拉·彼得罗芙娜是个情感极其充沛的人,体现在生活的各个方面。她圆肩驼背,浓眉下的一双黑眼睛大而有神,额头又宽又低,脸上的皮肤粗糙,有不少麻点子,嘴很大,显得肉感又严厉,举止傲慢而任性无常。她像个孩子一样固执,当然,像许多丑陋的女人一样,她也可以变得很迷人,让朋友们很喜欢,而且很风趣。她的一生过得很可怜。

传记作者提到传主时使用的语调是讲述传记故事时必不可少的一环。传记作者有时会问自己,他们觉得传主比真实的年长还是年轻,需要给予同情的保护还是敬畏的仰慕。现代传记作家往往采用一种幽默的、讽刺的、处变不惊的语气,清楚地表明人性的任何一面都不会让他们厌恶。约翰·哈芬登在那部非凡卓越又特立独行的《燕卜荪传》的一开始便回忆往昔,讲起自己1960年代曾在都柏林圣三一大学听过他读书,声音太小,谁都听不清:

一个女人在教室后面愤怒地喊道:"大声点儿,你这个愚蠢的老东西!"因为尴尬,整排整排的脖颈缩进肩膀,但后来我被暗中告知,那个大声说话的女人是燕卜荪的妻子——所以还好。

有性描写时,常常会用到这种冷静而带有喜感的语气。安德

鲁·莫申在描写拉金对色情作品的兴趣时,讲了这么一个故事:

> 有一次,看见拉金怯懦地在店外犹豫,老板走上前谨慎地问道:"要捆绑片吗,先生?"

菲奥娜·麦卡锡在确定自己对埃里克·吉尔与(他的)孩子和动物进行性行为的态度时,大胆地写道:

> 就连他……付诸实践的兽性实验本身也不算特别可怕或惊人,虽然它们让人觉得古怪。更奇怪的事情已经被记录下来了。

传记

更加庄重的传记视角把传主的故事变成了原型悲剧,例如迈克尔·雷诺兹在史诗性的海明威传记的结尾写道:

> 他的故事是一个经典的美国故事:年轻人按照自己的雄心壮志改造自己,成功地超越了梦想,最终因竭力忠于那个已经成为的自己而筋疲力尽。……这是个古老的故事,比任何文字都要古老,古希腊人想必会认出故事里的这个人。

不那么富有同情的传记用传主来练习打靶,试图把他们拉下神坛:

> 那些对贝娄的霸权构成威胁的作家们总是被他冷眼相待;那些在文坛稳稳落于下风的作家则被他看成"艰辛工

作"中的同志,贝娄喜欢那么称呼他的职业。

贝娄……抨击宽松的六十年代不加管制的性行为,与此同时,他可没有错过任何一次纵容自己的机会……他似乎希望自己喋喋不休的说教能在某种程度上缓和他放荡不羁的性冲动……无力的超我总是不停地责备内疚的本我。

传记必然会涉及作者与传主的关系,哪怕是下意识地。完全中立的传记叙事是不存在的。并非每个人都赞同安德烈·莫洛亚的观点,即任何传记的传主都是"传记作家表达个人情感的媒介"。并非每一位传记作家都选择说"我"。并非每个人都愿意将自己的生活与传主的生活等同起来,像以下这位梭罗的心理传记作者那样亲密无间:

在过去几年里,我与梭罗的"婚姻"的发展出现了新的、意想不到的动向……记录……我自己与梭罗之间的"对话"……让我深入了解了我们之间关系的这些动向……我最初写下这些对话时,受到妻子和我会孕育新生命这个可能性的启发,感觉到自己即将进入新的人生阶段。确认了我们的确即将有个孩子之后,我毫无疑问进入了一个新阶段……我现在很好奇,自己将为人父之事是否会对我与梭罗的关系产生影响,是怎样的影响……我希望还能与梭罗保持和发展这种持久的"你我"的关系。

传记或许的确是一种婚姻关系。如果传记作家认识或见过他们的传主,他们对传主的个人感情就会在某种程度上影响作品的

134　**基调**。塞琳娜·黑斯廷斯与罗莎蒙德·莱曼建立了艰难的友谊,后者对她的传记作家越来越苛求和急躁,这样的关系给她对传主的看法蒙上了阴影。萨缪尔·贝克特对他的传记作家戴尔德丽·拜尔的典型反应——"他说他不会帮助我,但也不会妨碍我"——让她十分自由,但也因为觉得"他不希望我写这本书,如果我放弃,大概会令他十分愉快"而十分困扰。就算传记作家没有见过传主,他们也会遇到阻力或妨碍,朱迪丝·瑟曼发现科莱特[①]正是如此:"她强烈鄙视一切形式的共情,根本不想为人所知。"

一切传记都试图占有传主(A. S. 拜厄特的小说《占有》和《传记作家的故事》充满激情地探讨了这个观点),但某些传记作家占有得更多,或者说占有欲更强。有些人试图爬到他们的表皮之下,与他们同床共枕,穷尽一生探求他人的生平。诺曼·谢里花了好几十年时间追踪格雷厄姆·格林和堆积如山的资料,在传记故事中处处留下自己的痕迹,甚至包括他本人"追踪""我们的人"[②]的插图,以至于谢里看似已经变成了"这部传记的事实上的传主,而格林更像是谢里自我描述的一个载体"。有些传记作家要与那些坚信传主属于自己的竞争对手角逐数年。有些像主人一样占有传主,以至于他们的人生永远和传主联系在了一起;博斯韦尔的约翰逊、埃德尔的詹姆斯和埃尔曼的乔伊斯都是这样。但传记作者应该清楚,如罗伯特·格雷夫斯所说:

[①] 西多妮-加布里埃尔·科莱特(1873—1954),法国20世纪上半叶作家,于1948年获得诺贝尔文学奖提名。

[②] "我们的人"指格雷厄姆·格林的小说《我们在哈瓦那的人》(1958)中所讽刺的英国情报部门人员。

让死人复活
并非什么精彩的魔法……
规训你的笔写出他的笔迹
直到签下他的名字时
和签自己的一样自然。
像他一样跛行,
说出他说过的脏话;
如果他穿黑色衣服,你也一样;
如果他的手指粗壮,
设法让你的也变得肿胀。
收集他的私密物件——
戒指、风帽或书桌:
围绕着这些元素建起
一个让贪婪的亡灵
熟悉的家。
就这样让他复活,但切记
那埋葬他的坟茔
如今或许不再空虚:
你裹着他污渍斑斑的外衣
孤独地躺在那里。

　　完全占有的传记作家,也就是那些知晓一切的人,其所遭遇的叙事问题不同于那些几乎一无所知的传记作家。莎士比亚就是明显的例子。他的许多传记作家在视角选择上差异极大,可以说是天差地别,有浪漫的猜想、顽固的侦察、历史背景论、后现代不确定论等等。试举两个21世纪的实例来说明这有着怎样广阔的可能性。查尔斯·尼科尔像个侦探那样,从莎士比亚出庭作证的一份1612年的诉讼案件记录中寻根溯源,查到他一度住在克里泼盖特的一座房子里,那时他公开的身份"不过是个住户,是住在楼上房间里的先生:一位莎士比亚先生"。追查莎士比亚的踪迹到锡尔弗大街只不过需要细读几个分散的线索,一些猜想,再加上创造:结果是打开了"窥见莎士比亚生活的一扇意想不到的小窗"。与之相反,乔纳森·贝特在《时代的灵魂》中采纳了一种广阔、全面而包容性的视角,那是一部精彩的莎士比亚学术传记,并非严格按照时间顺序写作,而是按照"人生的七个阶段",来揭示他所谓的莎士比亚的文化基因。

詹姆斯·夏皮罗在他撰写莎士比亚生命中的一年的"微型传记"中指出,要从莎士比亚的作品中追溯他的情感,仿佛那些戏剧是一面"双面镜",最终难免会陷入"循环和武断"。然而莎士比亚的传记作者们总会面对无法抵制的诱惑,要从他们所知的一星半点中挖掘出尽可能多的宝藏。拿莎士比亚一生中众多令人困惑而难以理解的事实之一,也就是他年仅11岁的儿子哈姆内特在1596年夭折之事来说吧,莎士比亚就此事没有任何言论被记录下来。哈姆内特和哈姆雷特这两个名字的相似,以及莎士比亚在剧中扮演哈姆雷特父亲的鬼魂之事,曾引发大量近乎虚构的猜测,从乔伊斯的《尤利西斯》中斯蒂芬·迪达勒斯[①]关于父亲身份的理论,到安东尼·伯吉斯在1970年的一部关于吟游诗人[莎士比亚]的通俗图画书中随便地宣称"莎士比亚把

[①] 《尤利西斯》中的重要人物,是詹姆斯·乔伊斯在文学上的另一个自我。

自己的儿子变成了疯狂的丹麦王子"。夏皮罗的传记是这样讲述哈姆内特之死的：他弄清了莎士比亚在1596年8月听到这个噩耗时的精确所在（在巡演）；他告诉我们会是斯特拉福德的哪个邮差带给他这个噩耗，以及邮差是否知晓莎士比亚其人。他确定莎士比亚不会有时间回家参加葬礼，并告诉我们莎士比亚对儿子知之甚少，可能都很少见儿子。"这不是说，"夏皮罗接着说，"他没有发自内心地感到悲痛。这甚至能够解释他为何在那一两年里作品数量都减少了。只是我们不知道。"在讨论《哈姆雷特》时，他仔细探究了这部剧的文本版本、伦理、文化参考、制作、表演和观众反应，却只字未提这部剧可能会与莎士比亚死去的儿子有何关系。

其他传记作家采用了不同的基调。帕克·霍南1998年的传记逐条追溯了一切已知事实和公认观点的源头，自称"公正客观"，却还是容忍自己做一点情绪化的猜测。以莎士比亚1596年之后的创作为依据，霍南猜想哈姆内特之死"改变了他"，"他似乎从未走出丧子之痛的阴霾"，以及这件事"让他变成了一个更深刻的艺术家和思想家"。不过与斯蒂芬·格林布拉特那部大胆的畅销传记《尘世间的莎士比亚：莎士比亚如何成为伟大的剧作家》（2004）相比，霍南的猜测还算温和。格林布拉特先是说"至少没有理由认为莎士比亚只是草草埋葬了儿子，毫发无伤地继续生活"，随即就跳跃到毫无根据的猜测，说"深深的伤口再次撕裂"，导致"一场哀悼和回忆的危机"，"心灵所受到的困扰或许能够解释《哈姆雷特》巨大的爆发力和内在性"。对格林布拉特来说，"只是我们不知道"显然是不存在的。彼得·阿克罗伊德2005年的传记则平衡了两方的观点：

图20 威廉·莎士比亚?

就这样，莎士比亚失去了唯一的儿子……此事对剧作家的打击当然是无法估量的。他或许变得极度沮丧，也或许并非如此。他或许也曾像许多其他人一样在不间断的辛勤写作中寻求逃避。尽管如此，人们在解读他这个时期的剧作时，一直把这个死去的儿子考虑在内……的确，莎士比亚此后受到启发写出了哈姆雷特的悲剧，不可能是纯粹的巧合。

每一位传记作家都会偶尔有猜测和推论。如果他们的研究工作做得出色，对传主的了解足够深入，那么他们的猜想就值得一听。但纯粹主义者或许会说，传记应该把有些东西留给小说，或者像《恋爱中的莎士比亚》或《成为简·奥斯汀》这样的传记片：想象中的交谈、虚构的梦境和幻象、没有证据的情感危机、未经证实的精神创伤。无论传记怎么努力把鱼放回水流中，提供详细的资料，探求文化背景和社会特性，尽可能地诠释人物，传记写作中还是会有模糊和缺失的部分。传记作家或许——而且多半应该——在自己的写作完成时，仍然觉得有许多事情是他们永远也发现不了的。

传记的最后一页往往透着一股依依不舍的气息，仿佛写作的结束也意味着一段关系的终结。传记作者很难在叙述其传主去世时不带任何情感，只把那当成故事的下一个、最后一个事件而已。大多数传记作家觉得有必要做出告别的姿态。写作一部传记的最后一个阶段是分离和放手，是认识到这个被建构出来的版本注定是片面的、暂时的。在那么多辛苦的重构和表述工作即将结束时，传记作家留在那里，看着他们曾经痴迷之人离他们而去，渐行渐远，消失在无声的往昔。

索 引

(条目后的数字为原书页码，见本书边码)

A

Ackroyd, Peter 彼得·阿克罗伊德 7, 91, 138

Addison, Joseph 约瑟夫·艾迪生 48

Aelfric 埃尔弗里克 25

Alcibiades 阿尔西比亚德斯 22—23

Alfred the Great 阿尔弗雷德大帝 28

Alexander the Great 亚历山大大帝 19—20, 21, 29, 78

alternative or hidden lives 另类或隐蔽的人生 126—127

Amin, Idi 伊迪·阿明 111

Amis, Kingsley 金斯利·埃米斯 99

'ana' "语录" 37, 44—46, 73

anecdotes 传闻，逸闻 6, 19—22, 31, 36—38, 44—48, 55—56, 59, 61

Aristotle 亚里士多德 22, 23

Arnold, Thomas 托马斯·阿诺德 58, 76—77

Aubrey, John 约翰·奥布里 36—38, 78

Auden, WH W. H. 奥登 8, 104

Augustine, Saint 圣奥古斯丁 103

Austen, Jane 简·奥斯汀 44, 87, 91, 129—131

Austin, John 约翰·奥斯汀 16

authenticity 本真性 10, 11, 43, 46—49

authorized biographies 授权传记 10, 12, 58

B

Bacon, Francis 弗朗西斯·培根 30, 38, 102

Baker, Carlos 卡洛斯·贝克 91

Barnacle, Nora 诺拉·巴纳克 127

Barnes, Julian 朱利安·巴恩斯 15, 87—88, 99—100

Barrett Browning, Elizabeth 伊丽莎白·巴雷特·勃朗宁 6, 81—82

Barthes, Roland 罗兰·巴特 94

Bate, Jonathan 乔纳森·贝特 136

Bates, Walter Jackson 沃尔特·杰克森·贝特 91

Baudelaire, Charles 夏尔·波德莱尔 93

Beatles 披头士乐队 105

Beckett, Samuel 萨缪尔·贝克特 135

Bede 比德 10, 25

Bellow, Saul 索尔·贝娄 134

Bentham, Jeremy 杰里米·边沁 15

Bhutto, Benazir 贝娜齐尔·布托 123—124

Bible《圣经》19—21, 44

Biko, Steve 史蒂夫·比科 107

Biography Channel "传记频道" 18

biopics "传记片" 17—18

Bair, Deirdre 戴尔德丽·拜尔 135

Boccacio, Giovanni 乔万尼·薄伽丘 29

154

Boehmer, Elleke 埃利克·伯默尔 107

Bolokowsky, Jake 杰克·博洛托夫斯基 98

biography 传记
   attitudes to 态度 2, 12, 15—17, 30, 52, 68—71, 93—100, 105
   beginnings in 最初 12—26
   changes in 变化 67, 72
   criticisms of 批评 27—28, 93—100
   definitions of 定义 1, 5—6, 56, 73—74, 78
   definitive 权威性 18, 89—90, 124
   form of 形式 13—14, 18, 21, 34, 40, 42, 46—48, 54, 63, 66, 72, 79, 82—83
   history of 历史 11, 13—14, 24, 30, 123—125, 127
   methods of 方法 89, 76, 82, 87, 90
   national approaches to 国家视角 12, 63—66, 68—69
   origins of 起源 11—12, 21—25, 32—33
   rules for 规则 6—18, 123—124
   tone of 基调 80, 124, 126, 132—134
   types of 类型 8—10, 14, 33—34, 72—92, 125—132

Boswell, James 詹姆斯·博斯韦尔 3, 11, 34, 39—58, 80, 82, 135

Boyle, Robert 罗伯特·波义耳 34

Bradford, Gamaliel 加梅利尔·布拉德福德 79

Brontë, Charlotte 夏洛蒂·勃朗特 59—62, 91

Brooke, Rupert 鲁珀特·布鲁克 73

Browning, Robert 罗伯特·勃朗宁 68—69, 102

Bruccoli, Matthew 马修·布鲁科利 91

Bullock, Alan 艾伦·布洛克 111

Burckhardt, Jakob 雅各·布克哈特 112

Burgess, Anthony 安东尼·伯吉斯 137

Burney, Fanny 范妮·伯尼 43, 44, 45

Burns, Robert 罗伯特·彭斯 58

Butler, Samuel 萨缪尔·巴特勒 72

Byatt, AS A. S. 拜厄特 135

Byron, George 乔治·拜伦 58

C

Caligula 卡利古拉 20—21

Campion, Edmund 埃德蒙·坎皮恩 25—26

Capote, Truman 杜鲁门·卡波特 17

Carlyle, Thomas 托马斯·卡莱尔 3, 13, 55—57, 69—73, 79—80

Catherine, Saint 圣凯瑟琳 26

Cavendish, George 乔治·卡文迪什 30

Cavendish, Margaret 玛格丽特·卡文迪什 45

Cavendish, William 威廉·卡文迪什 45

celebrities 名人 17, 68—69, 116—121

Cellini, Benvenuto 本韦努托·切利尼 31

censorship 审查 9—10, 55, 57, 86, 98

characterization 人物塑造 22—24, 46, 90

索引

Chatwin, Bruce 布鲁斯·查特温 125

chronology 编年史 8, 42—43, 62—63, 122—124

Churchill, Winston 温斯顿·丘吉尔 107

Churchwell, Sarah 萨拉·切奇威尔 118

citation of sources 引用资料来源 10—11

cities 城市 6

Clarke, James 詹姆斯·克拉克 109

classical lives 古典人物传记 22—23, 29—34

Cleopatra 克莱奥帕特拉 7, 78

Clough, Arthur Hugh 阿瑟·休·克拉夫 76—77

Coleman, Terry 特里·科尔曼 111

Coleridge, Samuel Taylor 塞缪尔·泰勒·柯勒律治 13, 55—56, 91

Colette 科莱特 135

collective lives 集体传记 6, 31, 34—37, 62—65, 126, 128

comedy 喜剧 38, 42, 50—51, 55, 75, 81, 133

Compton-Burnett, Ivy 艾维·康普顿-伯内特 91

concealment and omissions 隐瞒和省略 9—10

Constant, Benjamin 邦雅曼·贡斯当 82

contents pages 目录页 130

conventions 惯例 123—124

conversation 对话 24—25, 42—43, 46, 52—53, 55, 111

Cousin, Victor 维克托·库赞 68

Cross, John 约翰·克罗斯 63

culture 文化 18, 48, 68, 73, 136—138

Curll, Edmund 埃德蒙·柯尔 48—49, 95

Cuthbert, Saint 圣人卡斯伯特 10, 25

Cyrus 居鲁士 22

D

da Vinci, Leonardo 列奥纳多·达·芬奇 15, 84—85

De Gaulle, Charles 夏尔·戴高乐 107

de Vere, Edward 爱德华·德·维尔 38

De Voto, Bernard 伯纳德·德·沃托 88

death 死亡 12, 23, 87, 94—95, 138, 140

Defoe, Daniel 丹尼尔·笛福 44

deities 神祇 6

Descartes, René 勒内·笛卡尔 103

detail 细节 3, 8, 17, 59, 61, 78

detective work 侦探工作 1, 81—82, 136

dialogue 对话 22, 44—46

diaries 日记 23, 36—37, 62—63

Dickens, Charles 查尔斯·狄更斯 58—59, 91, 125, 127

dictionaries 辞典 34, 64—68, 80

Dictionary of National Biography (DNB)《国家人物传记辞典》66—68, 80, 107, 109, 129

Diogenes 第欧根尼 19—20

disciples 门徒 21—22, 52, 58, 72

Donne, John 约翰·多恩 11, 13, 34—36

double identity 双重身份 118—119

Dowden, Edward 爱德华·道登 58

传记

156

dramatization 戏剧化 6—7
Dryden, John 约翰·德莱顿 5, 24—25, 28, 34, 48, 102
Duffy, Carol Ann 卡罗尔·安·达菲 98—99

E

eccentricity 怪人 62
Edel, Leon 利昂·埃德尔 10, 88—89, 132, 135
education 教育 16—17, 18, 22, 65, 94
Edward IV 爱德华四世 30—31
Edward the Confessor 忏悔者爱德华 11
Ehrenpreis, Irvin 欧文·埃伦普赖斯 91
elegy 哀歌 107
Eliot, George 乔治·艾略特 63, 68—69, 129—130
Eliot, TS T. S. 艾略特 93
Elizabeth I 伊丽莎白一世 17, 30, 38, 78, 84
Ellison, Ralph 拉尔夫·埃里森 125
Ellison, Richard 理查德·埃里森 14
Ellmann, Richard 理查德·埃尔曼 7, 88, 90, 101, 102, 135
email 电子邮件 10
Emerson, Ralph Waldo 拉尔夫·沃尔多·爱默生 54
empathy 共情 2, 55, 62, 135
Empson, William 燕卜荪 133
encomium "颂文" 22
encyclopaedias and dictionaries 百科全书与辞典 34, 64—68, 80
Epstein, Brian 布赖恩·爱泼斯坦 105
Erikson, Eric 埃里克·埃里克森 88
executors 遗嘱执行人 2, 10, 96
exemplary lives 榜样传记 16—17, 23—31, 36, 52, 90, 109, 119
experimental biography 实验性传记 16, 28, 73—83, 90, 122—123
exposure 曝光 17, 57, 68—69, 96, 99, 120

F

facts 事实 5, 7, 21, 80—81, 88, 117, 123, 137
Fairholt, Frederick 弗雷德里克·费尔霍尔特 62
fame 名气 17—18, 68—69, 105, 117—121
family 家庭 2, 9, 58—59, 96, 111—112; 参见 fathers
fathers 父亲 75, 86, 89, 119
Fay, Laurel 劳雷尔·费伊 113—114
feelings about subject 对传主的感情 134—135
feminism 女性主义 14, 82, 117, 126, 129
fiction 虚构 7, 15, 43, 80—82, 98—100, 132, 137—138
Fielding, Henry 亨利·菲尔丁 44
Fitzgerald, Scott 斯科特·菲茨杰拉德 91
Flaubert, Gustave 居斯塔夫·福楼拜 10, 87, 93, 99—100
footnotes 脚注 10—11, 130—131
Ford, Ford Madox 福特·马多克斯·福特 91, 93
Forster, EM E. M. 福斯特 79

Forster, John 约翰·福斯特 58—59
Foster, Roy 罗伊·福斯特 91, 123
Foxe, John 约翰·福克斯 27
Frank, Anne 安妮·弗兰克 112
Frazier, Adrian 阿德里安·弗雷泽 130
Frederick the Great 腓特烈大帝 56
Freud, Sigmund 西格蒙德·弗洛伊德 15, 27, 73, 75,77—79, 83—90
friends 朋友 7, 43, 54, 58—60, 62—63, 75,80, 82, 132, 135
Froude, John Anthony 约翰·安东尼·弗劳德 70—71, 73
Fry, Roger 罗杰·弗赖伊 80, 122
Fuller, Thomas 托马斯·富勒 28, 34, 64

G

Gandhi, Mahatma 圣雄甘地 107
Garrick, David 戴维·加里克 49—50
Gaskell, Elizabeth 伊丽莎白·盖斯凯尔 59—62, 91, 129
Gay, Peter 彼得·盖伊 84
gender 性别 12, 14, 45, 59—62, 65, 72, 81, 89, 119, 126—129
Genet, Jean 让·热内 87
genre 文类 18, 34, 49, 52, 75, 79, 82, 127
Gérin, Winifred 威妮弗雷德·热兰 91
Gilgamesh 吉尔伽美什 22
Gill, Eric 埃里克·吉尔 91, 133
Gladstone, William 威廉·格莱斯顿 63
Glendinning, Victoria 维多利亚·格伦迪宁 87, 91, 124—125

Godwin, William 威廉·戈德温 45
Goethe, JW von 歌德 54, 79
Goffman, Erving 欧文·戈夫曼 101—102
Golding, William 威廉·戈尔丁 99
Gordimer, Nadine 娜丁·戈迪默 96, 98
Gordon, George 乔治·戈登 76, 77
Gosse, Edmund 埃德蒙·戈斯 28, 73, 75, 78—79
Gosse, Philip 菲利普·戈斯 75, 78
gossip 八卦 17, 36—38, 44, 55, 95—98, 118
grave-robbers, biographers as 传记作家被比作掘墓贼 2
Graves, Robert 罗伯特·格雷夫斯 135—136
Great Men 伟人 24—25, 29, 44—45
Greenblatt, Stephen 斯蒂芬·格林布拉特 137—138
Greene, Graham 格雷厄姆·格林 135
Greer, Germaine 杰梅茵·格里尔 96
Grey, Jane 简·格雷 65
group or collective lives 群体或集体传记 6, 31, 34—37, 62—65, 126, 128
Grove, George 乔治·格罗夫 66
Grub Street 格拉勃街 43—44, 47—48
Guevara, Che 切·格瓦拉 107—108

H

Haffenden, John 约翰·哈芬登 133
hagiography (saints' lives) 圣徒传记 (圣人生平) 8—16, 20—21, 24—30, 34, 52, 63—65, 78, 107
Hamilton, Emma 艾玛·汉密尔顿 109

Hamilton, Ian 伊恩・汉密尔顿 7, 96
Hardy, Thomas 托马斯・哈代 6
Hart-Davis, Rupert 鲁珀特・哈特-戴维斯 73
Hastings, Selina 塞琳娜・黑斯廷斯 135
Haydon, Benjamin 本杰明・海登 8
Hayter, Alethea 阿莱西娅・海特 8
Hazlitt, William 威廉・黑兹利特 3, 55—56, 80
Heidegger, Martin 马丁・海德格尔 103
Heilbrun, Carolyn 卡罗琳・埃尔布兰 61—62, 127
Hemingway, Ernest 厄内斯特・海明威 91, 133
Herbert, George 乔治・赫伯特 11, 34—35
Herder, JG J. G. 赫尔德 54
heroes 主人公 51—52, 63—64, 68, 105—111
hidden lives 隐蔽的人生 126—127
Hitler, Adolf 阿道夫・希特勒 12, 111—112
Hobbes, Thomas 托马斯・霍布斯 38
Hogarth, William 威廉・霍格思 49, 91
Holbein, Hans 汉斯・霍尔拜因 31
Holcroft, Thomas 托马斯・霍尔克罗夫特 56
Holmes, Richard 理查德・霍姆斯 13, 48, 91, 124
Holroyd, Michael 迈克尔・霍尔罗伊德 91, 111
Honan, Park 帕克・霍南 137

honesty 诚实 9, 47
Hooke, Robert 罗伯特・胡克 34
Hooker, Richard 理查德・胡克 34
Hughes, Ted 特德・休斯 95, 100
Hutchinson, John 约翰・哈钦森 45
Hutchinson, Lucy 露西・哈钦森 45

I

icons and iconoclasm 偶像与偶像崇拜 18, 107—109, 117
idealization 理想化 9, 55—56, 73, 86, 107
identity 身份认同 14—16, 52, 54, 88, 102, 118—119
illness 疾病 63, 86, 87, 89
indexes 索引 7, 130—131
individualism 个人 16, 28—29, 31, 54
information 信息 21, 37, 66

J

Jackson, William 威廉・杰克逊 65—66
Jacobus de Voragine 雅各・德・佛拉金 25
James, Alice 艾丽斯・詹姆斯 126—127
James, Henry 亨利・詹姆斯 2, 10, 15, 69, 88—89, 93, 95, 102, 104, 126—127, 132, 135
Jerome, Saint 圣杰罗姆 20—21
Jesus 耶稣 7, 20—21, 25
John, Augustus 奥古斯塔斯・约翰 91
Johnson, Samuel 萨缪尔・约翰逊 3, 9, 11, 34, 39—44, 45, 46—53, 56—58, 77, 135
Jones, Ernest 厄内斯特・琼斯 84

journalism 新闻报道 43, 47—48, 68
journals 日记 44, 54, 58, 73
Joyce, James 詹姆斯·乔伊斯 90, 93—94, 135, 137
Joyce, William 威廉·乔伊斯 111
Jung, Karl 卡尔·荣格 90

K

Kaplan, Justin 贾斯廷·卡普兰 91, 96
Keats, John 约翰·济慈 3, 58, 91, 130
Kelley, Kitty 凯蒂·凯利 96
Kennedy, Jackie 杰基·肯尼迪 119
Khaikin, Boris 鲍里斯·海金 116
King, Martin Luther 马丁·路德·金 26, 107, 123—124
Kingsley, Charles 查尔斯·金斯利 58
Kinsey, Alfred 阿尔弗雷德·金赛 17

L

Larkin, Philip 菲利普·拉金 98, 133
Lawrence, DH D. H. 劳伦斯 6
Lee, Sidney 西德尼·李 66
Lehmann, Rosamund 罗莎蒙德·莱曼 135
length of book 书的篇幅 131
Leonardo da Vinci 列奥纳多·达·芬奇 15, 84—86
Lessing, Doris 多丽丝·莱辛 98
letters 信件 10, 31, 44, 49, 54, 62—63
Lewis, RWB R. W. B. 刘易斯 91
Lewis, Sinclair 辛克莱尔·刘易斯 91
life-writing 生平写作 5—6, 12, 24, 28, 30, 46—47, 52, 55—56, 73, 79—80
Light, Alison 埃里森·莱特 127
Lively, Penelope 佩内洛普·莱夫利 99
Locke, John 约翰·洛克 34
Lockhart, John Gibson 约翰·吉布森·洛克哈特 10, 57—58
Louis XIV 路易十四 78
love 爱 12—13, 54, 57—59, 86, 89, 119
Ludwig, Emil 埃米尔·路德维希 73, 79
Lurie, Alison 艾莉森·鲁里 99
Luther, Martin 马丁·路德 88
Luxembourg, Rosa 罗莎·卢森堡 107
Lydgate, John 约翰·利德盖特 29

M

Macaulay, Thomas 托马斯·麦考利 42, 58
MacCarthy, Fiona 菲奥娜·麦卡锡 133
MacIntyre, Alasdair 阿拉斯代尔·麦金泰尔 104
Mack, Maynard 梅纳德·麦克 91, 125
Maddox, Brenda 布兰达·马多克斯 127
Mailer, Norman 诺曼·梅勒 118
Malamud, Bernard 伯纳德·马拉默德 99
Malcolm, Janet 珍妮特·马尔科姆 95—96
Malcolm, Robert 罗伯特·马尔科姆 62
Malone, Edmond 埃德蒙·马龙 46
Mandela, Nelson 纳尔逊·曼德拉 14, 107
Manning, Henry Edward 亨利·爱德华·曼宁 76

Marsh, Edward 爱德华·马什 73
Marshall, Megan 梅根·马歇尔 6
martyrs 殉道者 9, 16, 25—26, 52
Marx, Karl 卡尔·马克思 15, 87
Matisse, Henri 亨利·马蒂斯 91
Maurois, André 安德烈·莫洛亚 73, 79, 101, 134
Maxentius 马克森提乌斯 26
McArthur, John 约翰·麦克阿瑟 109
McCarthy, Fiona 菲奥娜·麦卡锡 91
McMillan, Margaret 玛格丽特·麦克米伦 129
media 媒体 9, 17—18, 68, 97
metaphors for biography 传记的比喻 1—5, 13
Michaud, Louis-Gabriel 路易-加布里埃尔·米肖 64
Middlebrook, Diane Wood 戴安娜·伍德·米德尔布鲁克 129
Milton, John 约翰·弥尔顿 27—28
Mizener, Arthur 阿瑟·迈兹纳 91
modernism 现代主义 12—13, 74, 78—79, 82, 86, 90—94
monarchs 君主 26, 30—31, 34, 126
Monk, Ray 雷·蒙克 103—104
Monroe, Marilyn 玛丽莲·梦露 117—121
Montaigne, Michel de 米歇尔·德·蒙田 31—32
Moore, GE G. E. 穆尔 16
Moore, George 乔治·穆尔 130
morality 道德观 16—17, 23—24, 29, 48, 52, 57—59, 68—70, 78, 93
More, Thomas 托马斯·莫尔 11, 30—32
Morgan, JP J. P. 摩根 106

Morley, John 约翰·莫利 63, 66
Morris, Edmund 埃德蒙·莫里斯 7
Morris, William 威廉·莫里斯 91
Morrison, Blake 布雷克·莫里森 75
Moses 摩西 19, 21
Mosley, Nicholas 尼古拉斯·莫斯利 111
Mosley, Oswald 奥斯瓦尔德·莫斯利 111
Motion, Andrew 安德鲁·莫申 133
motives 动机 8, 12—13, 17, 21, 47—49, 84, 111
Mugabe, Robert 罗伯特·穆加贝 111
music 音乐 113—117
myth 神话, 迷思 7, 107—111, 117, 121, 123

N

names 姓名 129—130
narrative 叙事 5, 10—18, 29, 103—104, 122—123, 130—140
national biographies 国家人物传记 63—69
National Portrait Gallery 国家肖像画廊 64—65
nationalism 国家主义, 民族主义 63—66, 68—69, 107—111
Nelson, Horatio 霍雷肖·纳尔逊 63—64, 107, 109—111
Nero 尼禄 111
Newman, John Henry 约翰·亨利·纽曼 76
Nichols, John 约翰·尼科尔斯 45—46
Nicholls, Charles 查尔斯·尼科尔 136

Nicholls, Christine 克莉丝汀·尼科尔斯 67

Nicolson, Harold 哈罗德·尼科尔森 73, 78—79

Nightingale, Florence 弗洛伦斯·南丁格尔 76—77

North, Roger 罗杰·诺思 47

North, Thomas 托马斯·诺思 24, 32

Northcote, James 詹姆斯·诺思科特 46, 55

novels with indexes, biographies as 传记是"附有索引的小说" 7

O

Oates, Joyce Carol 乔伊丝·卡罗尔·欧茨 118

obituaries 讣告 34, 67, 113

objectivity 客观性 12—13

obscure lives 无名之人 9, 14, 66—68, 80, 82, 125—127

Oedipal biography "俄狄浦斯式传记" 75—76

Oliphant, Margaret 玛格丽特·奥利芬特 45, 62, 69—70

Oman, Carola 卡萝拉·欧曼 110

omissions or concealment 省略或隐瞒 9—10, 79

oral dimension 口述层面 5—6, 107, 112

over-involvement 过度介入 13

P

pain, biography as cause of 传记带来痛苦 2, 70, 95, 100, 111

Painter, George 乔治·佩因特 88—89

Paisley, Ian 伊恩·佩斯利 123—124

panegyric 赞辞 22, 45, 47, 48, 51

paratexts 类文本 130

Parker, Tom 汤姆·帕克 105

Pater, Walter 沃尔特·佩特 73, 79, 82

Paulson, Ronald 罗纳德·保尔森 91

Pepys, Samuel 萨缪尔·佩皮斯 36, 45, 91

performance 表演 15, 30, 10—25, 102—104, 116—117

Petrach 彼特拉克 31—32

Pettigrew, Thomas 托马斯·佩蒂格鲁 109

Phaedo 斐多 21

Phillips, Adam 亚当·菲利普斯 84

philosophy 哲学 16, 10—24, 103

Picasso, Pablo 巴勃罗·毕加索 82, 83, 91

Plath, Sylvia 西尔维娅·普拉斯 95, 129

Plato 柏拉图 16, 21, 23, 44

Plutarch 普鲁塔克 3, 5, 10, 11, 21, 22—25, 32—34, 52, 102

poetry 诗歌 15, 34—35, 43—44, 47—48, 56, 58, 69, 93, 106

Pol Pot 波尔布特 111

politics 政治 14, 56, 63—64, 77, 104—105, 107—116, 123, 126

Pope, Alexander 亚历山大·蒲柏 45, 48—49, 52, 91, 125

Popper, Karl 卡尔·波普尔 8

popular biography 通俗传记 6, 11, 14,

17—18, 62, 66, 68, 79, 90—95, 125, 137—138

portrait metaphor 肖像的比喻 2—4

posthumous scrutiny 死后细察 2

post-mortems 尸检 1—2, 5

Powell, Anthony 安东尼·鲍威尔 36—37

Presley, Elvis 埃尔维斯·普雷斯利（"猫王"）105, 117, 119

Pritchett, VS V. S. 普里切特 132

privacy 隐私 9—10, 17, 57—58, 68—71, 95—96

professionalization 专业化 10, 68, 82—84, 91, 128—129

Proust, Marcel 马塞尔·普鲁斯特 15, 79, 88—90, 130

psychoanalysis 精神分析 12, 15—16, 72—73, 78—79, 83—90, 111—112

psychobiography 心理传记 84, 87—88, 134—135

public life 公共生活 9, 17—18, 22, 26, 68—69, 101—121

R

race 种族 12, 14, 104, 112

Raleigh, Water 沃尔特·雷利 30, 38

Rampersad, Arnold 阿诺德·兰佩萨德 125

Reagan, Nancy 南希·里根 96

relation to subject 与传主的关系 11—12, 47, 58—62, 70—71, 134—140

Renan, Ernest 欧内斯特·勒南 68

Reynolds, Joshua 乔舒亚·雷诺兹 3, 49

Reynolds, Michael 迈克尔·雷诺兹 133

Richard III 理查三世 11

Richardson, John 约翰·理查森 91

Ricks, Christopher 克里斯托弗·里克斯 62

Robbe-Grillet, Alain 阿兰·罗布-格里耶 94

Roberts, Ronald Suresh 罗纳德·苏雷什·罗伯茨 96, 98

Rolfe, Frederick 弗雷德里克·罗尔夫 82

romantics 浪漫主义者 54—56, 79

Roosevelt, Theodore 西奥多·罗斯福 104

Roper, William 威廉·罗珀 11, 30—31

Roth, Philip 菲利普·罗斯 75, 99

Rousseau, Jean-Jacques 让-雅克·卢梭 44, 52, 54

rulers 统治者 26, 30—31, 34

Russell, William 威廉·拉塞尔 62

S

Sackville-West, Vita 维塔·萨克维尔-韦斯特 82

Sainte-Beuve, CA C. A. 圣伯夫 15

saints' lives (hagiography) 圣人生平（圣徒传记）8—16, 20—21, 24—30, 34, 52, 63—65, 78, 107

Salinger, JD J. D. 塞林格 96

Sallust 萨鲁斯特 22

Sand, George 乔治·桑 69

Sanderson, Robert 罗伯特·桑德森 34

索引

Sandford, Mrs John 约翰·桑福德夫人 65

Sartre, Jean-Paul 让-保罗·萨特 10, 15, 87, 102

Savage, Richard 理查德·萨维奇 47—48

scandal 丑闻 9, 17, 37—38, 34, 68—69, 73, 96, 117

Schorer, Mark 马克·肖勒 91

Schwob, Marcel 马塞尔·施瓦布 37, 73, 78

Scott, Geoffrey 杰弗里·斯科特 73, 82

Scott, Walter 沃尔特·斯科特 10, 57

Sebag-Montefiore, Simon 西蒙·塞巴格·蒙蒂菲奥里 112

secrecy 秘密 7, 10—11

Selden, John 约翰·塞尔登 44—45

self-expression 自我表达 15—16, 54

Seward, William 威廉·苏厄德 45

sex 性 9, 70, 76—78, 80—81, 86, 89, 91, 118, 133—134

Sexton, Anne 安妮·塞克斯顿 129

Shakespeare, Nicholas 尼古拉斯·莎士比亚 125

Shakespeare, William 威廉·莎士比亚 2, 7, 8, 17, 24, 46, 130, 136—140

Shapiro, James 詹姆斯·夏皮罗 8, 136—137

Shaw, George Bernard 萧伯纳 72, 91

Shelley, Percy Bysshe 珀西·比希·雪莱 13, 58, 79, 91, 124

Sherry, Norman 诺曼·谢里 135

Shore, Jane 简·肖尔 30—31

shortlives 短篇生平故事 36—38, 64—65

传记

Shostakovich, Dmitri 德米特里·肖斯塔科维奇 113—117

Sitwell, Edith 伊迪丝·西特韦尔 91

Smiles, Samuel 萨缪尔·斯迈尔斯 65—66

Smith, George 乔治·史密斯 66

Socrates 苏格拉底 19, 20—21, 22, 23, 44, 103

sources 资料来源 10—12, 47

Southey, Robert 罗伯特·骚塞 63—64, 109

Spence, Joseph 约瑟夫·斯彭斯 45

Spender, Natasha 娜塔莎·斯彭德 96

Spender, Stephen 斯蒂芬·斯彭德 96

spirit of the age 时代精神 13

Spurling, Hilary 希拉里·斯珀林 91

Stalin, Joseph 约瑟夫·斯大林 12, 111, 112—114

Stanley, Arthur Penrhyn 阿瑟·彭林·斯坦利 58, 77

Stansfield, James 詹姆斯·斯坦斯菲尔德 55

Steedman, Carolyn 卡罗琳·斯蒂德曼 127

Stein, Gertrude 格特鲁德·斯泰因 6, 82—83

Steinem, Gloria 格罗丽亚·斯泰纳姆 118—119

Stephen, James Fitzjames 詹姆斯·菲茨詹姆斯·斯蒂芬 58

Stephen, Leslie 莱斯利·斯蒂芬 50, 58, 66—68, 79—80

Sterling, John 约翰·斯特林 56

Stevenson, Robert Louis 罗伯特·路易斯·史蒂文森 69

Storr, Anthony 安东尼·斯托尔 86—87

Strachey, Alix 阿里克斯·斯特雷奇 84

Strachey, James 詹姆斯·斯特雷奇 84

Strachey, Lytton 利顿·斯特雷奇 37, 72, 73—79, 84, 90—91

Strouse, Jean 琼·施特劳斯 106, 126—127

style 风格 49, 63, 74

Suetonius 苏埃托尼乌斯 21, 22—23, 32

Sugden, John 约翰·萨格登 109

Summers, Anthony 安东尼·萨默斯 119

Swift, Jonathan 乔纳森·斯威夫特 91

Symons, AJA A. J. A. 西蒙斯 7, 73, 82

sympathy 同情 30, 47—48, 55—60, 66, 76, 90

T

Tacitus 塔西佗 22, 32

Tadié, Jean-Yves 让-伊夫·塔迪耶 130

television 电视 9, 17—18

Tennyson, Alfred 阿尔弗雷德·丁尼生 58, 68—69, 72, 95

Tennyson, Emily 艾米丽·丁尼生 58

Tennyson, Hallam 哈勒姆·丁尼生 58

Ternan, Ellen 艾伦·特南 127

texting 短信 10

Thackeray, William 威廉·萨克雷 69

Thatcher, Margaret 玛格丽特·撒切尔 107

Theophrastus 泰奥弗拉斯托斯 22, 32, 34

theory 理论 15, 18, 78—79, 88, 94

Theresa, Mother 特蕾莎修女 26, 107

Thoreau, Henry 亨利·梭罗 54, 134

Thrale, Hester 海斯特·思罗尔 43, 45

Thucydides 修昔底德 22

Thurman, Judith 朱迪丝·瑟曼 135

Timbs, John 约翰·廷布斯 62

time 时间 122—124

titles 书名 130

Toklas, Alice B 艾丽斯·B.托克拉斯 6, 82

Tomalin, Claire 克莱尔·托马林 87, 91, 127

tragedies 悲剧 117, 133

Trevelyan, GO G. O. 特里维廉 58

Trollope, Anthony 安东尼·特罗洛普 87, 91

truth 真实 3, 6—9, 17, 37, 43, 46—47, 51—52, 75, 84, 88, 103, 106, 118

Turgenev, Ivan 伊万·屠格涅夫 132

Twain, Mark 马克·吐温 91

U

Uglow, Jenny 珍妮·厄格洛 6, 62, 91, 126

unauthorized biographies 未授权传记 10, 70, 96

unknown figures 不知名的人物 125—127

universality 普世性 16—18, 30, 34, 64, 89
university courses 大学课程 18, 94
Updike, John 约翰·厄普代克 7
ur-biographies 初始传记 21, 24

V

Valéry, Paul 保罗·瓦莱里 123
value of story 故事的价值 16—17
Vasari, Giorgio 乔尔乔·瓦萨里 31—32
Vespasiano da Bisticci 韦斯帕夏诺·达比斯蒂奇 31
Victoria, Queen 维多利亚女王 73, 77—78
Villani, Filippo 菲利波·维拉尼 31—32
vitalspark 生命活力 3
Volkov, Solomon 所罗门·伏尔科夫 113, 115

W

Walpole, Horace 霍勒斯·沃波尔 42, 73
Walton, Izaak 艾萨克·沃尔顿 11, 34—36
Warhol, Andy 安迪·沃霍尔 119
'warts and all' 如实描述 3
Watts, GF G. F. 沃茨 64
Waugh, Evelyn 伊夫林·沃 25—26, 72
Wells, HG H. G. 威尔斯 72
West, Rebecca 丽贝卡·韦斯特 91, 111—112, 124—125
Wharton, Edith 伊迪丝·沃顿 69, 91
Wilde, Oscar 奥斯卡·王尔德 7, 8, 69, 71, 73, 76
Wilhelm II 威廉二世 79
Wilkes, John 约翰·威尔克斯 50—51
Wilson, Henry 亨利·威尔逊 62
Winter, Simon 西蒙·温特 21
witnesses 证人 7, 10, 11, 117
Wittgenstein, Ludwig 路德维希·维特根斯坦 8, 16, 103—104
Wollstonecraft, Mary 玛丽·沃斯通克拉夫特 56
Wolsey, Thomas 托马斯·沃尔西 29, 30
women, lives of 女性传记 12, 14, 45, 59—62, 65, 72, 81, 89, 119, 126—129
Wood, Anthony 安东尼·伍德 37
Woolf, Virginia 弗尼吉亚·伍尔夫 13—14, 58—59, 73—75, 79—82, 122—123, 127, 129
working class 工人阶级 65—66, 127—128
Wotton, Henry 亨利·沃顿 34

X

Xenophon 色诺芬 22

Y

Yeats, WB W. B. 叶芝 91, 93, 123

Hermione Lee

BIOGRAPHY
A Very Short Introduction

For Jenny Uglow

Biography

Who turned the page?
When I went out last night
his Life was left wide-open,
half way through, in lamplight on my desk:
The Middle Years.
Now look at him. Who turned the page?

Ian Hamilton

Contents

Acknowledgements i

List of Illustrations iii

A Very Short Introduction v

1 The Biography Channel 1
2 Exemplary Lives 19
3 Warts and All 39
4 National Biography 54
5 Fallen Idols 72
6 Against Biography 93
7 Public Roles 101
8 Telling the Story 122

References 141

Bibliography 163

Publisher's Acknowledgements 167

Acknowledgements

I am grateful to the following for various kinds of help, advice, inspiration, and information: John Barton; Dinah Birch; Elleke Boehmer; Michael Burden; Robert Faber; Roy Foster; Alex Harris; Hugh Haughton; Kathryn Holland; Ann Jefferson; Benjamin Lee; Amanda Lillie; Stephen Mulhall; Lucy Newlyn; Chris Pelling.

My deepest gratitude goes to my critical and affectionate readers, Julian Barnes and Jenny Uglow; my late, and much mourned, agent and friend, Pat Kavanagh; my editor at OUP, Andrea Keegan; the students with whom I have discussed biography and life-writing, at York and Oxford; and my husband John Barnard, for his unflagging encouragement of, and interest in, this book.

List of Illustrations

1. *The Art of Painting*, c. 1665/6, by Jan Vermeer **4**
   © akg-images/Erich Lessing

2. *The Anatomy Lesson* of *Dr Nicolaas Tulp*, 1632, by Rembrandt **5**
   © The Granger Collection/TopFoto.co.uk

3. *The Martyrdom of St Catherine of Alexandria*, c. 1505, by Lucas Cranach the Elder **27**
   © akg-images/Erich Lessing

4. *Sir Thomas More*, by Hans Holbein **32**
   © The Frick Collection, New York

5. Title page of the first edition of Sir Thomas North's English translation of Plutarch's *Lives*, London, 1579 **33**
   © The Granger Collection/TopFoto.co.uk

6. John Donne **35**
   © The Granger Collection/TopFoto.co.uk

7. *Dr Samuel Johnson*, by Sir Joshua Reynolds **40**
   © The Granger Collection/TopFoto.co.uk

8. Title page of the first edition of Boswell's *Life of Johnson* **41**
   © The Granger Collection/TopFoto.co.uk

9a. Charlotte Brontë **60**
   © The Granger Collection/TopFoto.co.uk

9b. *Elizabeth Gaskell*, 1832, by W. J. Thomson **60**
   Courtesy of the University Librarian and Director, The John Rylands University Library, University of Manchester

10. Virginia Woolf and Lytton Strachey, 1923 **74**
   National Portrait Gallery, London

List of Illustrations

11 *Gertrude Stein*, 1906, by Pablo Picasso **83**
© Succession Picasso/DACS 2009. Photo: © The Granger Collection/TopFoto.co.uk

12a Sigmund Freud in 1938 **85**
Courtesy of the Library of Congress

12b Self-portrait by Leonardo da Vinci **85**
© The Granger Collection/TopFoto.co.uk

13 Screen grab from *www.biography.com* **97**

14a Che Guevara poster **108**
© Jim Fitzpatrick

14b Corpse of Che Guevara **108**
© 1999 TopFoto.co.uk

15a Nelson's Column **110**
© iStockphoto

15b Nelson medallion **110**
© TopFoto.co.uk

15c Nelson mug **110**

16 Shostakovich writing at his desk **114**
© Underwood & Underwood/Corbis

17 *Marilyn Diptych*, by Andy Warhol **120**
© The Andy Warhol Foundation for the Visual Arts, Inc./Artists' Rights Society (ARS), New York and DACS

18 'Pit Brow' girls, Wigan, 1893 **128**
© Public Record Office/HIP/TopFoto.co.uk

19a Jane Austen sketch, by Cassandra Austen **131**
© 2004 TopFoto.co.uk

19b Jane Austen engraving **131**
Courtesy of the Library of Congress

20 Shakespeare's portrait on the First Folio, engraved by Martin Droeshout **139**
Folger Shakespeare Library

A Very Short Introduction

Biography has gone through many centuries of change, many variants and embodiments, and this book looks at a few of these in order to try and understand what biography does and how it works. Given the confines of a 'very short' book, it concentrates—though not exclusively—on British literary biography. Up to a point, it is structured chronologically. But it does not attempt to give a comprehensive survey of the genre, which would be a mind-numbing exercise.

Books or essays on biography often trace an evolutionary graph that goes from exemplary Lives or 'hagiographies', through to the vivid realism and intimacy of 18th-century portraits, to the conservative solidity of Victorian 'Lives and Letters', to modernist experiments with life-writing as an art form, and then rejoicingly on to the 'Golden Age' of long, professional, candid, post-Freudian 20th-century biography. Although these lines can, to an extent, be drawn, I find that kind of progressive model for biography misleading. What I see, rather, is the continual recurrence, in different contexts, of the same questions of definition, value, and purpose.

Chapter 1
The Biography Channel

Metaphors for biography

Biography is often compared to some other kind of thing, as though it is difficult to fix it within a neat, single definition. The terms used to describe what it is include Life, Life-history, Life-writing, memoir, profile. Biography gets compared to history (oral and written), to quests or journeys, detective work, criminal trials, scenes in a play or the backstage of the theatre, obituaries, encomiums, gossip, psychoanalysis, documentaries, hauntings, burglary, embalmings, excavations, Oedipal conflicts, betrayal, revenge, a broken bridge, a fishing-net, a work of fiction.

Of the many metaphors for biography, two make useful starting points. One – a disturbing image – is the autopsy, the forensic examination of the dead body which takes place when the cause of death is unusual, suspicious, or ambiguous. The medical examiner trained as a forensic pathologist opens up the corpse (sometimes stripping the skin of the face right off the skull) and employs his or her expertise in anatomy and pathology to investigate, understand, describe, and explain what may have seemed obscure, strange, or inexplicable. As one writer on postmortems puts it, 'The property rights of the deceased to their bodies terminate at the moment of death.' This process may not be conclusive. Though the medical examiner is trained in scientific methods and interpretation of the evidence, such expertise may not 'completely erase subjectivity...' 'The body does not lie – but the cause of death can still remain ambiguous.'

The metaphor of the autopsy invokes biography as a process of posthumous scrutiny, applied to a helpless subject from which life – or the soul, if you believe in a soul – has gone. The process cannot injure the person who is no longer there, but it can certainly change our posthumous view of them, depending on what is ascertained from the examination. And it can cause pain to surviving relatives and friends. The image of biography as a forensic process also suggests its limitations, since an autopsy can have nothing or little to say about the subject's thoughts, intelligence, emotions, temperament, talents, or beliefs. It may not even be able conclusively to prove the cause of death.

There is something gruesome about this metaphor. It is used when commentators on biography want to emphasize its ghoulish or predatory aspects. Henry James, shortly before his death, told his nephew (who was his executor) that his 'sole wish' was to 'frustrate as utterly as possible the postmortem exploiter' by burning a large number of his papers. Typically of those who think of biography as 'adding a new terror to death', he links the metaphor of the 'postmortem exploiter' to that of the grave-robber, adding that he had 'long thought of launching, by a provision in my will, a curse not less explicit than Shakespeare's own on any such as try to move my bones'.

A contrasting metaphor for biography is the portrait. Whereas autopsy suggests clinical investigation and, even, violation, portrait suggests empathy, bringing to life, capturing the character. The portraitist simulates warmth, energy, idiosyncrasy, and personality through attention to detail and skill in representation. Yet these two metaphors do have something in common. Portraits taken from life and posthumous autopsies both make an investigation of the subject which will shape how posterity views them. Both must pay precise attention to detail. Both can be revelatory. And the success of both depends on the practitioner's expertise and judiciousness.

When Hazlitt said in 1814 that 'portrait-painting is the biography of the pencil', he was using a commonplace analogy. The highest praise for a portrait (or a portrait-bust, or statue) is that 'the very life seems warm upon her lip', that it might be warm to the touch, 'looking as if she were alive'. So, 'catching a likeness' is a common phrase for what a biographer is trying to do. 'Warts and all' is another favourite phrase for what the ideally truthful biography should present. The subject of a biography, like that of a portrait, should seem to be alive, breathing, present in all the totality, there-ness, and authenticity of their being.

Biographers frequently use portraiture as an image for what they are doing. Plutarch compared his method of working to portrait-painters' concentration on the faces, and especially the expression in the eyes, of their subjects. Boswell said of Johnson, to their mutual friend the painter Joshua Reynolds, that Johnson 'has a peculiar art of drawing characters, which is as rare as good portrait-painting'. When he was writing his own *Life of Johnson*, Boswell drew on and made use of Reynolds' portraits of Johnson, and famously called his work 'the Flemish picture which I give of my friend...in which...I mark the most minute particulars.' The metaphor suggests biography's need to capture the 'vital spark' of the human subject, what Keats meant when he said 'The creature hath a purpose and its eyes are bright with it.' Thomas Carlyle, writing in the 1830s about the human sympathy that should fuel an ideal biography, spoke of catching the 'light-gleams' that make up a person's character.

The image of the portrait, though a more appealing one than the autopsy, also suggests what can go wrong with biography – flattery, idealization, flatness, inaccuracy, distortion. It makes us think, too, about the viewer's dependency on the artist's approach and technique. Another portrait might have given us a completely different idea of the subject. The possibilities for the representation of a self are infinitely various.

The metaphor has its limits. There are obvious differences between portraiture and biography: 'Biographical subjects... rarely stand still.' They speak, they change, they grow old, and they die.

1. An image for biography: the portrait taken from life

2. An image for biography: the forensic examination of a dead body

Definitions of biography

Is it possible to define biography without using metaphors or analogies? *The Oxford English Dictionary* of 1971 gives two definitions. The first, which now reads rather quaintly, is: 'The history of the lives of individual men, as a branch of literature' (the earliest example is from 1683, in Dryden's introduction to the *Lives* of Plutarch). The second is: 'A written record of the life of an individual' (first citation 1791). The *New Oxford Dictionary of English* of 2001 gives 'An account of someone's life written by someone else'. Here is another possibility: Biography is the story of a person told by someone else. Why 'story' rather than 'account'? Because biography is a form of narrative, not just a presentation of facts. Why 'told' rather than 'written'? After all, the word 'biography' literally means 'life-writing'. The two halves of the word derive from medieval Greek: *bios*, 'life', and *graphia*, 'writing'. But all biography involves an oral dimension – the recounting of memories, witness-testimony, much-repeated anecdotes. And some forms of biography, such as documentary film, are not written.

Even this basic definition, 'the story of a person told by someone else', is unstable, and liable to exceptions. A biography could be written by the person whose story is being told, pretending to be someone else. Thomas Hardy, for instance, wrote his own biography, under the pretence it was being written by his wife. She finished it after his death, and it was published under her name. Gertrude Stein wrote her own biography as if it were being written by her partner, Alice B. Toklas, and called it *The Autobiography of Alice B. Toklas*. A biography of someone could be written by more than one person (the three-volume 1990s Cambridge University Press *Life of D. H. Lawrence* has a different author for each volume). A biography could be the story of several lives, not of one person. 'Group Lives', popular biographical enterprises in recent years (as in Jenny Uglow's *The Lunar Men*, or Megan Marshall's *The Peabody Sisters*) have a long history, though their predecessors usually took the form, not of several stories woven together in one narrative, but of short separate accounts of lives collected in a series or volume. A biography might tell the story of an animal or a thing rather than a person: there are biographies of cities, deities, and diseases, of Elizabeth Barrett Browning's spaniel Flush, of the Bayeux Tapestry, and of the River Thames.

Ten rules for biography

If definitions of biography need qualifying, what about rules? Here are ten possibilities.

1. The story should be true

Biographies of human beings are generally about real people, not fictional or mythological characters. Therefore the biographer has a responsibility to the truth, and should tell us what actually happened in the life. This looks like a solid, unarguable rule for biography. But there are many ways of breaking it. Plenty of biographers dramatize their narratives with descriptions of emotions, highly coloured scene-setting, or strategies of suspense. Some go further, and deploy full-scale fictional methods: invented meetings between author and subject, imaginary episodes, musings on the identity of the biographer, hypothetical conversations. Examples are A. J. A. Symons's *The Quest for Corvo: An Experiment in Biography* (1934), Ian Hamilton's *In Search of J. D. Salinger* (1988), Peter Ackroyd's *Dickens* (1990), and Edmund Morris's *Dutch: A Memoir of Ronald Reagan* (1999). Some biographies read more like fiction than history. This can attract readers, but can also give the genre a bad name. John Updike once remarked that most biographies are just 'novels with indexes'.

Even in the most sober and factual of biographical narratives, 'what actually happened' can be ambiguous or obscure. For some lives – such as the life of Jesus, or Shakespeare, or Cleopatra – there may be a vast mass of written or recorded utterances and a host of stories and legends, but little or no primary evidence. Where there is more first-hand or accredited evidence, there may often, also, be lies, exaggerations, and secrets. Biographers can spend a great deal of time sorting out the myths or false trails their subjects have created about their own lives. Witnesses, friends, and enemies have their own agendas, or misremember events, or embroider their anecdotes over the years. Biographers have to treat all testimony with scepticism and care. Untruths gather weight by being repeated and can congeal into the received version of a life, repeated in biography after biography until or unless unpicked. Some biographers settle on a single, possibly shaky hypothesis to explain a whole life: Richard Ellmann was criticized, for example, for maintaining on rather little evidence that Oscar Wilde had syphilis. Sometimes the truth about a person's life cannot be accessed: the evidence has been made away with, the witnesses are not there, the subject is mute. Then the true story would have to take the form of unanswerable questions or gaps in the record.

2. The story should cover the whole life

If a biography is to give you your money's worth ('A shilling life will give you all the facts', as Auden wrote), the expectation is that it will cover the whole story, or, in the case of a living subject, will go as far as it can. But attitudes have changed towards coverage. Until the 20th century, little detail was given about the childhood of the subject, unless to give anecdotes which pointed towards their behaviour in later life. The emphasis has shifted in the relative coverage of public achievements and domestic behaviour. Contemporary readers of biography expect to be given details about a subject's motives and fears, sexual habits, dealings with money, behaviour as a partner or parent, illnesses, peculiarities, even dreams or fantasies. Some, not all, biographers, spend time on their subjects' ancestors; some, not all, biographers track their subjects' posthumous lives and reputations.

If covering a 'whole life' implies that biography should proceed chronologically from cradle to grave, then this rule has been so often broken as not to count. Biographies can run backwards, can be organized by themes, can choose to dwell on certain key moments in a life, or can inter-cut their narratives with passages of history, literary criticism, description, or autobiography. Some biographies use a small part of a life-story to open out into the whole life. In *A Sultry Month: Scenes of London Literary Life in 1846* (1965), Alethea Hayter told the life-story of the Romantic painter Benjamin Haydon and of the group of writers and artists he knew by concentrating on the month in which Haydon died. *Wittgenstein's Poker* (2001) provided a dual mini-biography of Wittgenstein and Popper in 'the story of a ten-minute argument between two great philosophers'. James Shapiro chose the year 1599, 'a year in the life of William Shakespeare', as a way of capturing 'some of the unpredictable and contingent nature of daily life too often flattened out in historical and biographical works of greater sweep'. But this is not exclusively a modern method of writing biography. Lives of saints often spent far more time on their martyrdoms than on their daily lives. Biographers who knew their subjects tended to concentrate on the parts of the life they had witnessed. Total coverage is not an invariable rule.

3. Nothing should be omitted or concealed

Contemporaneous readers of Western biography generally believe that there should be no censorship and no idealization, and that the value of the exercise of life-writing depends on its honesty and its thorough-going investigativeness. Even if it is hard to distinguish, at times, between a dislike of hypocrisy and a delight in scandal, the ethics of our society entail a belief in openness. This has partly to do with an increasing resistance to authority. We no longer want to treat leaders, monarchs, priests, or doctors with reverence, and we think their lives should be open to inspection. And the line we draw between the private and the public has changed. The ambivalent overlap between the 'public sphere' and the private life has been a contentious issue since the rise of mass media. In the late 20th and the 21st centuries, the presentation of the ordinary person's (as opposed to the famous person's) everyday private life for public consumption in Western culture has developed rapidly and dramatically out of new affordable technologies and media trends. Reality television, social networking websites, artwork dedicated to the banality of the private life, point to changing attitudes to what can be exhibited in public. These changes impinge on the writing of biography, always an index of its time. Mid to late 19th-century biography tended (with some exceptions) to censor sexual matters and what Johnson called 'domestick privacies'. We now regard such discretion, or hypocrisy, as unthinkable, unless a biography is being written of a recently dead subject with still-living relatives or close connections whose feelings have to be considered or who may threaten legal proceedings against the biographer if they feel they have been libelled. In such cases, exceptions to our codes of openness may be made.

Changing concepts of privacy and changing attitudes to censorship are not the only factors that affect biography's inclusiveness. Life is accumulation and repetition; narrative has to entail shaping and selection. Even a biography that appears to be omitting nothing – like Sartre's gigantic existential commentary on Flaubert's life, or Lockhart's voluminous, venerating life of Walter Scott, or Leon Edel's 'definitive' critical life of Henry James – has emerged from a process of choices.

4. All sources used should be identified

Biography is not a free zone. It is often involved with legal issues of property, permission, and copyright. A biography may be written at the request of an individual executor, or of a firm of publishers or agents acting for the subject's estate. Terms and conditions may be set up for the biographer which involve permission to use and quote certain materials. 'Unauthorized' biographers, who have not been asked to write about their subjects or who have not been granted such permissions, may find themselves unable to quote from, or having to paraphrase, key materials. Long before the concept of the authorized biography came into being, reputable biographers have preferred to authenticate their stories by referring to their sources or citing witnesses. So Plutarch would compare the different versions of a life-story he had derived from various authorities; Bede described the death of Saint Cuthbert by quoting at length from an eyewitness. From such early biographies right through to 20th-century biographies, witnesses are named and quoted, passages of testimony are infiltrated into the main narrative, the subject's own autobiographical writings are cited as evidence, and letters are used extensively, so much so that a genre called 'Life and Letters' emerged in the 19th century. (Biographers are often asked what effect the superseding of letters by email and texting will have on their work.) It was not until the 20th century, with the professionalization of biography and the emphasis on authenticity and verification, that extensive footnoting became the norm for biography, so that every reference could be checked. This professional convention, which is less than a hundred years old, seems to be on its way out. Trade publishers dislike footnotes: too academic, too space-consuming. Some historical biographers are solving this problem by putting their footnotes online, some popular biographers are minimizing their notes.

Citing one's sources is not always possible. An unauthorized biography of a still-living subject may make use of statements by witnesses who do not wish to be named. A biographer who has obtained materials from a source on condition of secrecy may not be able to disclose the name of the source. Authentication is desirable in biography, but it is not always the rule.

5. The biographer should know the subject

In early examples of biographical writing, centuries might elapse between the life of the subject and the writing of the Life. Plutarch was writing between about AD 98 and 125 about Greek leaders who lived in the 300s BC. Some medieval saints' Lives reached back over many centuries for the stories of their legendary subjects. Others – like a biography of Edward the Confessor commissioned by his widow – were written by near-contemporaries. Sir Thomas More wrote his critical history of Richard III, who died in 1485, in about 1513, only one generation on; More's son-in-law William Roper used his intimate knowledge of More in his memoir of him, written twenty years or so after his death. In the mid-17th century, Izaak Walton claimed a special virtue for his Lives of the Divines (including Donne and Herbert), written between 1640 and 1678, because he had either known them personally or had talked to those who did. A hundred years on, the belief that a biography could only be really valuable and useful if it were written by someone who had known the subject intimately was firmly held both by Dr Johnson and his biographer Boswell. 'Nobody can write the life of man', Johnson told Boswell, 'but those who have eat and drunk and lived in social intercourse with him.' Such personally connected biographical writing was much practised, and discussed, for good and ill, in the 19th century, when biography was often kept in the family. Not so now, when personal knowledge of or connection to the subject is not necessarily seen as an advantage or a requirement. The biographer who is asked to write the Life by the subject or by the subject's relations may find the authorization a heavy burden.

6. The biographer should be objective

The notion that biography can and should be impersonal and authoritative has always been in question. Early Lives of saints, martyrs, heroes, leaders, and thinkers frequently expressed opinions about their subjects, for good and ill. Life-writing from the 16th to the 18th centuries tended to be opinionated and partial, 19th-century biography often over-praised, 20th-century biography was often committed to a particular approach – notably the psychoanalytical method – which skewed the evidence. It has been argued – especially in the modernist period when an authoritative, public style for biography was being reacted against – that all biography is a form of autobiography. Even biographers who resist the notion that the story they are telling has anything to do with them, and put themselves in the narrative as little as possible, have to admit that their choice of subject has been made for a reason, and that there is no such thing as an entirely objective treatment. We write from a certain position, constructed by our history, nationality, race, gender, class, education, beliefs. More specifically, there is likely to be some shared experience between the writer and the subject. A drama critic might well write the life of an actor, a musicologist of a composer. It would be hard, if not impossible, to write a life of a mountaineer or a gardener, a chemist or an architect, with no experience – or at least no understanding at all – of those professions.

Biographers are often asked whether they like or love their subjects. If you are writing a biography of Hitler or Stalin or Attila the Hun, this is evidently not likely to be the case. Yet there will always be some emotion. The passion may be for the historical period or for the victims of the subject. The driving energy for the book may come from loathing or fear, a need to understand some monstrous career, or a revisionary desire to set the record straight.

Over-involvement, either way, can be counterproductive. Biographies written out of uncritical adulation can be as distorted as those that are motivated by punitive or revengeful motives. But biographies written without involvement, just as a money-making job or a duty, may fall flat. There must be some involvement, but there must also be detachment. Richard Holmes, the 'romantic' biographer of Coleridge and Shelley, put it memorably when he described biography as a broken bridge into the past:

> You stood at the end of the broken bridge and looked across carefully, objectively, into the unattainable past on the other side... For me, it was to become a kind of pursuit... You would never catch them; no, you would never quite catch them. But maybe, if you were lucky, you might write about the pursuit of that fleeting figure in such a way as to bring it alive in the present.

7. Biography is a form of history

'No man is an island, entire of it self; every man is a piece of the Continent, a part of the main.' 'No man lives without jostling and being jostled; in all ways he has to *elbow* himself through the world, giving and receiving offence... To paint a man's life is to present these things.' Donne is teaching his congregation about the individual's social responsibility, Carlyle is complaining about the over-delicate discretion of English biography, but both carry a message for biographers. There is no such thing as a life lived in isolation. In her 1920s, modernist spoof of 19th-century biographical conventions, *Orlando*, Virginia Woolf had fun with that biographical cliché 'the spirit of the age'. But, though she satirized the concept, she knew that one of biography's tasks is to place its subject in its 'age': the question is how best to do it. When she was thinking aloud about the difficulty of writing her memoir in her unfinished 'Sketch of the Past', in the late 1930s, she said of her own life: 'I see myself as a fish in a stream; deflected; held in place; but cannot describe the stream.' Biography, even more than autobiography (where the writer can choose how much to talk about the world surrounding the self), has a duty to the stream as well as to the fish.

This is not only a matter of perspective or of narrative tactics. The relation of the individual to the age is also a political issue. Historians sometimes complain that biography is a misleading way of writing about the past. Concentration on an individual life distorts historical processes and can trivialize or over-personalize events. The political implications of prioritizing the life of an individual have been much debated. To set one Great Life centre-stage can be read as promoting a particular political agenda or as consolidating a hierarchical, anti-egalitarian social structure. The venerating and celebratory 19th-century lives of public figures have been called (by Michael Holroyd) 'part of the machinery for preserving the status quo'. The history of feminism, and of movements for racial equality, have a great deal to do with whose life-stories have been thought worth telling and how a life is told. Biography always reflects, and provides, a version of social politics, whether it is the nationalist agenda behind the collective biographical encyclopaedias of 19th-century France and England, or the post-Apartheid-era reactions which led to the biographical idealization of Nelson Mandela, or the changes in black cultural history in 20th-century North America which finally produced a full life of Ralph Ellison – whose *Invisible Man* was published in 1953 and who died in 1994 – in 2007. The popularity of certain kinds of biographies in different countries, periods, and cultures – biographies of saints or of naval heroes, of religious leaders, of footballers or rock-stars – provides an insight into that society. What does that society value, what does it care about, who are its visible – and invisible – men and women?

8. Biography is an investigation of identity

Since biography tells the story of a person, it requires, or assumes, a way of thinking about identity and selfhood. Writers of, and about, biography often discuss the best ways for biography to represent a self: shall it be through anecdote, revelatory incidents, description, conversation, encounters with others, moments of decision-making, single acts, preferences, peculiarities, repeated habits? Any biographer must give some thought, even if not explicitly, to the relation of nature and nurture in the formation of a self, and to the negotiation between interior existence and the self's public performance.

It is not necessary for a biographer to have a theory or a set of general rules about identity – in fact, it can be a disadvantage. Biographers who succumb to the occupational temptation of using their subjects as a peg for generalizations about human behaviour can sound ponderous. Biographies that apply a specific theory of human behaviour – derived from Freud, or Bentham, or Marx, or Sartre – to the telling of a life-story, can retrospectively seem limited or simplifying. But in the writing of a life-story, some idea of how human beings function and what identity consists of is bound to emerge, though more often than not in an unsystematic or unexamined way.

Biography rubs up all the time against rival ways of understanding and explaining human beings and the nature of identity – psychoanalysis, philosophy, fiction, poetry, sociology, ethnography, history. Practitioners of those disciplines often have a hostile or sceptical attitude to biography: there are many examples of poems written against biography, especially in the 19th and 20th centuries, or of novelists treating biography with ironical suspicion or distaste (as in Henry James's *The Aspern Papers* or Julian Barnes's *Flaubert's Parrot*). Freud feared and distrusted biography (especially any that might be written of him) for its simplifications and over-conclusiveness. Proust argued against the critic Sainte-Beuve for belittlingly interpreting the works of his chosen writers through their life-stories. Yet Freud was fascinated – as in his case-study of Leonardo – by the possibilities of psychoanalytical biography, and Proust made his life's work a fiction which both resisted and invited biographical interpretation.

Biographers are not usually as explicit as philosophers such as Plato, Wittgenstein, Austin, or Moore on questions of the existence of an essential self, the extent to which a life can be lived according to a philosophical system, or the relation between acts and emotions. That is not their job – unless they are writing the Life of a philosopher. But biography is bound to reflect changing and conflicting concepts about what makes a self, what it consists of, how it expresses itself. The idea that there is such a thing as an innate, essential nature often vies in biographical narrative with the idea that the self is formed by accidents, contingencies, education, and environment. The idea that character can be designated as a type, or that human beings can be labelled by general, universal categories of identity, is more dominant in early biographies, and tends to give way, from the mid-18th century onwards, to an investment in individualism, originality, and specialness. The belief in a definable, consistent self, an identity that develops through the course of a life-story and that can be conclusively described, breaks down, to a great extent, in the late 19th and early 20th centuries, at a time when psychoanalysis, scientific discoveries such as the theory of relativity, and experiments in art forms, are producing a more indeterminate approach to identity. Western biography from this time has more to say about contradictions and fluctuations in identity, and about the unknowability of the self. But such contrasting ways of describing the self overlap and conflict, rather than following each other in a neatly chronological order.

9. The story should have some value for the reader

Biography raises moral issues. Its early, classical and Christian versions, presented their subjects as moral examples. A good life or a martyrdom provided a model for good behaviour or spiritual aspiration; a bad ruler or a fall from greatness provided an awful warning. This 'exemplary' strain in biography has never disappeared. A recurring argument is made for the usefulness of the genre. If biography can teach us how to live our lives, or can open our minds to lives very unlike our own, then it has an educational purpose: it is a branch of history and of knowledge. There are different and shifting opinions about how it can best fulfil this purpose. Biographers differ in their dedication to candour or 'veracity'; they ask whether small details or large acts are more eloquent ways of communicating character; they have varying views on whether the reader should be led to identify with recognizable, universal traits, or should be stirred or excited by examples of exceptional, unrepeatable behaviour. Is biography of more use if it provokes recognition and sympathy, or a sense of awe and unfamiliarity?

The opposite – and equally recurrent – approach to biography is to attack it for immorality. Words such as betrayal, violation, shame, prurience, intrusion, and exposure are applied to biography over a very wide historical time-span. Biography is attacked for breaching trust, violating privacy, trivializing a life's work, preying on its victim, simplifying a person's complexity, playing to our appetites for gossip and sensation. If biography is a form of scandal-mongering, then it is a low branch of the media and entertainment industry, and has no moral or educational value.

These opposing versions of the genre are not, in fact, mutually exclusive. Biography hovers between the two, sometimes within the same Life. Similarly, readers' motives may veer rapidly, almost simultaneously, between a high quest for inspiration and base, greedy curiosity. But whether biography is regarded as mainly moral or mainly immoral, what is not in doubt is its contemporary popularity. The telling of life-stories is the dominant narrative mode of our times. The popularity of Western biography has lasted for over two centuries, but in the last forty or fifty years – keeping pace with the relaxing of social conventions, increased social egalitarianism, the blurring of high and low art forms, and the cult of media celebrity – it has occupied new spaces. Biographies of politicians, sports and media stars; 'biopics' dramatizing the lives of Shakespeare or Elizabeth I, Kinsey or Truman Capote; television and film documentaries about a huge range of public figures; and the successful American cable television 'Biography Channel' are indications of how iconoclastic, socially wide-ranging, and non-literary biography has become. At the same time, biography has begun to be taken seriously by academics and literary theorists, and biography courses are offered in university departments of literature and history. Biography's current crossings-over between popular culture and literature, mass media and scholarship, may be due to social envy or social levelling, a media-fed gluttony for feeding off private lives, a longing for latter-day saints and heroes in an increasingly secularized society, a dumbing-down of readers who prefer the accessibility of a life-story to the hard work of poetry or literary fiction, or a desire to understand at least one individual's behaviour in a period of global confusion and uncertainty. Or to all or none of the above: perhaps, simply, to a persisting and universal appetite for stories.

10. There are no rules for biography

The instability of definitions and rules for biography suggest that it is a shape-shifting, contradictory, variable form. Yet, paradoxically, it can look like the most solid, conventional, and resistant to change of all forms of narrative. The adjective 'definitive' is often attached to biographies by hopeful publishers or enthusiastic reviewers. There is a lingering idea of biography as the complete, true story of a human being, the last word on a life. But if it is, rather, a mixed, unstable genre, whose rules keep coming undone, then perhaps the only rule that holds good is that there is no such thing as a definitive biography.

Chapter 2
Exemplary Lives

Here are some memorable episodes from the lives of six famous figures.

Moses, having led the people of Israel out of Egypt and given them the word from God over many years, is taken up to the top of Pisgah and shown the promised land. 'I have caused thee to see it with thine eyes' [the Lord says to him] 'but thou shalt not go over thither.' So he dies 'in the land of Moab' at the age of 'a hundred and twenty years', and there is 'weeping and mourning' for him for thirty days.

Socrates, who has been condemned to prison and death for introducing strange gods and corrupting the young, asks for the cup of hemlock to be brought. One of his disciples tells him there is plenty of time: many others have taken the poison late on their last day. 'Socrates said: It's reasonable for those you speak of to do those things – because they think they gain by doing them; for myself, it's reasonable not to do them; because I think I'll gain nothing by taking the draught a little later: I'll only earn my own ridicule by clinging to life... Go on now; do as I ask, and nothing else.'

Alexander, Greek conqueror of the known world, goes to see the philosopher Diogenes, whose support he is seeking, and finds him 'relaxing in the sun'. He asks Diogenes if there is anything he wants. 'Yes,' replied Diogenes, 'move aside a little, out of my sunlight.' As Alexander is leaving with his retinue (who are all mocking the philosopher), he is heard to say: 'As for me, if I were not Alexander, I would be Diogenes.'

Just before he is captured, Jesus is praying in the garden of Gethsemane, asking his Father, 'if it be possible, to let this cup pass from me'. He has told his disciples to watch with him, but they fall asleep. 'And he cometh unto the disciples, and findeth them asleep, and saith unto Peter, What, could ye not watch with me one hour? Watch and pray, that ye enter not into temptation: the spirit indeed is willing, but the flesh is weak.'

The Roman Emperor Caligula, whose sadism, sexual appetites, extravagance, and perversity 'outdid that of all other prodigals ever', treats his horse Incitatus as a favourite. 'Apart from the marble stable, the ebony manger, the purple blankets and the gem-studded collar, he also gave him a house and a household of slaves and furniture... It is said, too, that he meant to make him consul.'

Saint Jerome is sitting with his brother-priests in Bethlehem, hearing the holy lesson, when a lion suddenly comes limping into the monastery. All the other priests run away, but Saint Jerome receives the lion as if he were a guest. 'Than the lyon shewde his foot that was hurte to Seynt Jerom. Wherfore he callyd his brederyn ayen and badde hem waisshe the lyons foot and seke bysily where the sore was and so they dyd and they fonde that the sole of his foot was as hit had be woundyd and kut wyth knyves.' After they have cured him with their medicines, 'the lyon, levynge all his wyldnesse and fersnesse, dwellyd amonge theym as a tame best'.

These narratives cover many centuries. In some cases, there is a vast span of time between these versions of the story and the date of the story's origins; in others, only a few decades. Both the biblical stories are taken from the 1611 Authorized Version of the Bible. The earliest surviving versions of the Old Testament date from the 5th century BC; Matthew's gospel (which gives one of the several versions of the scene at Gethsemane) was written in the second half of the 1st century AD. Complete manuscripts of the New Testament have survived from the 4th century AD. Phaedo's account of the death of Socrates in 399 BC was written down by Plato between 371 and 367 BC. Alexander lived from 356 to 323 BC; his life-story is told by Plutarch between about AD 100 and 125. Caligula ruled Rome between AD 37 and 41; his horrifying regime is described by the Roman writer Suetonius in his *Lives of the Caesars*, written between AD 117 and 138. The cult of Saint Jerome began to take shape, long after his life in the 3rd to 4th centuries, in 9th-century Latin writings. This version is from Simon Winter's early 15th-century vernacular life.

The narratives these anecdotes are taken from could be classified as 'ur-biographies', primal forms of a genre that has not yet evolved. They all contain information about the births, dates, lives, and deaths of the subjects. But their structures are not what we would call biographical. They emphasize certain features – the teaching or the lessons provided by the subject, their legendary sayings, achievements, or crimes – and completely ignore others. They deal with time in a way that would be alien to more realistic life-stories, covering huge sweeps or marking only key events. They contain amazing 'facts' – such as Jesus's conversations with God, Moses' age at his death, or Jerome's friendship with his lion – which are presented without qualification or demurral. Of course, the Old Testament's poetic utterance of inscrutable events, Plutarch's sophisticated illustration of the weakness in pride and the split in one man between tyrant and philosopher, Suetonius's gleefully piled-up details about depravity, and the Jerome-historian's simple telling of the miraculous made ordinary, are very different from each other. But these narratives do have features in common. They describe human behaviour without providing motives or explanations. They want to impress the reader with the sense of a personality or an event of importance. All are interested in the effects of a life on others, whether disciples, victims, a nation, or posterity. They all use speech-acts to bring their messages home. There is no conception of a private or interior life: moments of solitude are witnessed by God; statements of belief or defining acts are performed in public. They all present their central figures, for good or ill, as exceptional and influential.

Western biography has its origins in such educational stories of remarkable men. (Or in stories from long before these examples, if you take the *Epic of Gilgamesh*, the tragic life and loves of the legendary Assyrian king who ruled in about 2600 BC, or the commemorative accounts of the Egyptian Pharaohs, as the first biographies.) The subjects of the classical writers are public figures, judged by their peers and posterity for their behaviour. Other classical life-writers whose work has endured are Xenophon, the 5th- to 4th-century BC Athenian who wrote a semi-fictional biography of the Persian king Cyrus and wrote vividly about Socrates; Theophrastus, Aristotle's pupil, who in about 319 BC wrote his *Characters*, short prose sketches of imaginary types like the Coward, the Drunkard, the Bore, and the Superstitious Man; and the Latin writer Cornelius Nepos, who, ahead of Plutarch, wrote some short *Lives of Illustrious Men* in the late 20s BC, also pairing Romans and Greeks. There are strong character-drawings by the Athenian historian Thucydides (c. 460–395 BC) and by the Roman historians Tacitus and Sallust. Greek and Roman literature contained many examples, also, of 'encomium', praise of the dead, and 'panegyric', praise for the living, two rhetorical forms of address which had a lasting effect on biography.

The main events of classical lives are battles, conquests, victories in government and argument, dominance over the populace, the imparting of wisdom, influential deeds and sayings. (Though Plutarch, a richly varied writer, is also interested in personal detail and domestic anecdotes.) Sometimes, as in Plutarch, they are paralleled, so that one character stands out in relief against another: so the mercurial Greek charmer Alcibiades is paired with the stubborn, proud Roman Coriolanus. Sometimes, as in

Suetonius, good and bad characteristics are piled up in turn. But there is a standard pattern, beginning with early signs of character revealed in childhood incidents, followed by a rising trajectory, illustrated by exploits, sayings, or revealing examples of behaviour. The Lives reach a plateau of status, influence, success, wealth, or power, and then fall or decline, through errors of judgement, unpopularity, conspiracy, defeat, exile, betrayal, disgrace, or senility. The death scenes – like Plato's of Socrates or Suetonius's of Nero – can have a powerful impact. These lives are written with a moral purpose, but also to entertain. They have a political agenda – Plutarch's, for instance, to consolidate links between the Greeks and the Romans.

Plutarch, much influenced by Aristotle, is a writer with a moral purpose. In his *Life of Pericles* he says that 'actions arising out of virtue ... immediately put one in a frame of mind such that one simultaneously admires the acts and desires to emulate the agents'. He constantly drew exemplary, generalized lessons from individual lives. He showed that character could be shaped and changed through accidents, catastrophes, and successes. But he also believed there was such a thing as innate character. His treatment of that brilliant slippery character Alcibiades is a case in point:

> Of the many skills Alcibiades possessed, we hear in particular of one which was a useful tool for captivating men, and that was that he could assimilate and adapt himself to their habits and lifestyles ... In Sparta he took exercise, lived frugally, and wore a frown on his face; in Ionia he was fastidious, companionable, and easy-living; in Thrace he went in for hard drinking and hard riding ... It was not that he actually changed personality so readily, or that his character was infinitely mutable, but ... he assumed and took refuge in whatever appearance and image was appropriate for [the people he was with].

Not all Plutarch's subjects lead to a single moral: many are complicated, inconsistent, and profoundly flawed.

Plutarch was writing about long-past lives, which he wanted to bring vividly to life, but he famously distinguished what he was doing from the work of a historian.

> I am not writing history but biography, and the most outstanding exploits do not always have the property of revealing the goodness or badness of the agent; often, in fact, a casual action, the odd phrase, or a jest reveals character better than battles involving the loss of thousands upon thousands of lives... Just as a painter reproduces his subject's likeness by concentrating on the face and the expression of the eyes... I must be allowed to devote more time to those aspects which indicate a person's mind.... while leaving their major exploits and battles to others.

This kind of life-writing had a lasting influence. Between the 15th and the 17th centuries, Plutarch was translated into Latin, then French, then English. Shakespeare based his Roman plays on Thomas North's 1579 translation. His popularity in Britain continued all through the 18th and 19th centuries. Dryden explained Plutarch's appeal in 1683, in the preface to a new translation, not primarily as a moralist, but as a creator of character who takes you behind the scenes:

> Here you are led into the private lodgings of the hero: you see him in his undress, and are made familiar with his most private actions and conversation. You may behold... Augustus playing at bounding-stones with boys; and Agesilaus riding on a hobby-horse among his children. The pageantry of life is taken away; you see the poor reasonable animal, as naked as nature ever made him; are made acquainted with his passions and his follies, and find the Demi-God a man.

Plutarch's achievement, according to Dryden, is to have humanized his great men. That is not the main aim of the other major strand of 'ur-biographies', the saints' Lives, or hagiographies. (The term derives from Late Latin *hagiographa*, from Greek '*agios*', holy, and '*graphia*', writing.) These are lives lived in imitation of Christ, in retreat from the world, dedicated to God, providing lessons in exceptional godliness and purity. In the standard pattern, they start with early signs of spirituality shown through childhood incidents, followed by a break, often violent and difficult, with worldly connections (family, society, politics, government), perhaps a conversion, and a commitment to a holy life. The narrative then settles down to giving examples of the holy person's sayings, conversations, visions, and miracles, culminating in a farewell address, a holy death or martyrdom, miraculous posthumous proofs of sainthood, and evidence of lasting influence. The saints' trials – testing of virginity, conflicts with pagan authorities, torture, imprisonment – are always emphasized, and a good death is a key part of the story. As classical Lives emphasized traits and provided 'exempla' of types of behaviour, saints' Lives displayed prototypical virtues.

Hagiography was 'one of the dominant literary genres in Europe from Late Antiquity to the end of the Middle Ages'. It covers an enormous time-span, from Latin and Greek texts written by, and for, monks, to vernacular versions, probably for a lay audience, between the 13th and the 15th centuries. Saints' Lives run from early examples such as the anonymous Life of Cuthbert, written in about 699 by a monk of Lindisfarne (improved on by Bede when he came to write his Life of Cuthbert in the 720s) and Aelfric's Old English *Lives of the Saints*, written around AD 1000; to 11th- and 12th-century Anglo-Norman saints' Lives in verse; and 13th- and 14th-century collections such as the *South England Legendary* or Jacobus de Voragine's *Legenda Aurea, The Golden Legend*. They generally become more psychologically complex over time, more interested in the saints' conversions and self-doubts than in lists of miracles. After the 15th century, the dominance of hagiography fades away, but it persists in 19th-century collections of Protestant martyrs, such as *English Female Worthies*; 20th-century compilations of *Saints and Sinners*; modern lives of Catholic heroes such as Evelyn Waugh's Life of

Edmund Campion; and sanctified accounts of contemporary public figures like Martin Luther King or Mother Theresa. The most famous saints' Lives were repeatedly rewritten, collecting additional anecdotes along the way. Saint Catherine, the daughter of a king who challenged and defeated the Emperor Maxentius and his philosophers in arguments over sacrificing to pagan gods, who refused to marry Maxentius or to be worshipped as a statue, who was to be tortured on a knife-studded wheel except that angels broke it in bits, and who when eventually beheaded spouted milk, not blood, was supposedly martyred in 4th-century Alexandria. But her cult as the 'pre-eminent virgin martyr', bride of Christ, and patron of nuns, philosophers, wheelwrights, and wet-nurses, only developed from the 10th century, when the earliest known Greek and Latin versions of her story were written, coinciding with the discovery of relics and the building of shrines. As she became increasingly popular, later versions embroidered her qualities. Those written for clerics spent more time on her philosophical arguments; lay versions concentrated on her routing of the opposition and her miracles. In some retellings, she was courtly, witty, and brilliant; in others, she was rude and fierce – as here, refusing to be made into an object of worship: 'Be stylle, thou fool! I saye to thee,/Thou redes me to ful mekyl synne!/What man wolde idampnyd be/In helle for ony worldys wynne?/I have to Jhesu Cryst my love:/He is my spouse, bothe oute and inne.'

Saints' Lives served many purposes. They boosted cults, shrines, and the sale of relics. They encouraged piety and spirituality. They created links, in their vernacular versions, between ordinary people and the church. They had complex political and social agendas, including critiques of contemporary life, lessons in manners, sexual roles, and economics, and even religious dissent. Their subjects were 'rebels, failed monarchs, disobedient children, virginal spouses, social radicals and cross-dressers'. Like Catherine, they could be caustic, defiant, and bossy. There were many 14th-century examples in which 'witty, resilient saints make fools of the bumbling authorities who try to intimidate or to harm

3. A famous saint's dramatic martyrdom

them'. These lives were 'often more exemplary than imitable'. They are the starting point for the tension that biography produces between wanting to identify and emulate, and wanting to know about a life inconceivably different to one's own.

In Reformation England, hagiography became contested territory. Protestantism created its own saints (as in John Foxe's gigantic *Actes and Monuments*, better known as the *Book of Martyrs*, begun in 1563, or Milton's Sonnet of 1655 on the 'slaughtered saints',

Protestants massacred in Piedmont). The humanism and scepticism of the Renaissance or Early Modern period, its explorations and experiments in the arts and sciences, its passion for classical learning, and its interest in individualism, belief systems, and political structures involved fresh ways of thinking about life-writing. Hagiography came under attack as a form of superstitious ideology. By the 17th century, Thomas Fuller, in his Protestant biographical compendium of English types, *Worthies of England* (1662), was pouring scorn on the 'forgeries' and 'grand abuse' to be found in the Lives of Saints, due to the 'want of honest hearts in the *Biographists* of these saints' – and the profit they earned for pilgrimage sites. His prejudices come through strongly in his account of King Alfred, who 'loved religion more than superstition; favoured learned men more than lazy monks; which, perchance, was the cause that his memory is not loaded with miracles, and he not solemnly sainted with other Saxon kings who far less deserved it'.

Hagiography became a bad word. Especially for historians of biography at the start of the 20th century, reacting against what they saw as the Victorians' resurrection of saintly Lives, pre-Reformation life-writing looked like a black hole. Edmund Gosse's entry on 'Biography' in the 11th edition of the *Encylopaedia Britannica* (1910–11) pronounced: 'Biography hardly begins to exist in English literature until the close of the reign of Henry VIII'. Later commentators followed suit. Recent surveys refer to 'the darkness of hagiography' holding biography in thrall over 'a thousand years of saints' lives', of the 'dark ages' of 'a church-policed culture of veneration'. Modern readers do not expect biography to be programmed and polemical. We prefer, retrospectively, the classical strain of life-writing as described by Dryden, the revelation of the 'poor reasonable animal' in undress, and are frustrated by hagiography's 'conventional formulas, polemical exaggerations, and shameless borrowings'.

Exemplary Lives came to be seen as narratives of representative types, and it is often said that biography develops into the genre we know with the emergence of an interest in individualism in the 16th and 17th centuries. The range of subjects thought appropriate for a Life broadened with the rise of the middle classes and with social movements towards democracy. By the later 17th and 18th centuries, more 'private' Lives were being written and much more emphasis was being placed on ideas of selfhood and the autonomy of the individual.

But these tidy progressive histories of biography are not fool-proof. Neither classical Great Men's lives nor medieval saints' Lives presented uncomplicated models of exemplarity. They are also interested in providing moral instruction through dramatic examples of bad behaviour and unsuitable models for ordinary life, accompanied by awful warnings. Secular collections like Lydgate's *Fall of Princes*, derived from Boccaccio in the 1430s, told ominous stories of great men tumbling down as the Wheel of Fortune turns. *The Mirour for Magistrates*, a collection of verse-lives (in editions from 1555 to 1587), provided 'tragicall examples' of how 'this weltring world, both flowes and ebs like seas'. Destinies were summed up ('How Thomas Wolsey did arise unto great authority and government, his maner of life, pompe, and dignity, and how hee fell down into great disgrace, and was arested of high treason'), characters lamented their own fates as if from beyond the grave, and bitter lessons were drawn: 'How frayle al honours are, how brittle worldly blisse.'

As in *The Mirour for Magistrates*, the two strands of worldly classical Lives and Christian hagiography did not form clear-cut, separate influences on modern biography. The complicated intertwining of pagan and Judaeo-Christian stories is seen, for example, in the strange biographical mutations of Alexander, via Greek, Latin, Hebrew, Arabic, Spanish, and French sources in late antiquity and the early Middle Ages, from Greek conqueror of the East to chivalric Christian hero of medieval romances. A mixed lineage of classical leaders' speeches and Christian saints' oratory combined to influence the 'rhetorical performances' of 17th-century life-writings. The pre-history of biography leaves a complicated and long-lasting legacy. It is misleadingly neat to argue that classical models were overturned by the dark ages of hagiography, thankfully superseded by secular, democratic candour and idiosyncrasy. Exemplary representations of lives with universally recognizable traits did not suddenly disappear; they persisted into the 18th and 19th centuries. The idea of an exemplary life has never gone away.

Francis Bacon, politician and philosopher under Elizabeth and James I, famously divided History into three branches: Chronicles of the age, Lives, and Narrations of specific actions. He preferred Lives. Because they told of a single person 'in whom actions both greater and smaller, public and private, have a commixture', they ought, if well written, to contain 'a more true, native, and lively representation'. But he found it strange, in 1605, 'that the writings of lives should be no more frequent...yet are there many worthy personages...that deserve better than dispersed report or barren eulogy'.

There were a few exceptions which could have proved him wrong, but some of them were only circulating in manuscript: it was dangerous to publish accounts of recently dead monarchs and leaders. Sir Walter Raleigh, writing his *History of the World* from the Tower, knew that 'whosoever in writing a modern Historie shall follow truth too neare the heeles, it may haply strike out his teeth'. George Cavendish's lavishly descriptive tragic life of his employer Cardinal Wolsey (who died in 1561) was circulating long before it was printed in 1641. Sir Thomas More's *History of Richard III*, written in the 1510s but not published in full until 1557, made a vigorous, ironic, highly dramatized critique of the wicked monarch and in passing gave a sympathetic character-sketch of Jane Shore, Edward IV's 'concubine', with a note defending the value of setting so 'slight a thing' 'among remembrances of great matters'. Its story broke off before getting too close to the present. William Roper's memoir of his father-in-law Thomas More was written in the 1550s, about twenty years after More's death in 1535, and was privately circulated before being printed in 1626. Because he had lived in his household for many years, Roper could give an inward, authentic picture of More's character, with all his turns of speech. So we hear More trying to explain to his wife Alice why she should not mind his imprisonment. Clearly not his intellectual equal, she meets his philosophy with her usual kind of 'homely' brush-off: '"Is not this house," quoth he, "as nighe heaven as my owne?" To whom shee, after hir accustomed homely fashion... awneswered, "Tylle valle, Tylle valle!"'. And we see him going wisely and humorously to his death: 'I pray you, master Leiuetenaunte, see me salf [safe] uppe, and for my cominge downe let me shifte for my self.'

By the end of the 17th century, those sorts of vivid individualistic lives, almost a match for Thomas More's portraitist Holbein in depth, intensity, and telling detail, were no longer the exception in English and European life-writing. Montaigne's autobiographical writings of the 1580s and 1590s about the self and its complexities (first translated into English in 1603), preceded a flurry of vividly individualized 17th-century French memoirs, letters, and literary anecdotes, running alongside the formal, classical tradition of the *éloge*, which were increasingly being written in French rather than in Latin – a collection of *Éloges des hommes savants*, for instance. In Italy, Benvenuto Cellini's autobiography, though not published until 1730, was being written, between 1558 and 1566, at a time when vernacular collections of biographies – like the Florentine Vespasiano da Bisticci's lives of leaders and writers, or Giorgio Vasari's *Lives of the Most Excellent Italian Architects, Painters and Sculptors* (1550, 1568) – were displacing the earlier, classically influenced collections of short 'illustrious' lives in Latin by 14th-century writers such as Petrarch and Villani. Vasari's *Lives* established a

4. Depth, intensity, detail: a great 17th-century-biographical portrait

powerful convention of talking about works of art biographically, through the personality of the artist.

Biographical writing in 17th-century England was energized, just as much as Petrarch or Montaigne or Vasari, by classical models, through Thomas North's translation of Plutarch's *Lives* in 1579 and new translations of Theophrastus, Tacitus, and Suetonius. But it

THE LIVES OF THE NOBLE GRECIANS AND ROMANES, COMPARED

together by that graue learned Philosopher and Historiographer, Plutarke of Chæronea:

Translated out of Greeke into French by IAMES AMYOT, Abbot of Bellozane, Bishop of Auxerre, one of the Kings priuy counsel, and great Amner of Fraunce, and out of French into Englishe, by *Thomas North.*

Imprinted at London by Thomas Vautroullier and Iohn VVight.
1579.

5. Classical lives: the rise and fall of great men

reached beyond its origins. It covered a wide, contemporaneous range of subjects – rulers, magistrates, worthies, artists, poets, churchmen, thinkers – and took many forms. There were individual Lives, collective group Lives, biographical dictionaries, obituaries, 'memoirs, diaries, epistolary collections, hagiographies, character-sketches and royal lives'. Praise and eulogy were mixed with criticism and satire, universal types with curious individuals, formal rhetorical patterns with eccentric deviations. Empirical scientific discoveries and explorations of the natural world, notably by members of the Royal Society such as Robert Hooke and Robert Boyle, impinged on ideas of how a human life might be investigated. Locke's enquiries towards the end of the century into the workings of the mind changed the next generation's thinking about the formation of identity. Hierarchies of high and low, public and private, were shifting. The traditions of saints' Lives and classical Lives began to mingle in life-writing with quite different genres: scandal-sheets, crime reports, satirical poetry, family portraits.

As the writing of Lives became more diverse, the word 'biography' came into general use – first with Fuller's use of 'biographist' in 1662, then with Dryden's category, in his 1683 introduction to Plutarch, of 'biographia, or the history of particular men's lives'. Biography began to be discussed as a genre. Two famous examples of collective Lives show how differently it could be done. Izaac Walton's serious celebrations of the poet-priests Donne and Herbert, the politician Henry Wotton, and the theologians Richard Hooker and Robert Sanderson, written and much re-written between 1640 and 1678, fused together a number of the available ways of thinking about 'good men': hagiographies and martyrologies, panegyrics and encomiums, funeral sermons, commemorations, and portraiture, Theophrastian character-sketches, and books on '*ars moriendi*', the art of dying, giving advice on 'Dyenge Well' or 'Good Deaths'. Walton was carefully read by both Johnson and Boswell. Later, he came to be over-idealized as a saintly writer, and then dismissed for inaccuracy. One 19th-century biographer of Herbert attacked Walton's Lives

6. Donne: the death-bed portrait

as a 'mingle-mangle of unhistoric statement and mendacious zeal'. But his loving respect and, in some cases, personal feeling for his subjects, and his copious use of their own words, gave his exemplary Lives an intimate sense of personality. He did not make high claims for his own work; he was making 'the best plain Picture' that he could, and he thought what he was doing was 'usefull'.

Walton ends his *Life of Donne* with visual comparisons. On his death-bed, Donne asked to be wrapped in his winding-sheet, to have a portrait made of his 'lean, pale and death-like face', which he kept by him till the hour of his death. Walton compares this image to Donne's portrait as a young man and to his commemorative marble statue in St Paul's, so like Donne that 'it seems to breath faintly'. He ends with his own 'picture' of Donne, drawn according to the science of physiognomy: 'His aspect was cheerful, and such as gave a silent testimony of a clear knowing soul... His melting eye showed that he had a soft heart, full of noble compassion.' Walton concludes with a pious hope which also sums up what he has been trying to do. The body which he has been describing 'is now become a small quantity of Christian dust'. 'But I shall see it reanimated.'

Those eloquently written, carefully structured, reverential memoirs could not be more different from *Brief Lives*, the amoral, forthright, energetic, and scrappy life-writings of John Aubrey, dating from the 1670s and 1680s. Typically of an inquiring man of his time – like Pepys, whose diaries were contemporaneous – Aubrey was interested in everything: antiquarianism, archaeology, astrology, horticulture, mathematics, folklore, dreams, ghosts, horoscopes, heraldry. Biography, for him, was just another branch of natural science. But Aubrey was, also, wildly disorganized. He called his four hundred or so biographical sketches, a mixture of anecdotes, gossip, memories, and observations, 'skediasmata', 'scattered things' (or, in the phrase of his later biographer, the novelist Anthony Powell, 'pieces written on the spur of the moment'). They were written in no particular order, often in bits or unfinished, as a collaboration with the antiquarian Anthony à Wood (the most vain and vindictive of Oxford scholars) for his *Athenae Oxonienses*, an encyclopaedia of all the writers and bishops educated at Oxford from 1500 to 1690. Aubrey told Wood in 1680 that he thought life-writing should be candid and truthful, but that there were risks attached.

> I here lay-downe to you...the Trueth...the naked and plaine trueth, which is here exposed so bare that the very pudenda are not covered, and affords many passages that would raise a Blush in a young Virgin's cheeks. So that after your perusall, I must desire you to make a Castration...and to sowe-on some Figge-leaves...These Arcana are not fitt to lett flie abroad, till about 30 yeares hence, for the author and the Persons (like Medlars) ought to be rotten first.

Wood betrayed his trust and got Aubrey into hot water. They quarrelled bitterly, and Aubrey's work was published only piecemeal or in expurgated form until the 20th century. Even so, his commitment to the naked truth played an important part in biography's long debate between 'veracity' and discretion; his lively, gossipy miniaturism had an influence on later 'short lives' like Marcel Schwob's *Vies Imaginaires* or Lytton Strachey's *Eminent Victorians*, and his magpie eye for revealing details of behaviour and speech anticipated the 18th century's passion for anecdotes and 'ana'.

Aubrey liked to mix up his life-stories with theories about human behaviour, superstitions, general opinions, and accounts of how he came by his information. One Brief Life ends: 'He dyed of a broaken heart.' Telling of a youthful drunken exploit by the poet John Denham, who once blotted out with ink all the road-signs between Temple Bar and Charing Cross, he noted that he 'had [the story] from R. Estcott, Esq., that carried the Inke-pott'. A life of a famous beauty, Venetia Digby, whose memorial bust he later spotted standing outside a shop in Newgate Street, with the gilding peeled off, provoked the comment: 'How these curiosities would be quite forgott, did not such idle fellowes as I am putt them downe.' He had a brilliant gift for rapidly invoking character. Francis Bacon, baldly described (in Greek lettering) as a paederast, had 'a delicate, lively, hazel Eie; Dr Harvey told me it was like the Eie of a viper'. Hobbes, who gets the longest Life, had a habit of singing aloud at night, when 'he was sure nobody heard him' from his book of prick-songs (vocal music): 'He did beleeve it did his Lunges good, and conduced much to prolong his life'. Aubrey could get carried away with a particularly juicy story (of the kind that had to be fig-leafed by his 19th-century editor):

> [Sir Walter Raleigh] loved a wench well; and one time getting up one of the Mayds of Honour up against a tree in a Wood... who seemed at first boarding to be something fearfull of her Honour, and modest, she cryed, sweet Sir Walter, what doe you me ask? Will you undoe me? Nay, sweet Sir Walter! Sweet Sir Walter! Sir Walter! At last, as the danger and the pleasure at the same time grew higher, she cryed in the extasey, Swisser Swasser Swisser Swasser. She proved with child, and I doubt not but this Hero tooke care of them both, as also that the Product was more than an ordinary mortal.

And he could not resist a good joke:

> Edward de Vere. Born 1550. He was a courtier of Queen Elizabeth, who lost his friends by his insolence and pride, and his fortune by his extravagance... This Earle of Oxford, making of his low obeisance to Queen Elizabeth, happened to let a Fart, at which he was so abashed and ashamed that he went to Travell, 7 yeares. On his returne the Queen welcomed him home, and sayd, My Lord, I had forgott the Fart.

We have come a long way from the fate of Moses to the fart of Edward de Vere: but biography continues to mix together those contradictory strains, the epic and the absurd, legends and gossip, the elegiac and the anecdotal, gravity and foolishness.

Chapter 3
Warts and All

Samuel Johnson (aged 64) and James Boswell (aged 33) are travelling together in the Hebrides, in the autumn of 1773. It is ten years since they first met in London. They are staying, in company, on the Isle of Skye.

> We danced tonight to the musick of the bagpipe, which made us beat the ground with prodigious force. I thought it better to endeavour to conciliate the kindness of the people of Sky, by joining heartily in their amusements, than to play the abstract scholar. I looked on this Tour to the Hebrides as a copartnership between Dr. Johnson and me. Each was to do all he could to promote its success; and I have some reason to flatter myself, that my gayer exertions were of service to us. Dr. Johnson's immense fund of knowledge and wit was a wonderful source of admiration and delight to them; but they had it only at times; and they required to have the intervals agreeably filled up, and even little elucidations of his learned text. I was also fortunate enough frequently to draw him forth to talk, when he would otherwise have been silent. The fountain was at times locked up, till I opened the spring.

This is from Boswell's *Journal of a Tour to the Hebrides*, published in 1785, a year after Johnson's death, and twelve years after their journey. Johnson had published his own version of the tour, *A Journey to the Western Islands of Scotland*, in 1775. The two versions are – as Boswell's biography would be – a form of

7. Reynolds' Johnson: The man of letters, warts and all

THE LIFE

OF

SAMUEL JOHNSON, LL.D.

COMPREHENDING

AN ACCOUNT OF HIS STUDIES
AND NUMEROUS WORKS,

IN CHRONOLOGICAL ORDER;

A SERIES OF HIS EPISTOLARY CORRESPONDENCE
AND CONVERSATIONS WITH MANY EMINENT PERSONS;

AND

VARIOUS ORIGINAL PIECES OF HIS COMPOSITION,
NEVER BEFORE PUBLISHED.

THE WHOLE EXHIBITING A VIEW OF LITERATURE AND LITERARY MEN
IN GREAT-BRITAIN, FOR NEAR HALF A CENTURY,
DURING WHICH HE FLOURISHED.

IN TWO VOLUMES.

BY JAMES BOSWELL, ESQ.

——— *Quò fit ut* OMNIS
Votiva pateat veluti defcripta tubella
VITA SENIS.——— HORAT.

VOLUME THE FIRST.

LONDON:
PRINTED BY HENRY BALDWIN,
FOR CHARLES DILLY, IN THE POULTRY.
M DCC XCI.

8. Boswell's Johnson: still the most famous of all British biographies

'copartnership', often giving different accounts of the same events. Boswell's *Journal* was also a trailer for his long-awaited *Life* of Johnson. He noted in the *Journal* that in 1773 he was asking Johnson 'particulars of his life, from his early years', and was planning to 'collect authentick materials for *The Life of Samuel Johnson, LLD*'. He had 'a vast treasure of his conversation', and planned to make up for not having known him earlier by 'assiduous enquiry'. The *Life* finally appeared in 1791, twenty-eight years after their first meeting and seven years after Johnson's death.

Boswell dancing and Johnson talking on the Isle of Skye introduce the dynamics, and the comedy, of their biographical relationship. Those who (at the time and later) found Boswell chattering, prancing, and self-promoting, and Johnson uncouth, severe, and overbearing, always made fun of the 'copartnership'. Boswell has been much blamed for dancing in front of his subject. The *Tour*, said Horace Walpole, making Johnson and Boswell into Don Quixote and Sancho Panzo, was the story of 'a mountebank and his zany'. The *Life*, said the hostile Thomas Macaulay, forty years after its publication, was a great book inexplicably written by a feeble-minded laughing-stock about 'a mind at least as remarkable for narrowness as for strength'. Boswell's absurdity and Johnson's grotesqueness have always been mixed up with the epic, even tragic, dimensions of what is still the most famous (even if, now, not the most widely read) biography in the English language.

It is such a strange book to stand as the classic example of the genre. Why should an eccentric, passionately opinionated, bullying, neurotic 18th-century lexicographer, biographer, and journalist be the most famous hero of British life-writing? And why should an enormous, garrulous hold-all of a narrative be the pre-eminent model of biography? Though the *Life* is chronological, it spends far more time on the period during which Boswell knew Johnson than on the preceding fifty-four years of Johnson's life: half the book covers Johnson's last eight years. Because Boswell was a slow and disorganized worker, several other accounts of

Johnson were published before his, so he is constantly slapping down his rivals and promoting his own account as the most 'authentick'. Because his 'assiduous enquiry' produced a mountain of testimonies and documentation, he puts chunks of Johnson's letters and other people's letters and anecdotes in between his own stories of Johnson's behaviour, descriptions of social occasions, and transcriptions (or imitations) of Johnson's conversation and sayings. His own relationship with Johnson is much the most prominent of Johnson's friendships. Though he promises 'veracity' – about himself as well as his subject – he also omits some details, for instance about Johnson's peculiar marriage or his feelings for women.

Since the discovery of an amazing cache of Boswell's papers in the 1920s, and the growth of a huge scholarly industry on Boswell and Johnson, much work has been done to show how carefully and artfully shaped the *Life* really is. Meanwhile, Johnson has been rescued from Boswell, in biographical works that go back to the young, pre-Boswellized Samuel Johnson, or look at him through other eyes – for instance, those of his women writer friends such as Hester Thrale and Fanny Burney – or in editions of his works, notably of his own major biographical enterprise, the *Lives of the English Poets*. Yet Boswell continues to dance at the centre of the British biographical stage.

Boswell's Life of a man of letters emerged from a century in which there was a massive expansion of print and reading in Britain. The democratization and secularization of knowledge, the growing dominance of realistic fiction as a popular genre, the increasing variety of available reading materials, involved a book trade and a literary market place (mainly centred on London) of the utmost energy, competitiveness, brutality, and complexity. Boswell and Johnson were both deeply embedded in this Grub Street world of professional, money-making hack-work, and part of the interest of Boswell's *Life* is that it gives such a detailed account of, yet seems to rise above, its context. Literary patronage, literary rivalry, and literary reputations were the driving forces, and also, often, the subject matter, for many writers. A highly socialized, gossipy, backbiting, and rivalrous literary world structured itself through clubs, magazines, reviews, and literary groups. Writers met in public, sat in coffee houses, talked in salons, walked the streets and took journeys together, and then wrote everything up. In every form of art – poetry, portraiture, sculpture, theatre, essays, fiction, journalism – there was an intense interest in expressing and analysing selfhood. 'The proper study of mankind is man', Pope wrote in *The Essay on Man* in 1733. At the other end of the century, Rousseau's posthumous *Confessions* (published between 1781 and 1788) promised the display, with hitherto unrivalled frankness, of a unique, incomparable individual. From Fielding and Defoe to Jane Austen and Fanny Burney, fictional personages were represented as individuals vividly marked by particular character traits, exploring life and seeking satisfaction through their relationships with other people. The products and processes of the book trade were closely bound up with this interest in personality and character. Literary correspondence was being published (starting with Pope's letters), autobiographies were being written, journals were being kept, in bulk.

Boswell's annotation of Johnson's life was not unique. The literary disciple following the great man around and taking down everything he says has stayed with us as an almost parodic image of biography. (Boswell was unfairly caricatured for having taken notes in company while Johnson was talking: in fact, he relied more on a good memory and quick writing-up after the event – if he left it too long, it was like 'pickling long-kept and faded fruits' – and he congratulates himself on having become better at 'taking down' Johnson as he grew less in awe of him.) But the practice of collecting and publishing the 'ana' (sayings) or 'anecdotes' of famous wise men went back a long way. You might call Plato's books Socratiana, or the New Testament, Messiana. Lives in the 17th century made great use of 'sayings'. The lawyer and orientalist John Selden's 'table talk' was collected by his secretary and published in 1689. French literary history of the 18th century was crowded with collections of 'ana'. Such collections showed an intense interest in great men's spoken words.

Women were not such objects of interest. There were plenty of women writers producing poems, plays, novels, diaries, letters, travel writings, essays, and hymns in the late 17th and early 18th centuries. But memoirs or 'ana' of women were not being collected. Instead, Margaret Cavendish, Duchess of Newcastle, wrote a life of her (living) husband, William Cavendish, in 1667, praising him to the skies for his virtues. (The panegyric was mocked by Pepys, who thought her 'a mad, conceited, ridiculous woman, and he an ass to suffer her to write what she writes'.) Lucy Hutchinson wrote a self-effacing, loving memoir of her husband Colonel Hutchinson, the Protestant regicide, in 1664, referring to herself throughout in the third person and extolling him as a Protestant saint: 'His life was nothing else but a progress from one degree of vertue to another.' The 19th-century novelist and autobiographer Margaret Oliphant said of it, in 1882: 'There is never an "I" in the book from beginning to end.' Hester Thrale wrote *Anecdotes of the Life of the late Samuel Johnson* in 1786. Fanny Burney edited her father's *Memoirs*.

The 'Great Men' whose sayings were being written down by their admirers were often writers, painters, or actors. There was a deep interest in imagination and creativity, in the life of the mind. The literary Oxford clergyman Joseph Spence met Pope in the mid-1720s and noted down his sayings from 1727 until Pope's death in 1744. Spence's 'Popeana' or *Anecdotes* circulated in manuscript for many years. Johnson saw the manuscript in 1780, when he was writing his Life of Pope. Spence provided materials for biography: he never wrote his own Life of Pope, and his manuscript was not published until 1820 (nor fully edited until the 1960s). The fashion for 'ana' continued, linking the centuries: there were William Seward's *Anecdotes of Some Distinguished Persons* (1795) and John Nichols' nine-volume *Literary Anecdotes of the Eighteenth Century*

(1812–16). In the 1820s and 1830s, soon after Spence's *Anecdotes* were published, Hazlitt published his *Conversations with Sir James Northcote* (the portrait-painter who had been Reynolds's pupil and friend), Fanny Burney's anecdotal *Memoirs* of her father Dr Burney came out, and Drummond's *Conversations with Ben Jonson*, dating from 1618, were published. Speech acts were valued. Conversation was a vital part of life, an art, a form of entertainment, and – in Johnson's case – a brow-beating competition. But Boswell was unusual in turning 'ana' into a whole biographical narrative, while keeping the fragmentary quality of an anthology. He was pioneering, too, as one of the first to publish private conversations so fully and candidly, and he got into trouble for it. Critics, of both the *Tour* and the *Life*, objected to his having exhibited all Johnson's 'unhappy infirmities', thereby 'disgracing a character ... as wens and warts would do a statue or Portrait'.

The main ingredients of that scene on Skye, from the *Tour*, are all there in the *Life*. Boswell insists on his kind of biographical writing as a 'copartnership'. He takes pride in his own role. He stage-manages his main performer. He venerates, but is also wary of, his subject. He believes in conversation as the best way of 'displaying' character. He feels that the relationship he had with Johnson, which 'opened the spring' of that conversation, is of great value to himself and to the world. He is determined to write the truest version. 'Authenticity is my chief boast', he said of the *Tour* in 1785, to Edmond Malone, the Shakespeare scholar who gave him so much help and encouragement. In his 'Preface' and 'Advertisement' to the *Life* (addressed to Malone), Boswell used a cluster of words that are keys to his work, and to this phase of British biography: 'conversation', 'authenticity', 'fidelity', 'accuracy', 'intimately'. He believed – as Johnson did – that the point of life-writing was to be truthful and realistic: 'veracity' was one of their favourite words. Fidelity to the subject should not be a process of loyal concealment, but of accurate characterization. It was the 'minute particulars' that gave biography its usefulness.

'Authenticity', in the best sense, implied a moral standard, and a reaction against more dutiful or pious forms of life-writing. This reaction had set in well before Boswell. The lawyer and biographer Roger North, in a prescient unpublished manuscript dating from the 1730s, outlined all the arguments that would become familiar in the next two centuries, about the benefits of 'private lives' over public histories, the usefulness of ordinary men's life-stories, and the need for 'honesty' in biography. Johnson (who had not read North) made his own case for 'authenticity' long before he wrote most of his *Lives of the Poets*. His principles were set out, with typical confidence, in a famous essay written for his own magazine, the *Rambler*, in 1750. It claims that biography is the most 'delightful and useful' form of writing because 'the narrative of the lives of particular persons' allows us to sympathize with others. The 'judicious and faithful' story of almost any life is 'useful' because 'there is such a uniformity in the state of man', and we can recognize our own 'motives' and passions in the lives of others. Biographers need to choose the most important anecdotes to illustrate 'the manners and behaviour of their heroes'. Preferably, biography should be written from 'personal knowledge', but should not be dressed up with 'panegyrick'. 'If we owe regard to the memory of the dead, there is yet more respect to be paid to knowledge, to virtue, and to truth.' In a later essay in his magazine the *Idler*, Johnson argued that the most truthful life-writing is when 'the writer tells his own story', since only he knows the whole truth about himself. (He does not use the word 'autobiography', which only came into circulation in the early 19th century.) Those who write about another may want to over-praise him or 'aggravate his infamy'; those who write about themselves, he says – optimistically – have no 'motive to falsehood' except 'self-love', and we are all on the watch for that.

When Johnson wrote these essays he had already published, in his thirties, an extraordinarily pioneering *Life of Mr Richard Savage* (1744), the erratic poet and playwright, close friend of his twenties, whose struggles to survive in Grub Street included a criminal trial and an early death in the debtors' prison. Johnson's youthful sympathy for his strange friend inspired a fine book by Richard Holmes, which argues that the Life of Savage created a new, hybrid, 'romantic' non-fictional form, combining drama, romance, folk ballad, journalism, and morality. Writing it certainly crystallized Johnson's views on biography's ideal 'blend of sympathetic engagement and instructive detachment'. But Johnson's later *Lives of the Poets* were different. They were written, more than thirty years after the Life of Savage, not out of personal sympathy, but as commissioned prefaces to a new edition of 'the most eminent English poets', meant to analyse and place their works. Their main interest is in what makes a 'Genius' (especially in the Lives of Dryden and Pope). In the moral, realistic tradition of Plutarch, the *Lives* show off the 'usefulness' of anecdotes, a resistance to 'the mist of panegyric', powerful, strenuous, sometimes wilful critical attentiveness, and a clear sense of what can and can't be known about another person: 'Actions are visible, though motives are secret.' However, for all his earlier arguments that the value of biography is in the imaginative sympathy it can produce, Johnson's *Lives* can be ironic, opinionated, or brutally hostile, especially when he disapproves of a poet's politics:

> Milton's republicanism was, I am afraid, founded in an envious hatred of greatness, and a sullen desire of independence; in petulance impatient of controul, and pride disdainful of superiority ... He hated all whom he was required to obey.

Johnson's strong, principled, argumentative voice spoke out of an often ruthless and opportunistic literary culture. The use of the word 'authentic' might be a cheap form of advertisement or a warning-sign of predators at work, rather than an indication of high moral value. As early as 1716, the essayist Joseph Addison was complaining about 'Grub-street biographers' as vultures, 'who watch for the death of a great man, like so many undertakers, on purpose to make a penny of him.' The most notorious of these grave-robbers was the book dealer Edmund Curll, Pope's lifelong enemy and butt, notorious for his piratic literary thefts, his pornography, his unauthorized editions of writers' letters, and his quick, cheap, cobbled-together biographies, which led to his being famously described, in the 1730s, as 'one of the new terrors of Death'. Curll's shamelessly exploitative publications would always be prefaced with the words 'Genuine' and 'Authentic', as in his 1745 Life of Pope, rushed out after his old enemy's death, 'Faithfully Collected From Authentic Authors, Original Manuscripts, and the Testimonies of many Persons of Credit and Honour'.

There were dangers in authenticity. To some readers – and in some hands – it meant betrayal, not fidelity. Boswell venerated his subject and wanted to do well by him, but he was also trying to make his mark in a self-advertising literary world. So – as always in the history of biography – Boswell's *Life* involved both low and high motives. And, like all memorable biographies, it mixed together many different genres and approaches.

It is vividly visual, showing us the physical Johnson in every light and at every angle, often unflatteringly. 'I am so nice in recording him' (Boswell wrote in his Journal) 'that every trifle must be authentic. I draw him in the style of a Flemish painter. I am not satisfied with hitting the large features. I must be exact as to every hair, or even every spot on his countenance.' What this 'Flemish picture' provides is 'a sustained act of looking' (which owes as much to Hogarth and to Reynolds as to the Dutch painters). Once Johnson's huge, odd body has been sighted in its 'uncouth', 'slovenly' badly fitting clothes, we keep seeing it in our mind's eye: his convulsive tics, his savage, sweating eating habits, his obsessive-compulsive habits of counting steps and shaking his body and rubbing his left knee, the way he 'scraped the joints of his fingers with a pen-knife, till they seemed quite red and raw'.

We see him and we hear him; he comes on stage and talks like an actor in a play, with Boswell as stage-manager. Their friend the actor David Garrick is one of the most important figures in the biography, and the *Life* is as theatrical as it is painterly, arranged in scenes set up to display Johnson's character. We seem to hear his voice in our ear, pontificating and pronouncing like Humpty Dumpty, whether on remarriage ('Johnson said it was the triumph of hope over experience') or on a leg of mutton: 'It is as bad as bad can be: it is ill-fed, ill-killed, ill-kept, and ill-drest'. We hear the strange sounds he makes when he is not actually talking, as if he is 'chewing the cud' or 'clucking like a hen' or – victorious over his opponent in conversation – blowing 'out his breath like a Whale'.

This pictorial drama also reads like a realist novel of its time. It keeps opening out into the surrounding texture of urban society, politics, manners, and domestic scenes, and provides a running commentary on the literary, theatrical, legal, artistic, and journalistic professions. Boswell's eager, proprietary attempts to get Johnson going, his inexhaustible curiosity in 'soliciting particulars' of Johnson's life, his fixing up of encounters which will produce the best Johnsonianisms, his rebuffs when Johnson rounds on him ('Don't you know that it is very uncivil to *pit* two people against one another?'), or sulks in his corner like the 'bear' he is often compared to, are funny. Part of the comedy is that Boswell knows how ridiculous he is. 'I know not how so whimsical a thought came into my mind, but I asked, "If, Sir, you were shut up in a castle, and a newborn child with you, what would you do?"' (Leslie Stephen, in his own *Life of Johnson* of 1879, called this 'exquisitely ludicrous': 'But a man capable of preferring such a remark to silence helps at any rate to keep the ball rolling.') The famous scene of 1776 in which Boswell manipulates Johnson into meeting the radical political writer John Wilkes, in the hopes of a conflagration, only to find Johnson treating Wilkes with humorous civility, is a fine example of the wit and brio (and the careful structuring) of Boswell's 'novel', and of his chameleon-like ability to echo and imitate Johnson: 'If I had come upon him with a direct proposal, "Sir, will you dine in company with Jack Wilkes?" he would have flown into a passion, and would probably have answered, "Dine with Jack Wilkes, Sir! I'd as soon dine with Jack Ketch."'

But there is more to this relationship than comedy, and part of the interest is that we want to see how the asexual but tender attachment between the biographer and his subject develops. Boswell's own depressions and anxieties, his veneration for Johnson as an alternative to his own disapproving father, and Johnson's ability to teach and advise him, make an affecting story: as when Boswell fusses over a small domestic problem, and Johnson 'laughed, and said, "Consider, Sir, how insignificant this will appear a twelvemonth hence"'. Though Boswell insists that he is following Johnson's example in not giving us 'panegyrick', he also wants to 'infuse every drop of genuine sweetness into [his] biographical cup', citing others to show how 'few persons quitted his company without perceiving themselves wiser and better than they were before', and insisting that Johnson could be 'civil, obliging, nay, polite' as often as he could be 'violent', 'with a club in his hand, to knock down everyone who approached him'. '"Well, (said he), we had good talk." BOSWELL: "Yes, Sir; you tossed and gored several persons."' He takes care to contrast, with all the conversational tossing and goring, moments when Johnson shows a wistful, tender, affectionate side, as when, talking of a young man who is 'running about town shooting cats', Johnson 'in a sort of kindly reverie... bethought himself of his own favourite cat, and said, "But Hodge shan't be shot; no, no, Hodge shall not be shot."'

Boswell's Johnson is the man of letters as epic hero (as well as comic grotesque), and it is one of the new features of this late 18th-century biography that secular, bourgeois, everyday life should be the vehicle for heroic qualities. The heroism lies in Johnson's commitment to truth, his endurance, his philosophic stoicism wrestling with his dark, lonely, troubled, passionate mind, his struggle with the fear of death: 'So much so, Sir, that the whole of life is but keeping away the thoughts of it.' When Boswell compares

Johnson's mind to the Coliseum at Rome, with his judgement at the centre like a 'mighty gladiator' doing battle with the 'apprehensions' that assail him like 'wild beasts', he makes his rationalist secular hero into a Christian martyr. This is not a saint's life, but Boswell gives Johnson spiritual victories, disciples, intellectual influence, and a good death.

The Life mixes genres, and it also mixes ways of thinking about the self. Johnson and Boswell both believe in the usefulness of biography in displaying moral values. In that sense they continue the exemplary tradition in life-writing derived from Plutarch and from Christian hagiography. But the presentation of identity in the Life is complicated, subtle, and new. There are at least two kinds of selfhood on display, two lines of behaviour. Broadly speaking, one line derives from Pope, Johnson's hero, and the other from Rousseau, whose novels Boswell much admired when he was young, and whom Johnson detested. The kind of behaviour on show that links to Rousseau is sentimental, tender, tearful, and confessional – as when, 'such was his sensibility', Johnson weeps when reading poetry. The line that can be associated with Pope is robust, satirical, observant, stoic: 'He advised me... when I was moving about, to read diligently the great book of mankind.' 'Let us endeavour to see things as they are', Johnson writes to a friend in 1758, 'and then enquire whether we ought to complain.'

That complex sense of what personality consists of will have a profound effect on biographical writing. Johnson is not a fixed entity, and nor is his biographer. In the dance of conversation and copartnership between the two, the figures seem to move about, talk, and think in front of us, embodied and immediate, though so long vanished into the past – as here, when Boswell, about to leave England for Utrecht, is saying goodbye to Johnson at Harwich:

> My revered friend walked down with me to the beach, where we embraced and parted with tenderness, and engaged to correspond

by letters. I said, 'I hope, Sir, you will not forget me in my absence.' JOHNSON: 'Nay, Sir, it is more likely you should forget me, than that I should forget you.' As the vessel put out to sea, I kept my eyes upon him for a considerable time, while he remained rolling his majestick frame in his usual manner: and at last I perceived him walk back into the town, and he disappeared.

Chapter 4
National Biography

Conversation, friendship, collaboration, quarrels; letters telling of personal feelings and encounters, of work in progress and political opinions; confessional narratives of addiction, love, and weakness; journals of domestic life; manuscripts circulating between small groups: early 19th-century literature was criss-crossed with a spider's web of life-writing. 'Self-fashioning' took many forms. In Europe, Rousseau's confessional individualism and his linking of natural passion and virtue, Goethe's 'elective affinities' transcending social laws, Herder's philosophy of self-defining subjectivity, profoundly influenced the telling of life-stories. In America, the intellectual declarations of independence of Transcendentalist thinkers like Emerson and Thoreau insisted on 'self-reliance' and a connection to nature for the forging of a true identity. Self-expression ran through every literary genre. Biography, character-sketches, autobiography, memoirs, diaries, travel-writing, and correspondence overlapped. For the British Romantic writers there was a porous line between published work (often scandalously autobiographical, even if written in disguise) and private writings passed between friends. Interior lives were closely bound up with group relations. Writers described each other, worked and lived together (sometimes catastrophically), published and reviewed each other, agonized over the survival and publication of personal documents, and looked anxiously for the right biographers to do justice to the dead.

The emphasis in life-writing was on empathy. William Hazlitt called his 1820s *Conversations* with the old portrait-painter James Northcote 'Boswell Redivivus', but he was more impressionistic than Boswell: 'My object was to catch the tone and manner, rather than to repeat the exact expressions, or even opinions.' Coleridge thought that too much 'minutiae' in a biography or memoir could 'render the real character almost invisible, like clouds of dust on a portrait'. The first British book on biography, written by James Stansfield in 1813, argued for a mixture of 'sympathetic emotion', 'impartiality', and 'moral illustration' – and for censoring 'particulars' which 'do not reflect great honour on the deceased'.

But life-writing also involved gossip, gusto, satire, and comedy. Romantic biography had teeth. Descriptions, for example, of Coleridge's extraordinary conversational manner show how wicked such writings could be. Hazlitt (who met Coleridge in 1798, and wrote about him with mixed admiration and disappointment in the early 1820s) described a 'tangential' mind which spilt itself in talking: 'If Mr Coleridge had not been the most impressive talker of his age, he would probably have been the finest writer... he may be said to have lived on the sound of his own voice.' Thomas Carlyle, who saw Coleridge in old age, wrote a lethal description in the 1850s of his 'confused unintelligible flood of utterance, threatening to submerge all known landmarks of thought', his habit of corkscrewing from one side of the garden path to the other ('he never could fix which side would suit him best'), and his plaintive, snuffling, sing-song voice: ' "Ah, your tea is too cold, Mr Coleridge!" mourned the good Mrs Gilman once... handing him a very tolerable though belated cup. "It's better than I deserve!" snuffled he, in a low hoarse murmur, partly courteous, chiefly pious, the tone of which still abides with me: "It's better than I deserve!" '

That anecdotal sharpness, one of the vital qualities of biography, was fuelled by a dislike of Coleridge's hazy idealism. There were ideological wars going on in early 19th-century biography, reflecting – as biography always does – the politics of the time. Life-writing could be boldly radical. Hazlitt's commitment to civil liberties energized his character-sketches of politicians and poets in *The Spirit of the Age* (1825) and his editing of the *Memoirs* of the working-class Jacobin writer Thomas Holcroft. William Godwin's short biography of his wife Mary Wollstonecraft, published in 1798, soon after her death in childbirth, as *Memoirs of the Author of 'The Rights of Woman'*, caused outrage for its candid account of her feminism, atheism, and anti-establishment views. Biography of this sort was dangerous, and would produce a backlash of censoriousness.

But sympathy was the key for Godwin as, fifty years on, for Carlyle, in his late Romantic biography of 1851 of 'a brilliant human presence', the unsuccessful poet John Sterling, who died young in 1844. Unlike Carlyle's later epic, historical biography of Frederick the Great, this is biography as confession, brimful with elegiac melancholy for 'this most friendly, bright and beautiful human soul; who walked with me for a season in this world, and remains to me very memorable while I continue in it'. When Boswell's *Life of Johnson* was republished in the 1830s, Carlyle wrote about biography as a sacred enterprise.

> In Boswell's 'Life of Johnson', how indelibly and magically bright does many a little Reality dwell in our remembrance!... some slight, perhaps mean and even ugly incident, if *real* and well-presented, will fix itself in a susceptive memory, and lie ennobled there... with the pathos which belongs only to the Dead. For the Past is all holy to us; the Dead are all holy, even they that were base, and wicked while alive...

He instances the glimpse of Boswell and Johnson walking along the Strand arm-in-arm at night, and being accosted by a 'woman of the town':

Strange power of Reality! Not even this poorest of occurrences, but now, after seventy years are come and gone, has a meaning for us. Do but consider that it is *true*; that it did in very deed occur!...Johnson said, 'No, no, my girl; it won't do'; and then 'we talked'; – and herewith the wretched one, seen but for the twinkling of an eye, passes on into the utter Darkness.

How, he asks, can biography do this – invoke such 'light-gleams' of reality?

> One grand, invaluable secret there is...: *To have an open loving heart, and what follows from the possession of such*...This is it that opens the whole mind, quickens every faculty of the intellect to do its fit work, that of *knowing*; and therefrom, by sure consequence, of *vividly uttering-forth*.

It is one of the great justifications of biography as a humane discipline – and it is very much of its time. If asked what the key to biographical success is now, we probably would not reply: 'to have an open loving heart'. And 'a loving heart' is a risky basis for life-writing. The impulses of sympathy and veneration that dominated much 19th-century biography often solidified into hagiography. Though many different kinds of Lives were being written between the 1830s and the 1890s, the period has come to be retrospectively caricatured for white-washing and censorship. The hallmarks of Victorian biography – quite unlike the risky narratives of the generation before – were morality and reticence. Carlyle saw this coming, reviewing the critic John Gibson Lockhart's 1837 *Memoirs* of his father-in-law, Walter Scott, which was causing outrage for exposing the 'sanctities of private life'.

> How delicate, decent is English biography, bless its mealy mouth! A Damocles' sword of *Respectability* hangs for ever over the poor English life-writer (as it does over poor English life in general) and reduces him to the verge of paralysis.

But discretion increasingly became the norm, in a period when class-consciousness, religious belief, social aspirations, serious evangelical moral standards, work ethic, fears of European-style revolution, and national loyalties, were such central themes in fiction and poetry – and in everyday middle-class life. Literary remains and reputations were being tidied up, as in the apologetic tone of Lockhart's 1828 biography of Burns (excusing the poet's 'dissipation' by pointing to 'the moral influence of his genius'), or the burning of Byron's scandalous journals in his publisher's office in 1824, or the Shelley family's efforts to sanctify his posthumous life. When the real stories of dead poets' intense emotions burst through these safeguards, as with Shelley's shocking 'irregular relations', scorching the pages of a guarded, compromised 1888 biography by Edward Dowden, or the publication in 1878 of Keats's love-letters to Fanny Brawne, there was always an outcry.

Biography in the mid to late 19th century was often written by a descendant or a disciple. The essential materials – letters, diaries, secrets – were usually in the family's possession. If the biographer was commissioned by the family, he (or, much less often, she) could only read what was given out, and had to be careful not to cause offence. There were many examples of protective Lives written by friends or family. These included Arthur Penrhyn Stanley's 1844 Life of Dr Thomas Arnold, the headmaster of Rugby who had been his teacher; John Forster's of his revered friend Charles Dickens (1872–4); G. O. Trevelyan's of his uncle Macaulay (1876); and Hallam Tennyson's of his father, the Poet Laureate (1897), written under the censoring eye of his mother Emily Tennyson. Widows of famous men such as Charles Kingsley piously memorialized their late husbands. Family biographers were well aware of their compromised position: Leslie Stephen, setting out gloomily to write a dutiful, commissioned life of his older brother, the legislator James Fitzjames Stephen, whom he had always found unsympathetic, asked himself: what 'if Boswell had been Johnson's brother?' His daughter Virginia Woolf would satirize the writing of such family biography in her 1919 novel *Night and Day*, part of a whole literary generation's scathing reaction against Victorian Lives.

Yet there was a great deal to be said for affectionate, venerating biography. Forster's *Dickens* was censored and inaccurate, but it also gave a sympathetic, energetic close-up of its remarkable subject. Elizabeth Gaskell's Life of her fellow novelist Charlotte Brontë told a tender and moving story. Gaskell had few precedents in 1857 for the writing of a woman's life by a woman. She was six years older than her subject and admired her work. They met in 1850, when Gaskell was forty; she had recently published *Mary Barton*; Brontë, *Jane Eyre*. After Brontë's death in 1855 at the age of thirty-eight, Gaskell was asked by the Reverend Patrick Brontë (who had outlived all his children) to write the Life. She approached her subject with sympathy and respect, as an equal – and also as a woman with her own history of family bereavements. Brontë had lost her mother and all her siblings; Gaskell's parents had died when she was young and she had lost two children. Her approach was protective: she wanted to defend Brontë against the accusations of immorality and coarseness which had greeted *Jane Eyre*, and she did so by suppressing her knowledge of Brontë's passionate love-letters to the married M. Heger in Brussels, and by emphasizing her femininity and religious stoicism over her professional achievements.

Gaskell noted down three suggestive quotations to guide her. One read: 'If you love your reader and want to be read, get anecdotes!' One spoke of the need for a 'tender tie' between biographer and subject. And one, from a friend of Brontë's, noted her 'boundless sphere of feeling and intellect crammed into a silent existence'. Gaskell set out to write a narrative of tragic loss, loneliness, anguish, Christian fortitude, and 'dignified endurance', set with novelistic vividness in the dark, gloomy Yorkshire moorland setting of Haworth. Small domestic details of Brontë's life as a daughter and sister dominate the story. One eloquent example is the story of Charlotte's interrupting her writing of *Jane Eyre* to cut

9. Charlotte Brontë and Elizabeth Gaskell: Two women, two friends, two novelists: biography as the art of sympathy

out the eyes in the potatoes which Tabby, the housekeeper, was too old and blind to see.

> Miss Brontë was too dainty a housekeeper to put up with this; yet she could not bear to hurt the faithful old servant... Accordingly she would steal into the kitchen, and quietly carry off the bowl of vegetables... and breaking off in the full flow of interest and inspiration in her writing, carefully cut out the specks in the potatoes, and noiselessly carry them back to their place. This little proceeding may show how orderly and fully she accomplished her duties, even at those times when the 'possession' was upon her.

The very next paragraph begins with an account of the 'singular felicity' in Brontë's choice of words in her writing, as though precision and fastidiousness in writing and housekeeping go alongside each other, even though they may conflict.

When Gaskell describes her subject as an author rather than a private person, it is, specifically, as a woman author:

> When a man becomes an author, it is probably merely a change of employment to him. He takes a portion of that time which has hitherto been devoted to some other study or pursuit; he gives up something of the legal or medical profession... or relinquishes part of the trade or business by which he has been striving to gain a livelihood; and another merchant or lawyer, or doctor, steps into his place... But no other can take up the quiet, regular duties of the daughter, the wife, or the mother, as well as she whom God has appointed to fill that particular place: a woman's principal work in life is hardly left to her own choice... And yet she must not shrink from the extra responsibility implied by the very fact of her possessing [the most splendid talents that ever were bestowed]. She must not hide her gift in a napkin; it was meant for the use and service of others.

Later biographers of Charlotte Brontë have reproached Gaskell for (as Carolyn Heilbrun put it) restoring her 'to the safety of womanliness', and for promoting 'the myth of her unswerving faith'. But Gaskell's admirers have warmed to the biography's novelistic empathy and generosity. Margaret Oliphant called it a new kind of biography, a plea 'for every woman dropped out of sight'. Christopher Ricks thinks it 'the greatest life of a woman by a woman'. Gaskell's biographer, Jenny Uglow, says that 'with all its silences, large and small, *The Life of Charlotte Brontë* is profoundly expressive'.

Victorian biographies could be eloquent and vivid. And though respect and reticence shadowed them, quirks of temperament, oddity, and strangeness lurked in the margins. 'Eccentric Biography' was, indeed, a thriving popular genre all through the 19th century. Memoirs, group biographies, pamphlets, and 'Wonderful Magazines' told uncensored life-stories of the very odd. Henry Wilson's collection of *Wonderful Characters*, first published in 1821, was still going strong in the 1870s. Frederick Fairholt's *Remarkable Characters* (1849), John Timbs's *English Eccentrics and Eccentricities* (1866), William Russell's two-volume *Eccentric Personages* (1864), and Robert Malcolm's *Curiosities of Biography* (1865) were just as popular. There were collections of freaks, misers, clerical and medical eccentrics, remarkable females, and regional curiosities (*Three Wonderful Yorkshire Characters*). Timbs categorized his English Eccentrics under 'wealth and fashion, delusions, impostures and fanatic missions, hermits, fat people, giants, dwarfs and strong men...eccentric travellers, artists, theatrical people, and men of letters'. The eccentrics who did not fit into any of these categories had to go under 'miscellaneous'.

All the same, in mainstream biography, there was a generally stolid air to the 'Lives and Letters' of the period. They followed a formula of a lengthy chronological narrative, often, like the novels of the time, in several volumes, with extensive (but tactfully censored) extracts from letters and diaries. The stories told were of public achievement, professional challenges, friendships, travel, battles, political dilemmas, or crises of faith. Childhood problems, domestic privacies, affairs, and scandals were played down. The main characters were politicians and statesmen, military or naval heroes, churchmen, writers, and teachers. The trajectory led upwards and onwards, the tone was generally serious and uncritical. John Cross, George Eliot's widower, published a Life in 1885 of such decorousness that Gladstone complained: 'It is not a Life at all... It is a Reticence in three volumes.' Gladstone himself was venerated in a Life by his friend John Morley (1903), culminating, as Victorian biography often did, in a good death in the bosom of the family, which passed over (at the daughter's request) the horrible details of Gladstone's mouth cancer, and substituted a last page as from a Victorian novel:

> On the early morning of the 19th [May 1898], his family all kneeling around the bed on which he lay in the stupor of coming death, without a struggle he ceased to breathe. Nature outside – wood and wide lawn and cloudless far-off sky – shone at her fairest.

That sort of hagiography would be mocked by the next generation, as much for its ideology as for its prose style. But there were strong reasons for such biographical hero-worship. Biography is never just the personal story of one life. It always has political and social implications. The politics of 19th-century biography had to do with consolidating a national story. In North America, a distinctive national culture was being forged between the wars of Independence and the Civil War; in Europe, national identities were re-shaping themselves through a period of immense turbulence. In Britain, at the start of the century, great social changes, fears of unrest, political repression after the Napoleonic Wars, led to an investment in heroic Lives as a form of security. Later, they became expressions of imperial confidence and assertiveness. A biography which famously set the tone for life-writing as a form of patriotism was Robert Southey's *Life of Nelson* (1813), which excused all his personal weaknesses in order to immortalize 'a name and an example, which are at this hour inspiring thousands of the youth of England; a name which is our pride, and an example which will continue to be our strength and shield'.

But you did not have to be Nelson in order to contribute to the national story, and you did not have to be the subject of a three-volume Life in order to be remembered. In Europe and America, all through the 19th century, biographical dictionaries were being compiled of all those thought worthy of memorialization. Belknap's collective *American Biography* came out in the 1790s. In Europe, from the 1830s onwards, there were multi-volume dictionaries of illustrious Italians, Swedes, Dutch, Belgians, Austrians, and Germans. In France, Louis-Gabriel Michaud's 52-volume *Biographie Universelle Ancienne et Moderne*, published between 1811 and 1828, covered all kinds of public figures and spawned numerous French imitators, all aiming to create a universal national narrative out of individual life-stories.

In Britain, the National Portrait Gallery was founded in 1856, with a historical, patriotic agenda summed up by one of the great Victorian portrait-painters, G. F. Watts: 'The character of a nation as a people of great deeds is one...that should never be lost sight of.' Portraits – and, later, photographs – of British people of note made a visual biographical collection of, and for, the nation. The equivalent in print took longer to establish. Since Thomas Fuller's *Worthies of England* in 1662, and big biographical dictionaries like the multi-volume *Biographia Brittanica* (1747–66), there had been many collections of short biographies of worthy – or scandalous – lives, organized by county, region, type, or profession. In the mid-19th century, there were collections of 'Eminent and Illustrious Englishmen', 'Eminent English Judges', 'Famous Indian Chiefs', 'Notorious and Daring Highwaymen', 'Some of the More Celebrated Jewish Rabbis', 'Sundry Notorious Villains', 'Lives of Good Servants', admirals, apostles, bachelor kings, bigamists, bishops, martyrs, physicians, prophets, rakes, and regicides. 'Lives of Illustrious Shoemakers' (1883) told, for instance, the story of

'Samuel Drew: The Metaphysical Shoemaker', 'the self-taught Cornishman plying his lonely craft while he lays the foundation for his fame as a theologian'. Women featured in these collections as saints, poetesses, servants, criminals, and queens, under titles such as 'Stories of the Lives of Noble Women' or 'Memoirs of Several Ladies of Great Britain, who have been Celebrated for their Writings'. A collection called 'English Female Worthies', by Mrs John Sandford, published in 1883, consisting of hagiographies of Protestant 'saints' such as Lady Jane Grey, shows what terms were required for writing 'female biography':

> It is not to be expected that the lives of women should, in general, exhibit any peculiar striking incidents, or afford material for very animated narrative. Confined as the sex, for the most part, are to private life, they are not often participators in the stirring scenes which mark the period in which they live... Female biography, therefore, does not owe its chief interest to the events which it records... The quiet days of a woman usually present little more than a succession of private duties, or the ordinary events of domestic life... Yet may they not be the less worthy of notice on that account. To trace the development of character is the chief end in all biography.

The most famous – and best-selling – of these educational, nationalistic publications were Samuel Smiles' male-dominated *Self-Help* (1859) and *Lives of The Engineers* (1861–2), celebrations of the work and energy of the 'lesser-known' as heroic contributions to 'our power as a nation'. One example out of hundreds gives the tone: the story of William Jackson of Birkenhead ('the present member for North Derbyshire'), the seventh of eleven children, whose father died when he was little, who was put to work on the docks and then in the counting-house, and who, 'having obtained access to a set of the *Encyclopaedia Britannica*, read the volumes through from A to Z, partly by day, but chiefly by night. He afterwards put himself to a trade, was diligent, and succeeded in it. Now... he holds commercial relations with nearly every country on the globe.'

Smiles was part of educational movements such as the *Society for the Diffusion of Useful Knowledge*, which aimed to encourage self-help for the workers through education rather than revolution. His, and similar inspirational secular stories, were 'designed to be to the early machine age what collections of saints' legends had been to the Middle Ages'. There was a polemical agenda, also, behind popular late 19th-century series of cultural figures and national leaders like John Morley's *English Men of Letters* (from 1877), his *Twelve English Statesmen* (from 1888), and George Grove's *Dictionary of Music and Musicians* (from 1879).

In 1885, after many years of discussion on the need for a British equivalent to the *Biographie Universelle*, the *Dictionary of National Biography*, published by George Smith and edited by Leslie Stephen (and then by Sidney Lee, after Stephen gave up from strain and overwork), started its long history of publication. The first edition – containing the lives of almost 29,000 dead British people – was completed, in 63 volumes, in 1900, with three supplements in 1901. Supplements and revisions continued all through the 20th century until, in 1992, work began on a new, hugely expanded and thoroughly revised DNB, published as the *Oxford Dictionary of National Biography* in 2004.

Leslie Stephen set out to provide, in what he called (in imitation of the 18th-century prototype) his 'Biographia Britannica', 'the greatest possible amount of information in a thoroughly business-like form'. The entries had to be 'strictly biographical', factual, not 'overcrowded' with detail, impersonal but not hostile, 'written by persons who sympathize with the subject'. Grounds for inclusion in this collective national history were democratic and secular. The great names were all there, but also those whom Leslie Stephen called minor heroes: naval captains, country vicars, teachers, merchants, sportsmen. These were lives which had to be reconstructed from obituaries, memoirs, prefaces, letters, and 'who really become generally accessible through the dictionary alone'. And there were more dubious characters too: 'brothel-keepers, contortionists, gamblers, transvestites and centenarians'. Women made up only 4% of the entries, since there were relatively few in public life, and wives and mothers featured as mere appendages.

Time changes our concept of who deserves to have their life-story preserved, their biography written. In 1993, almost a hundred years after the original DNB completed publication in 1900, a volume of *Missing Persons* was published (with 1,074 additional names from all periods). The editor, Christine Nicholls, prefaced it with a thoughtful commentary on the exclusions of her predecessors. She notes that in the period from the end of the 17th century to mid-Victorian Britain:

> there often went unnoticed by the original editors, perhaps reasonably, those whose achievements, not always conspicuous, by deeds and invention... provided the secure underpinning of a society in constant rapid change and expansion in population and possessions. Here we find explorers, chemists, aeronauts, hydrographers, shippers, royal servants, architects, sailors, inventors, doctors, and practical men and women more often than visionaries or poets, speculators rather than speculatives, hard sloggers rather than loud mouths – without whom the smooth modulation of changing national structures would have been lost. The passage of time was necessary to establish their claims.

From the 1850s to the mid-20th century, 'there appear large numbers of businessmen, engineers, scientists, and women – all categories which had suffered some neglect'.

Yet, for all its historical blindspots, the 19th-century DNB provided a different kind of biography from the 'Lives and Letters' of Great Men. After his wife died in 1895, Leslie Stephen wrote an emotional essay called 'Forgotten Benefactors', celebrating the far-reaching influence of 'thousands who have long sunk into oblivion'. This Victorian theme, often used as an excuse for keeping women in the home, also provided an alternative concept of heroism, and a justification for writing the biographies of 'obscure' lives. It is found, too, on the last page of George Eliot's *Middlemarch* (1871) where Dorothea's obscure yet remarkable life is given as an example of those whose 'unhistoric acts' have an 'incalculably diffusive' influence: 'and that things are not so ill with you and me as they might have been, is half owing to the number who lived faithfully a hidden life, and rest in unvisited tombs'.

The great nationalistic production of the DNB came out of a prolific and increasingly professionalized 19th-century biographical industry. And its publication coincided with an intense and widespread debate about the ethics of life-writing. This was particularly vociferous in France, where biography was often despised as a low form of cultural life, and arguments raged over the relative merits of biography and history. The philosopher Victor Cousin maintained that individual life-stories reduced history to 'undistinguished trivia'. In his influential *Vie de Jésus* (1863), which presented its subject not as the Son of God but as an exceptional human being, Ernest Renan felt the need to justify a biographical approach as the best way of understanding the development of Christianity. The rise of a mass media, and the popularity of the journalistic, often scandalous, 'biographie' of the living, was viewed by some as a democratic plague, lowering literary culture to the 'exhibition of personality' and 'the squalor of personal data'.

The same anxieties were felt in America and Britain, as journalistic intrusion, the beginnings of celebrity culture, and the ever more shaky dividing line between private and public, gave rise to debates uncannily like our own, over a hundred years on, about the exhibiting of private lives for mass consumption. Public figures (like Parnell) could be toppled by personal scandal. Famous writers were aghast at the exposure of other writers' lives. Browning imagined the front of a house ripped off for people to peer inside.

Tennyson laid a public curse on the 'carrion vulture' who waits to tear the poet's heart 'before the crowd', and said, privately, that 'the lives of great men' were being 'ripped open like pigs'. George Eliot called biography 'a disease of English literature'. Thackeray warned his daughters that 'When I drop there is to be no life of me, *mind* this.'

Henry James wrote with horrified brilliance, in *The Aspern Papers* (1888) and elsewhere, about the violation of the writer's secret life by 'publishing scoundrels'. He passionately believed that 'a man's table-drawers and pockets should not be turned inside out', burned many private papers in the (useless) hope of 'frustrating' biographical intrusion, and resented the posthumous 'exhibition' of friends such as Robert Louis Stevenson. The trial and disgrace of Oscar Wilde in 1895 gripped and appalled him: 'Yes' (he wrote to Edmund Gosse), 'it is hideously, atrociously dramatic & really interesting – so far as one can say that of a thing of which the interest is qualified by such a sickening horribility.' He was as fascinated by the private lives of writers as he was horrified by their exposure. When he went on a motor-tour of France in 1907 with Edith Wharton, for instance, he couldn't wait to visit George Sand's house in Nohant to see the rooms where George and her lovers had, as he put it, 'pigged so thrillingly together'. And he read biography, memoirs, and letters with excitement.

'Ransacking', 'violation', 'betrayal', 'reticence', were key terms in the debate about biographical intrusion. The 'ethics of biography' became the subject of solemn discussion, as in an 1883 essay by Margaret Oliphant, who argued that the 'high-minded' biographer had a duty of responsibility to 'the helplessness of the dead', whose 'private drawers' could so easily be 'ransacked for evidence to their disadvantage'. Biographical betrayal, she concluded, was 'an offence against social morals'.

Oliphant was referring to the most notorious 'biographical betrayal' of the time, that of Carlyle, the greatly venerated Victorian sage. In the 1870s, Carlyle gave his friend, the historian John Anthony Froude, most of his papers, including his remorseful 'Reminiscences' of his late wife, Jane Welsh Carlyle, and the letters between them, with instructions to Froude to publish as he thought fit and to write his biography after his death. Froude saw that these materials revealed a shocking story of an unhappy marriage, but felt he owed it to his mentor to be as much of a truth-teller as Carlyle was himself. After Carlyle died in 1881, Froude immediately published the *Reminiscences*, followed by a respectful, vigorous Life in two volumes (1882, 1884), and the painful *Letters and Memorials of Jane Welsh Carlyle* (1883). He justified these publications by appealing to Carlyle's own belief that 'in proportion to a man's greatness is the scrutiny to which his conduct is submitted'. Howls of nationwide execration resulted. Biographical controversies always require someone to be blamed, and Froude was blamed for 'staining' the great man's name with these revelations of domestic cruelty, for getting his facts wrong, and for making unauthorized use of private papers. 'Froudacity' became a byword for treachery, immorality, and inaccuracy. After his death, his heirs published *My Relations with Carlyle* (1903), which explained that he had concealed the true reason Carlyle was so 'ill to live with', and Jane so discontented: Carlyle was impotent, 'one of those persons who ought never to have married'. Renewed outrage followed, spreading into medical and legal discussions about virility, marriage, and divorce. 'The frank biography has its limits', fulminated one critic in the pages of the *British Medical Journal*, 'and has not hitherto been held to include the history of a man's sexual experiences. It has been reserved for Froude to set a most pernicious example and inflict a stain on English literature by proclaiming abroad a genital defect in the man whose life he has been commissioned to write, and whom he affects to hold up to admiration...'

Froude's *Carlyle* is a good example of how closely biography is always involved with the social preoccupations of its time – and of how dangerous to the biographer personal intimacy with the subject can prove. 'It is always Judas who writes the biography', said Oscar Wilde in 1891. Froude, who never meant or wanted to be Judas, played a part, almost in spite of himself, in a shift towards more openness and directness in biography. A self-consciousness was developing about the practice of the craft, an interest in biography's aesthetic rather than its ethical implications, question marks about the extent to which it could ever be true to the private, inner self of the subject. Carlyle, the hero of this chapter, had thought about all that. He wrote in his journal in 1843:

> The world has no business with my life. The world will never know of my life, if it should write and read a hundred biographies of me. The main facts of it are known, and are likely to be known, to myself alone of all created men.

Chapter 5
Fallen Idols

George Bernard Shaw joked, in 1881, that what was needed for biography was a book called 'Queen Victoria: By a Personal Acquaintance Who Dislikes Her'. Lytton Strachey picked up the hint in the 1900s. He and other young British writers, who were living through catastrophic historical upheavals and startling social changes, preferred Shaw, H. G. Wells, and Samuel Butler to Carlyle or Tennyson, pacifism to patriotism, frankness to decorum, laughter to solemnity, secularism to religion. They sweepingly denigrated Victorian biography as a 'clumsy and laborious' monstrosity, 'dominated by the idea of goodness'. Evelyn Waugh, for instance, wrote in 1928 of the two-volume eulogy meant 'to assist with our fathers' decorum at the lying-in-state of our great men', 'their faces serenely composed and cleansed of all the stains of humanity'. The children of those fathers set out to change the way life-stories could be written (and writing about fathers was part of the story). The 'art of biography' used miniaturism, craft and craftiness, imaginative fictional tactics, irony, parody, and caricature. 'The corpse', Waugh noted, 'has become the marionette.' The biographer could be the equal, not the respectful or awe-struck disciple, of the subject. Biographers were self-conscious; biography might even be seen as a form of autobiography. Above all, biography aimed to uncover the inner self behind the public figure, with the help of the new tool of psychoanalysis.

Cultural shifts get over-simplified. Biography in the 19th century was not as monolithic and stolid as its detractors have claimed; biography at the start of the 20th century was not all candid, psychoanalytical, and experimental. Plenty of protective, decorous biographies went on being written, such as Edward Marsh's 1918 idealized memoir of the golden boy-poet Rupert Brooke, or Rupert Hart-Davis's *Hugh Walpole*, which, as late as 1952, omitted his homosexuality. But a surge of factors, great and small, local and global – the Carlyle-Froude and Wilde scandals, the death of Queen Victoria, suffrage campaigns, Freud, the War – all played their part in the shake-up. What Virginia Woolf called 'the new biography' had definable characteristics. They are on view, variously, over a period of about forty years, in Walter Pater's *Marius the Epicurean* (1885) and his *Imaginary Portraits* (1887); Marcel Schwob's 1895 short lives, *Vies Imaginaires*; Edmund Gosse's memoir *Father and Son* (1907), and his essays on biography; Lytton Strachey's four short Lives of *Eminent Victorians* (1918), and, less influentially, his *Queen Victoria* (1921) and *Elizabeth and Essex* (1928); Geoffrey Scott's *Portrait of Zélide* (1925); Virginia Woolf's essays on the art of biography, her fictional biographies, *Orlando* (1928) and *Flush* (1933), and her unfinished memoir 'Sketch of the Past' (1939–41); Harold Nicolson's *The Development of English Biography* (1928) and his whimsical portraits, *Some People* (1927); André Maurois' *Ariel: Ou La Vie de Shelley* (1923, translated 1924) and his *Aspects de la Biographie* (1928, translated 1929); Arthur Symons' experiment in biography, *The Quest for Corvo* (1934); and Emil Ludwig's *Die Kunst der Biographie* (1936).

The word 'biography' is coming under pressure here. As for the 18th century, with its mixture of 'ana' and satires, journals and conversations, 'life-writing' is a more useful term for this mixture of auto/biographical memoirs, satiric sketches, fictionalized or psychoanalytical quests, and investigations of how life-stories can be written. Virginia Woolf used the term in 'Sketch of the Past', talking about the need to place the individual life in the context of family, inheritance, environment, and 'invisible presences', to put

10. Woolf and Strachey. Irony, playfulness, and style: the modernists' approach to biography

'the fish in the stream'. In order to do this, she argued, there had to be new approaches. The blurring or breaking down of genres was part of the rethinking of biography.

Edmund Gosse (not usually known for adventurousness) produced a wonderfully uncategorizable book in *Father and Son*, his poignant, funny memoir of a very odd childhood. It was a pioneering genre, not a biography of his parents, nor an autobiography, but 'a study of two temperaments'. Gosse's account of his upbringing in a group of fundamentalist Calvinist 'Brethren', by his widowed father, Philip Gosse, a naturalist caught between his scientific curiosity and his religious beliefs, exposed a private family life with more candour than readers were used to. Gosse treats his father's scrupulous struggle to bring up a small boy according to rigid principles as at once admirable and pitiful. There are comic, rueful scenes where the son begins to doubt the father's infallibility, like his experiment with an 'act of idolatry', praying to the morning-room chair ('O Chair!'), as a fearful test of God's wrath ('but nothing happened... God did not care'), or his 'spiritual anguish' at having secretly had a mouthful of forbidden plum pudding at Christmas: 'Oh! Papa, Papa, I have eaten of flesh offered to idols!'. *Father and Son* was praised for its truthfulness, and also blamed for 'going too far'. But it has had a long afterlife as a vivid, humane account of a father–son relationship, setting a standard for many later novelistic memoirs such as Philip Roth's *Patrimony*, or Blake Morrison's *And When Did You Last See Your Father?*

Striking the father dead was part of the agenda for Lytton Strachey. *Eminent Victorians* has rightly been described as 'Oedipal biography'. Strachey, a child of the Empire's governing classes, was a brilliant, mannered, gangling, sickly intellectual, passionate in his friendships, in love with French and 18th-century literature, fascinated by Freudian psychoanalysis, a witty homosexual 'character' in his Cambridge and Bloomsbury circle. Though he wrote history, 'portraits', and criticism throughout his rather short life (he died at fifty-two), he became famous – and would be mainly remembered – for one book. *Eminent Victorians* had a powerful effect, now hard to re-imagine. It was a wartime book, written between 1912 and 1918. It chose four public figures, none of them writers: a headmaster of a great public school, the nation's favourite wartime nurse-heroine, a powerful, ambitious priest who crossed from the Church of England to Rome, and one of Britain's most famous, and catastrophic, military leaders. All four – Dr Arnold, Florence Nightingale, Cardinal Manning, and General Gordon – had already had venerating biographical coverage (sources which Strachey plagiarized and distorted). All were ripe for debunking as figures whose formidable public activities could be reread as sublimations of private traumas and repression, and as representatives of a period considered, by its sceptical descendants, responsible for the carnage and shambles of the Great War. .

Strachey set out his tactics in a Wildean preface which proposed to reject – and 'expose' – 'Victorian' heaviness, solemnity, and respect by light, ironic, irreverent methods. A 'little bucket' was to be lowered into the great ocean of the Victorian Age, which would 'bring up to the light of day some characteristic specimen, from those far depths, to be examined with a careful curiosity'. Scientific precision would lay bare what had been murky and hidden. Biography was to use unconventional angles of approach, attacking 'upon the flank, or the rear'. The military metaphors carried a knowing sexual nudge. This would be the Victorians unfrocked, with all their neuroses and secret appetites on show.

In fact, the essays were more emotional and sympathetic than the preface suggests. Strachey set Nightingale and Gordon, especially, as isolated, driven obsessives up against an incompetent English bureaucracy. He gave some touching pathos to defeated minor characters, like Cardinal Newman in the Manning essay and Arthur Hugh Clough in 'Florence Nightingale'. Certainly his tone was often sardonic, particularly with Dr Arnold, pillar of the single-sex public-school system, which Strachey's generation

abominated for its philistinism, patriotic smugness, muscular
Christianity, and unexamined sexual impact:

> Dr Arnold was never in any danger of losing his sense of moral evil.
> If the landscapes of Italy only served to remind him of it, how could
> he forget it among the boys at Rugby School? The daily sight of so
> many young creatures in the hands of the Evil One filled him with
> agitated grief.

But there were other tones in play, too. The family opposition
Nightingale encountered is fictionalized as if in the voice of a
fussing Victorian mother:

> It was very odd; what could be the matter with dear Flo?... the
> curious thing was that she seemed to take no interest in
> husbands... As if there was not plenty to do in any case, in the
> ordinary way, at home...

The administrative blunders that sent Gordon to the Sudan are
summed up with Johnsonian clarity:

> The whole history of his life, the whole bent of his character, seemed
> to disqualify him for the task for which he had been chosen. He was
> before all things a fighter, an enthusiast, a bold adventurer, and he
> was now to be entrusted with the conduct of an inglorious retreat.

The political agenda of *Eminent Victorians*, slyly expressed
through tone and structure, was, like all biographical experiments,
reacting against what came before. Now that we are not so familiar
with Dean Stanley's awestruck 1844 Life of Dr Arnold, or with the
post-Crimean War sanctification of Florence Nightingale as 'The
Lady with the Lamp', it is harder to see why Strachey's book
seemed so bold, funny, and shocking at the time. Later readers
became irritated by the book's inaccuracies, dandyism, and (as the
wise Iris Origo put it) its 'thinness' springing from 'condescension'.
Strachey's later biographical experiments, Freudian readings of

Queen Victoria, paralysed by mourning (with an irreverent and much-imitated deathbed scene which ran back through her whole life in the flash of an eye), and of the sexually 'warped' Queen Elizabeth, now seem curiously old-fashioned. But *Eminent Victorians* was a flamboyantly pioneering work which provided a blueprint for all the modernist theorizing about biography.

Gosse's 1910 entry on 'Biography' in the *Encyclopaedia Brittanica* defined 'true' or 'pure' biography, 'the faithful portrait of a soul in its adventures through life', told without a moral agenda, as a 'very modern' conception. Writing in 1925 about his 17th-century hero Tallemant des Réaux, France's John Aubrey, author of some wicked 'miniature' lives (full of sentences like 'The Chevalier is a kind of lunatic, and moreover the greatest blasphemer in France'), Gosse praises him for being – like Strachey – 'never astonished and never indignant'. 'He wishes to set down the truth, and is not afraid of the facts.'

These 'modern' biographical ideals were echoed by a range of writers. Well before Gosse and Strachey, the French writer Marcel Schwob argued that short lives, preferably of obscure or eccentric characters, were the most suggestive. Quirks and curiosities and telling physical details – Cleopatra's nose, Alexander's drinking, Louis XIV's fistula – could speak more loudly than large historical events. Schwob set biography against history, arguing for the significance of the particular and the contingent over 'generalities and continuities'.

Harold Nicolson, diplomat, diarist, and husband of Vita Sackville-West, also argued for, and practised, short, artful, playful biography. Like Gosse, Nicolson set two kinds of biography against each other, the 'impure' (hagiographical, Victorian) and the 'pure' (truthful, well constructed, modern). This opposition of right/wrong, old/new, is a frequent and continuing tactic in biographical theorizing. But biography is always spilling out of such neat patterns. Nicolson foresaw a split between 'scientific' (sociological, psychoanalytical) and 'literary' (imaginative, crafted) biography, a stand-off that has never really taken place.

The French critic and biographer André Maurois claimed equal artistic status for biography with other arts in his 1928 Clark lectures, which deliberately borrowed the word 'Aspects' from E. M. Forster's *Aspects of the Novel*. Maurois' *Ariel*, his Life of Shelley, was intensely romantic. He thought biography should work, like poetry, through recurrent motifs (*Ariel* is full of water) and, like fiction, through an empathetic inwardness which would intuitively unlock the key to the subject's inner self. Emil Ludwig, author of psychological biographies of great German figures such as Goethe, Bismarck, and Wilhelm II, was also driven by an intuitive search for the essence of character. In America, Gamaliel Bradford, author of popular biographies and themed collections like *Saints and Sinners* (1931) and *Wives* (1925), coined 'psychography' for 'the condensed, essential, artistic presentation of character' and for the capturing, in a 'scientific spirit', of the complicated 'variance' of 'men's souls'.

There was an acute sense of that 'variance', of the gaps and contradictions within human beings. Between 1913 and 1927, Proust was publishing *À la recherche du temps perdu* (first translated into English between 1922 and 1932), his modern epic of the self in society, which examined in depth and at length the intermittencies and gaps in memory and identity. 'Relativity' was a new idea in physics. Concepts of what lay buried and hidden beneath the publicly functioning, or malfunctioning, self were making their way from Freudian psychoanalysis into literature.

Virginia Woolf's writings on biography – though shadowed by Leslie Stephen, Carlyle, Pater, Gosse, Strachey, Nicolson, and Proust – were original, and influential. Like other contemporary commentators, she had an evolutionary concept of it as a genre that needed to throw off the past and move towards some as yet unattained form. As with her writings on, and experiments in, 'modern fiction', she thought life-writing had to change in order to meet the new conditions of the 20th century. Having grown up with Leslie Stephen and the *Dictionary of National Biography*, she liked to set the 'new' biography against a caricatured version of Victorian Lives. But she was also very interested in Boswell, Carlyle, Hazlitt, and other creative figures in British biographical history, and her fascination with 'obscure' and 'eccentric' Lives had something in common with her father's policy of inclusion in the DNB.

Woolf was as interested in life-writing as in fiction. While her novels were trying out radically experimental ways of telling a life-story, she read a great deal of biography, wrote many vividly evocative sketches of other writers (dead ones in her essays, living ones – often ruthlessly satirized – in her diaries and letters), experimented with fictional biography, and wrote eloquent essays on the topic. In 'The New Biography' (1927), she argued for fearlessness, brevity, and vividness as 'modern', anti-Victorian biographical qualities. Facts needed to be manipulated, the true life was the inner life, there could be artistry, choice, and laughter. Character could be displayed in 'the tone of a voice, the turn of a head, some little phrase or anecdote picked up in passing'. But contemporary biography was not yet 'subtle and bold' enough to master the 'queer amalgamation' of 'granite and rainbow' – fact and vision, truth and art – that was needed.

In 'The Art of Biography' (1939), she was still arguing that the biographer – unlike the novelist – could never be 'free'. She was writing this while working on a commissioned life of her friend, the painter and art critic Roger Fry, which she found an intensely frustrating experience. She put the reasons for her difficulties into the essay. Any attempt at 'vision' in biography was hampered by 'facts'. But facts, she added, were unstable entities. 'What was thought a sin is now known, by the light of facts won for us by the psychologists, to be perhaps a misfortune; perhaps a curiosity... The accent on sex has changed within living memory... Many of the old chapter headings – life at college, marriage, career – are shown to be very arbitrary and artificial distinctions.' So the biographer's job was to be a pioneer, to 'go ahead of the rest of us, like the miner's canary' (the very choice of image suggests how facts change through time), 'testing the atmosphere, detecting falsity, unreality, and the presence of obsolete conventions'. In an age of 'a thousand cameras', the biographer's job was to 'admit contradictory versions of the same face'. The angle was changing, and so were our ideas of 'greatness' and 'smallness'.

At the heart of Woolf's critique of the genre is her sense that the inner life we all lead is never adequately reflected in biography. This is her most eloquent statement of the case:

> Here is the past and all its inhabitants miraculously sealed as in a magic tank; all we have to do is to look and to listen and to listen and to look and soon the little figures – for they are rather under life size – will begin to move and to speak, and as they move we shall arrange them in all sorts of patterns of which they were ignorant, for they thought when they were alive that they could go where they liked; and as they speak we shall read into their sayings all kinds of meanings which never struck them, for they believed when they were alive that they said straight off whatever came into their heads. But once you are in a biography all is different.

One answer to this intractable difficulty, an evasive and playful one, was to rewrite biography as comic, parodic fiction. *Flush* (1933) told the story of Elizabeth Barrett Browning through the eyes – and nose – of her spaniel. *Orlando* (1928), also subtitled 'A Biography', came equipped with full apparatus – acknowledgements, illustrations, index. It took its biographer, who appears as an unnamed, ungendered character, on a wild goose chase in pursuit of its subject. Orlando resists biographical conventions, changing from a man to a woman, living through three centuries, and refusing any determinants about identity, gender, and chronological progress. ('For she had a great variety of selves to call upon, far more than we have been able to find room for, since a biography is considered complete if it merely accounts for six or seven selves, whereas a person may well have as many thousand.')

By subverting biographical conventions through fictional parody, Woolf found a way of writing a teasing, private memoir of her friend and bisexual lover Vita Sackville-West which could be at once coded and revealing, erotic and censored. This new form of life-writing was also a feminist enterprise (though she did not call it that), which implied – as Woolf always argued – that women's lives required new forms of writing.

Could such playful, stylized fictional methods work as serious biographical tools? Other examples of the time read now, like *Orlando*, more as intriguing experiments in genre-busting than precedents for professional biography. Gertrude Stein invented a new language for telling the lives of obscure American women in *Three Lives* (1908), and turned autobiography and biography upside-down in the intimate, garrulous, boastful, gossipy *Autobiography of Alice B. Toklas* (1933). (Picasso's great, sturdy 1906 portrait of Stein is another example of how modernist experiments in art could create a powerful sense of character.) The art historian and Boswell editor Geoffrey Scott created, in *The Portrait of Zélide*, an elegantly dramatized life of the Dutch 18th-century writer Isabelle van Tuyl, who was connected to Voltaire, proposed to by Boswell, and loved by Benjamin Constant. A. J. A. Symons, Paterian aesthete and admirer of Wilde, wrote a biography of Frederick Rolfe, alias Baron Corvo, author of *Hadrian the Seventh*, failed priest, exile, unhappy homosexual, and venomous letter-writer, in the form of a pursuit of its elusive subject. *The Quest for Corvo* is part detective story, part spiritual journey, and part meditation on biography. Steeped in arcane learning, queer encounters, and fanciful symbolist prose, it is a very peculiar operation indeed, leaving the reader unconvinced that there was ever such a real person as Frederick Rolfe – or, possibly, his biographer.

11. Picasso's Stein: a powerful sense of character

Aestheticism – shaping, impressionism, artfulness – took biography in one direction. Most biographers of historical, political, or literary figures, however, were not primarily interested in formal experiments. Where aestheticians and historians, professional biographers and experimental life-writers did find themselves converging, from early in the 20th century, was through the powerful doctrines of Freudian psychoanalysis.

Sigmund Freud began publishing his findings on hysteria and psychology in the 1890s, and was being translated into English by Strachey's brother and sister-in-law, James and Alix Strachey, for the Hogarth Press, from the 1920s onwards. Freud praised *Elizabeth and Essex*, which showed, he thought, that Strachey was 'steeped in the spirit of psychoanalysis', enabling him to 'touch upon [Elizabeth]'s most hidden motives'. The practice of psychoanalysis as defined by Freud, and narrated in case-histories such as Dora, Little Hans, the Rat Man, or the Wolf Man, paralleled (and influenced) some of biography's processes: following clues, building up a pattern of behaviour, interpreting a whole personality through attending to significant details, deciding what was relevant, finding the hidden causes of adult behaviour in childhood. Freud compared the process to archaeological excavation, a metaphor that works for both analysis and biography. Yet Freud was extremely hostile to the genre.

> Anyone who writes a biography is committed to lies, concealments, hypocrisy, flattery and even to hiding his own lack of understanding, for biographical truth does not exist, and if it did we could not use it.

Adam Phillips quotes this letter of 1936 in an essay which argues that Freud saw 'the genre... as a kind of rival of his own discipline'. Freud's 'misgivings' about biography 'may also be his own displaced misgivings about psychoanalysis itself', Phillips suggests. If the 'true' self is hard to track back, even in analysis, how could biography hope to discover it? 'Freud hated biography because it represented the dangerous and misleading claims one person might make about knowing another person.' This, as Phillips notes wryly, created difficulties for Freud's own biographers, Ernest Jones and Peter Gay.

In the first example of 'psycho-biography', *Leonardo da Vinci and a Memory of Childhood* (1910), Freud interpreted Leonardo's life

12. Sigmund Freud and Leonardo da Vinci. Psychoanalysis and the artist; a revolution in biography

and works as a story of neurosis, and homosexuality, produced by the repression of his childhood love of his mother. Part of that sexual repression was sublimated into 'a thirst for knowledge' – thus accounting both for Leonardo's strangeness, and his genius. This 'exhilaratingly speculative' analysis (based, notoriously, on the crucial mistranslation of a single word), shows a classic biographical tension 'between empirical observation and grand theory'. But, shaky or hypothetical though it may seem, it did throw down a forceful challenge to biographical censorship. Freud argued:

> If a biographical study really seeks to arrive at an understanding of the mental life of its hero, it must not – as most biographies do, out of discretion or prudery – keep silent about his sexual activity and sexual individuality.

Why should the exploration of a great man's pathology be felt to be distasteful? Because – he argued, weirdly – most biographers have an infantile fixation on their hero/subjects, and want to idealize them and turn them into their fathers. (Female biographers of female subjects do not exist for Freud.) Though their terms are different, Freud's claims for psychological investigation resemble the modernists' contemporaneous desire for a more daring, candid, and imaginative biographical practice.

Freud's influence on biography was immense. Even non-believers in psychoanalysis felt, post-Freud, a duty to deal with their subjects' sexuality, illnesses, dreams, and infancy. Anthony Storr notes:

> After psychoanalysis became established, biographers began to feel that, unless they had managed to uncover the emotional influences to which their subjects had been exposed during the earliest years of childhood, their portraits were incomplete.

Psycho-biography is out of fashion now, but vestigial traces of its language can be found (as in our everyday conversation), like a light scattering of snow, in contemporary biographies that are not remotely Freudian. So Claire Tomalin might speak of Jane Austen's 'childhood trauma' and 'depression', or Victoria Glendinning of Trollope's 'alienation'.

Psychoanalytical biography – sometimes fused with Marxist political analysis or sociological data – placed its subjects on the couch and fitted their behaviour into a pattern. Sartre's theory-driven literary biographies, indebted to both Freud and Marx, applied 'existential psychoanalysis' and sociological contextualizing to his subjects, in order to construct 'totalizing' accounts of the 'freedom and conditioning', which, for example, made Flaubert (*L'Idiot de la Famille*) both 'a neurotic and a great writer'. Sartre used his subjects to prove that 'a corpse is open to all comers'; or, to put it another way, 'that every man is perfectly knowable as long as one uses the appropriate methods and has available the necessary documents'. He applied a 'comprehensive synthesis which stopped only at death'. 'Total' biography could reveal a person's life 'as it was lived from within', and, at the same time, place the subjects 'as a product of their historical era, their class situation, and their childhood conditioning'. But Sartre's enormously detailed, controlling Lives of Genet and Flaubert, in which no illness is involuntary, no event contingent, no act inexplicable, leave many of his readers longing for 'inconclusiveness and disorder'. The narrator of Julian Barnes's *Flaubert's Parrot* comments:

> Look what happened to Flaubert: a century after his death Sartre, like some brawny, desperate lifeguard, spent ten years beating on his chest and blowing into his mouth; ten years trying to yank him back to consciousness, just so that he could sit him up on the sands and tell him exactly what he thought of him.

Erik Erikson's pioneering Freudian biography, *Young Man Luther* (1958), presented his subject in terms of 'a protracted identity crisis' arising from an Oedipal complex. Luther is 'beset with a syndrome of conflicts whose outline we have learned to recognize, and whose components to analyse'. So Luther's obsession with excrement is traced back 'to the beatings on his buttocks which he received as a child'. His 'identity crisis' began with a legendary fit he was supposed to have had in his twenties. Even if the fit did not actually happen, it could be accepted as 'half-history', provided it had a ring of truth and yielded 'a meaning consistent with psychological theory'.

From the 1920s to the 1960s (and even later), psycho-biography was a thriving genre. All sorts of writers, politicians, world leaders, composers, artists, scientists, and psychologists were put on the couch. Of course this aroused opposition. The American writer Bernard De Voto called psychoanalysis, in 1933, 'a preposterous instrument for the ascertaining of fact'. 'Psycho-analytical biography... does not tell us what did happen. It tells us instead what must have happened.' But Leon Edel maintained, in the 1950s, that the value of psychology, particularly for literary biography, was to show 'how the negatives were converted into positives', how the subject could overcome a 'wound' and turn it into art. His argument makes psycho-biography sound like medieval hagiography in its commitment to triumph over adversity. Richard Ellmann argued that psycho-biography could have its uses as long as 'it is the biographer manipulating psychological theory, not allowing psychological theory to manipulate him'. More recent commentators on psycho-biography tend to agree that its theory-driven, clinical approach had a distorting effect, and that the processes of psychoanalysis and biography have quite different aims.

Some of the most masterful literary lives of the mid-20th century – Leon Edel's *Life of Henry James* (1953–77), or George Painter's

Marcel Proust (1959) – now seem skewed by their psychoanalytical bias. Edel, reading James as formed by his father's subservience to his mother, rivalry with his brother, and a traumatic injury, analysed his fiction as often unconscious expressions of these experiences. So James's youthful observation of the dominance of women in his family is seen 'emerging' as a fictional 'vampire theme': 'Fear of women and worship of women: the love-theme plays itself out in striking fashion throughout Henry James's work. And usually love... is a threat to life itself.' Arguing at one point from a list of names in one of James's notebooks, 'Ledward', 'Bedward', and 'Dedward', Edel proposed: 'To be led to the marriage bed was to be dead. Henry James accordingly chose the path of safety. He remained celibate.' Edel's James sometimes seems not to have known what he was doing as a writer, 'yielding to dictates deeper than those of the craft of authorship... dictates of a psychological order'. 'The terms in which he talks of his father... and of his brother... tell a story the author never intended us to know, nor was fully aware of himself.' However rich and deep Edel's account of James's social, personal, and literary context, such moments in his biography seem over-schematic and infantilizing.

Painter's *Marcel Proust* was similarly theory-driven, unlocking the whole of Proust's life and work with the keys of 'mother' and 'illness'. Painter maintained that Proust 'invented nothing': his great literary achievement was not fiction but 'creative autobiography'. He drew on his own experience, synthesized and transformed it, to create 'a metaphorical representation of universal truths'. Working from internal evidence, Painter matched, with exhaustive and 'definitive' exactness, every piece of Proust's life to his work. (Strangely, he chose not to interview any of Proust's friends, many of whom were still alive while he was writing his biography.) The aim was 'to discover, beneath the mask of the artist's everyday, objective life, the secret life from which he extracted his work'.

Richard Ellmann's *Joyce*, another legendary mid-20th-century biography of literary 'genius', resisted such schematizing, and had fun with Joyce's mixed feelings about psychoanalysis. Joyce called Jung and Freud the Swiss Tweedledum and the Viennese Tweedledee, and had little time for Jung's analyses of *Ulysses*, or of his daughter Lucia, though he kept a dream diary and was deeply interested in the workings of the unconscious. Ellmann's method was not to psychoanalyse Joyce, though it happily used terms like 'Oedipal' and 'ambivalence'. It was to point everything in his life (and he tells us everything he can, in sympathetic, humorous, and eloquent detail) towards his work. His thesis is that of genius making shape and meaning out of the mundane and the messy. So there is a repeated note – as in more traditional, exemplary biography – of triumph and transcendence. At the end of *Ulysses*, 'the spirit is liberated from its bonds'. Such moments 'arise in quintessential purity from the mottled life of everyday'. Ellmann concludes his mighty book by insisting on the 'erratic and provisional' surface of Joyce's life and on what the 'splendid extravagance' of his work did with it, raising his life 'to dignity and high dedication'.

These three complex, intimate, supremely authoritative, much acclaimed biographies are now seen – as all biography comes to be seen – more as historical moments in the interpretations of those great writers' lives than as definitive monuments.

Modernist experiments and Freudian case-histories provided influential models for biography. Both fed into a thriving, rich, popular Anglo-American tradition of professional biography in the mid to late 20th century. Large-scale, realistic, thoroughly historicized Lives were energized by strong characterization and description, humour, candour, and intimacy. Many of them – like *Eminent Victorians* – took their subjects from the previous generation. It is an irony of biographical history that Lytton Strachey, the playful minimalist, should have been the subject of one of the first and biggest of these Lives. But it is apt, too.

Michael Holroyd's work (also on Augustus John and Shaw) followed Strachey's ethic of frankness, irony, impartiality, and vividness. His biography of Strachey echoed the sexual freedoms and political radicalism of the 1960s, and opened the door for a particularly strong phase of popular, respected British and Irish biography. Richard Holmes on Shelley and Coleridge; Claire Tomalin on Jane Austen and Pepys; Peter Ackroyd on Dickens; Victoria Glendinning on Rebecca West, Edith Sitwell, and Trollope; Hilary Spurling on Ivy Compton-Burnett and Matisse; Jenny Uglow on Gaskell and Hogarth; John Richardson on Picasso; Roy Foster on Yeats; Fiona McCarthy on William Morris and Eric Gill are a few outstanding examples.

At the same time, great numbers of solid, thoroughly researched professional and academic biographies of writers, artists, thinkers, politicians, scientists, and national leaders streamed out from (mainly) North American and European publishers. (Some magisterial specimens: Irvin Ehrenpreis's Swift (1962–83), Mark Schorer's Sinclair Lewis (1961), Walter Jackson Bates's Keats (1963), Justin Kaplan's Mark Twain (1966), Winifred Gérin's Charlotte Brontë (1967) and Gaskell (1976), Carlos Baker's Hemingway (1969), Ronald Paulson's Hogarth (1971, 1991–3), Arthur Mizener's Ford (1972), R. W. B. Lewis's Edith Wharton (1975), Matthew Bruccoli's Scott Fitzgerald (1981), Maynard Mack's Pope (1985).) No major – or, increasingly, minor – figure, in any field, now goes unbiographized. Many of these monuments to hard work and careful investigation are not self-consciously crafted, but set down, as fully and as accurately as possible, a chronological account of a significant life.

Though contemporary biography has not always been artful and selective, it does pay a debt to modernist discussions and practice of the genre, in its belief in truth-telling, humour, and realism, its emphasis on childhood and sexuality, its explorations of inner lives as much as public achievements, and its reluctance (with a few notorious exceptions) to moralize, take sides, or cast blame. Yet biography can still involve acts of piety. Though it wants to be truthful and frank, it can still find itself in thrall to censoring pressures, and may still have to grapple with stories that can only be partially told, disappearing evidence, reluctant or forbidding subjects. The same challenges and contradictions recur.

Chapter 6
Against Biography

The literary case against biography partly has its roots in aestheticism, in the idea of the separateness and purity – or amorality – of the work of art. The examples of Flaubert and the French symbolist poets fuelled an argument for art as an inviolable entity, set apart from the life, not to be degraded by biographical interpretation. For Baudelaire, for example, 'poetry is both distinguished from and elevated above the world in which it exists'. The artist-as-person – what Yeats famously called 'the bundle of accident and incoherence that sits down to breakfast' – was meant to be quite distinct from the artist in the work. 'The more perfect the artist, the more completely separate in him will be the man who suffers and the mind which creates.' T. S. Eliot's high claim for artistic separateness was shared by James, Yeats, Ford, and other modernist writers dedicated to constructing their own original, free-standing, authoritative aesthetic systems, masks, and patterns – however interested they might also be in biographies of other writers. Joyce, who invented the 'biografiend' or 'beogrefright' in *Finnegans Wake*, made the ultimate claim for artistic impersonality and invisibility in *A Portrait of the Artist*: 'The artist, like the God of creation, remains within or behind or beyond or above his handiwork, invisible, refined out of existence, indifferent, paring his fingernails.' Such modernist manifestos had a lasting effect on the Anglo-American academic school of 'new criticism', which rejected biography as a 'fallacious quest for the origins of works: fallacious, because anything relevant to an autonomous work was by definition contained within it'. Modernism's hostility to biography also influenced the French *nouveau roman*, whose authors, such as Alain Robbe-Grillet, argued for 'a conception of authorship defined purely in terms of formal awareness', and late 20th-century critical theories (notably voiced by Roland Barthes) of 'the death of the author'.

That theoretical separation of text and life created a long stand-off between biography viewed as a popular, impure, conservative, and unexamined product for consumption by the general reader, and the academic study of literature and history. From the mid to late 20th century, it was often noted (regretfully, or happily) that biography 'has remained notably untheorised', that it has had 'a lack of legitimacy in the worlds of contemporary critical theory [and] social historiography', and has 'seemed insufficiently substantial or scientific to merit study or teaching'. It is only recently that biography has become a regular subject for books and essays, and an established academic discipline. For example, the University of Hawaii has had a Center for Biographical Research since 1978; courses and departments of Life-Writing have been set up in several British universities; there is a Biography Institute at the Australian National University in Canberra, a Center for Biography at City University in New York, and an Institute in Vienna dedicated to the 'systematic' study of the History and Theory of Biography.

Meanwhile, biographies for the general reader, especially of non-literary figures, have largely ignored these critical arguments and academic debates. Popular biography, ranging from downmarket tabloid-style packages on media figures to solidly researched, lavishly illustrated lives of politicians or historical leaders, is a thriving industry (though every so often there will be predictions of doom from the publishing industry about 'the death of biography', as there used to be about 'the death of the novel'). But with the popularity and ubiquity of biography goes a good deal of fear and loathing. Hostility to biography can take the form not of an aesthetic critique, but of the same kind of ethical objections to its intrusiveness which might have been made against Edmund Curll, or by Tennyson or Henry James. This usually arises when there is a conflict between the 'keepers of the flame' and the 'publishing scoundrels'. The case against biography was forcefully made by the American writer Janet Malcolm in the 1990s, when she involved herself in the painful battle between Sylvia Plath's biographers and Ted Hughes, whose lifelong efforts to defend his and his children's privacy, to control the publication of Plath's archive, and to monitor what was published of Plath's or about Plath, led to much vilification from Plath's advocates:

> Biography is the medium through which the remaining secrets of the famous dead are taken from them and dumped out in full view of the world. The biographer at work, indeed, is like the professional burglar, breaking into a house, rifling through certain drawers that he has good reason to think contain the jewelry and money, and triumphantly bearing his loot away. The voyeurism and busybodyism that impel writers and readers of biography alike are obscured by an apparatus of scholarship designed to give the enterprise an appearance of banklike blandness and solidity. The biographer is portrayed almost as a kind of benefactor. He is seen as sacrificing years of his life to his task, tirelessly sitting in archives and libraries and patiently conducting interviews with witnesses. There is no length he will not go to, and the more his book reflects his industry the more the reader believes that he is having an elevating literary experience, rather than listening to backstairs gossip and reading other people's mail. The transgressive nature of biography is rarely acknowledged, but it is the only explanation for biography's status as a popular genre. The reader's amazing tolerance (which he would extend to no novel written half as badly as most biographies) makes sense only when seen as a kind of collusion between him and the biographer in an excitingly forbidden undertaking: tiptoeing down the corridor together, to stand in front of the bedroom door and try to peep through the keyhole.

Malcolm's rhetoric (of ransacking, burglary, voyeurism, violation) echoes 19th-century expressions of horror at the exposure of private lives. But biography has much more licence now, and often gets away with murder. Newspaper articles called 'Biography as a Blood Sport', or describing 'The Business of Biography' as 'digging up the traumatic, the indefensible, and the shameful and getting it all into print', regularly remind us of the genre's ancient, discreditable links to scandal and slander.

It is possible to talk about biography almost entirely in terms of exposure, titillation, and shock, as in a 1990s essay by Justin Kaplan, who maintains that 'by current standards, biographies without voyeuristic, erotic thrills are like ballpark hot dogs without mustard'. He cites several examples of sensational or vindictive Lives, like Kitty Kelley's book on Nancy Reagan, which he describes as essentially a 'drive-by shooting', and of outraged attacks on biography from its victims. Germaine Greer, for instance, threatened with an unwelcomed Life, called biography a form of 'rape... an unpardonable crime against selfhood', and described biographers of living writers as 'the intellectual equivalents of flesh-eating bacterium'. Natasha Spender bitterly protested at the 'prurient interest' and 'fundamental errors' of an unauthorized biography of her husband Stephen Spender, at the 'invasive techniques' of some biographers and the 'serious, incalculable injury' they can cause.

Efforts by living subjects or their relatives and executors to control the biographer can backfire. Salinger's court case against Ian Hamilton led to the withdrawal of the biography Hamilton wanted to publish, but then to a book which described in revealing detail Salinger's obstruction of the process. Nadine Gordimer's withdrawal of authorization from a biographer she had initially approved and encouraged, because of his violation of their agreement to address any objections she posed, and his refusal to remove passages of which she did not approve, exposed her to just the kind of gossipy publicity she had wanted to avoid. Ronald

13. Popular biography as media product: intrusion and sensation

Suresh Roberts's highly proprietorial, judgemental, anecdotal narrative, brimming with his own opinions on personal and political matters, as well as with close readings of her work and a great deal of interesting source material, was refused by Gordimer's publishers in New York and London, who had originally agreed to publish it, on the grounds that it was no longer 'authorized'. So Roberts placed it with a South African press (which exported copies), prominently incorporated into the book early expressions of enthusiasm for him by Gordimer and her publishers, and went public, in numerous interviews, with details of all the material she had not wanted him to include, and sarcastic remarks about the paradoxical contrast between Gordimer's own resistance to the repressive era of apartheid and her 'censoring' of his work: 'She is supposed to represent freedom of speech but she wanted complete control.' Gordimer withdrew into dignified silence on the matter, hoping, no doubt, that her work would outlast his.

When poets and novelists object to biography, it is often not so much for ethical or protectionist reasons as because biography seems to them a reductionist simplification, a grotesque travesty of what they do, and an interference with a writer's main ambition – which is to be judged by, and remembered for, their writing. Sometimes they make sure to get in first. Doris Lessing, in the first volume of her autobiography in *Under My Skin* (1994), said, with typical sharpness: 'You cannot sit down to write about yourself without rhetorical questions of the most tedious kind demanding attention.' One is 'Why an autobiography at all?' The answer was: 'Self-defence; biographies are being written.' When writers put imaginary biographers into their work, they are usually portrayed as monsters of cynicism, opportunism, tactlessness, or tin-eared stupidity. So Jake Bolokowsky in Larkin's 'Posterity' is a bored, crude young American using his subject, Philip Larkin ('One of those old-type *natural* fouled-up guys') as a necessary step to academic advancement, and Carol Ann Duffy's vain, shallow, and self-seeking biographer ruthlessly appropriates his 'Main Man': 'In all of your mirrors, my face;/with its smallish, quizzical eyes,/its cheekbones, its sexy jaw,/its talentless, dustjacket smile.'

Fictional biographers are usually characterized as parasites, obsessives, or stalkers. They turn up in contemporary novels such as (among many others) Penelope Lively's *According to Mark*, Alison Lurie's *The Truth about Lorin Jones*, A. S. Byatt's *Possession* and *The Biographer's Tale*, Kingsley Amis's *The Biographer's Moustache*, Bernard Malamud's *Dubin's Lives*, William Golding's *The Paper Men*, and Philip Roth's *Exit Ghost*. In *Exit Ghost* (2007), for example, the ageing novelist Nathan Zuckerman tries to protect the reputation of the long-dead hero and mentor of his youth, the reclusive writer E. I. Lonoff, from the predatory assault of a 'rampaging would-be biographer'. Both Zuckerman and the woman who cherishes Lonoff's memory express their dread of biography as a form of reductivism and exposure, the trespassing of an 'inferior' talent onto a major life, motivated by the desire 'to expose the writer to censure'. Zuckerman, asking himself if he will be the biographer's next target, after Lonoff, exclaims to himself: 'An astonishing thing it is, too, that one's prowess and achievement, such as they have been, should find their consummation in the retribution of biographical inquisition.'

When it is not being anathematized, biography in fiction is the subject of sceptical novelistic enquiry, most famously here in a much-quoted image from Julian Barnes's *Flaubert's Parrot*:

> You can define a net in one of two ways, depending on your point of view. Normally, you would say that it is a meshed instrument designed to catch fish. But you could, with no great injury to logic, reverse the image and define a net as a jocular lexicographer once did: he called it a collection of holes tied together with string.
>
> You can do the same with a biography. The trawling net fills, then the biographer hauls it in, sorts, throws back, stores, fillets and sells. Yet consider what he doesn't catch: there is always far more of that.

The biography stands, fat and worthy-burgherish on the shelf, boastful and sedate: a shilling life will give you all the facts, a ten pound one all the hypotheses as well. But think of everything that got away, that fled with the last death bed exhalation of the biographee.

To be 'against' biography, for moral or aesthetic, personal or professional reasons, is almost always to be involved in an argument about property, ownership, and control. Such arguments are liable to be fraught and painful, full of rivalry and jealousy, competitiveness and mistrust. Biography is not neutral ground: it arouses strong and passionate feelings. There is despair, anger, even hopelessness, in Ted Hughes's cry: 'I hope each of us owns the facts of his or her own life.'

Chapter 7
Public Roles

For the biographer, who himself represents the social world, the social self is the real self; the self only comes to exist when juxtaposed with other people. The solitary self is a pressure upon the social self, or a repercussion of it, but it has no independent life.

A great man... finds himself modelled by the function he has to perform; unconsciously he aims at making his life a work of art... and so he acquires... that statuesque quality that makes him a fine model for the artist.

Defensive and protective practices comprise the techniques employed to safeguard the impression fostered by an individual during his presence before others... The expressive coherence that is required in performances points out a crucial discrepancy between our all-too-human selves and our socialized selves. As human beings we are presumably creatures of variable impulse with mood and energies that change from one moment to the next. As characters put on for an audience, however, we must not be subject to ups and downs.

These observations by Richard Ellmann, André Maurois, and Erving Goffman all describe individual lives as constructed performances played out in a public arena, shaped by choices and functions, and dependent upon reception and recognition. The description does not only apply to 'great men': we all construct a 'presentation of the self'. The social anthropologist Erving

Goffman also talks about 'impression management' and 'the whole machinery of self-production'. Sometimes, as he observes, the performance breaks down, or is exposed as a cynical strategy, or is constructed at too great a cost. He cites Sartre's witty example of 'the attentive pupil who wishes to *be* attentive, his eyes riveted on the teacher, his ears open wide', who 'so exhausts himself in playing the attentive role that he ends up by no longer hearing anything'.

What is biography's relation to the performative aspect of identity, the individual's public role? The more public the subject of a biography, the more urgent the question becomes. The obvious answer – the one Plutarch gave, and commentators like Bacon and Dryden approved of – is that biography's job is to get behind the public performance and show us the real person at home in his 'undress'. But the quotations above suggest that a real self may be very hard to disentangle from a performed, public, social self. Richard Ellmann's insistence on biography as a record of the 'social self' implies that the biographer can have nothing to say about any other kind of self.

When Henry James met Robert Browning for the first time, in 1877, he was amazed at his unpoetic, vulgar, chattering, public self. He decided, half joking, that there must be '2 Brownings – an esoteric and an exoteric. The former never peeps out in society, and the latter hasn't a ray of suggestion of *Men & Women.*' This thought inspired, later, a story called 'The Private Life', where the narrator, baffled by the public performance of a much-admired writer, realizes that there are *two* of him: 'One goes out, the other stays at home. One is the genius, the other's the bourgeois.'

Literary biographers usually try not to split the performing, public, everyday self off from the private writing self, but to work out the connection between them. That is really the whole point of literary biography, though it can be done well or badly. For biographers of philosophers, the relation between the two performances, the life and the work, is a more contested area. It is often maintained that there can be only two schools of thought about this, as follows: 'The first contends that biography holds the secret to understanding the work of a philosopher, the second that the understanding of a philosopher's life is irrelevant to an understanding of his [sic] work.' It could be argued that a philosopher's writing may have as little to do with his, or her, private life as a set of mathematical propositions or a chemical formula might have to do with the mathematician's divorce or the chemist's breakfast. But it seems more plausible to argue for a middle ground. It could be the case that for certain kinds of philosophers – Augustine, Wittgenstein, Socrates – the life *is* the work, or the life has a bearing, if an oppositional one, to the work. So it could be said of Socrates (who wrote nothing) that 'his life is his work and his work is his life'. Philosophical commentators on Wittgenstein's work on language and ethics, the *Tractatus*, frequently point to the same kind of connection: 'No one who reads, or tries to read the *Tractatus*, can help wondering what kind of person its author was.... The more we know of him as a person, the more interesting become the connections, and disconnections, to his philosophical work.' 'He offered himself up in his philosophizing.' 'It would be hard to invent a life whose inner travails and self imposed adversities might better illustrate the perplexities that arise from Wittgenstein's philosophy of life.' Statements of Wittgenstein's such as 'If you are unwilling to know what you are, your writing is a form of deceit', or 'You cannot write anything about yourself that is more truthful than you yourself are', are likely to make his commentators want to connect a personal appraisal and a philosophical one. Ray Monk's biography of Wittgenstein shows that he 'neither wanted to, nor thought he could, separate the task of becoming the sort of human being he wanted to be from the task of being the sort of philosopher he wanted to be'.

Philosophy and biography are connected, too, because questions that occupy some philosophers (Descartes, or Heidegger) about the reality of the self and how we can make sense of ourselves, are questions with which biography is also concerned. Biography could be said to resemble philosophy in its aim. As Wittgenstein describes it, and as Ray Monk argues, that aim is to arrive at 'the kind of understanding that consists in seeing connections'. Biographical anxieties about how a narrative construction can represent a 'real' life or self may parallel, or come close to, philosophical arguments about how human actions can be presented and understood. Philosophy, indeed, can reassure biographers on this point. If, in the philosopher Alasdair MacIntyre's formulation, 'human actions' are 'enacted narratives', if 'we all live out narratives in our lives and... understand our lives in terms of the narratives that we live out', then 'the form of narrative is appropriate for understanding the actions of others'. It may be that the validity of such narratives will depend, as in philosophy, on how the story is constructed, 'with what degree of particularity'. But, whatever the specific qualities of the storyteller, biographers need not fear (as at least some philosophers argue) that 'to give a narrative account of a human life is necessarily to falsify it'.

Where a life is all action and narrative, rather than words or ideas, different kinds of challenges are presented to the biographer. What does biography do with subjects whose achievements consist entirely of public activities (politicians, bankers, doctors), whose life's work may be non-verbal (composers, painters, mathematicians, athletes), or who express themselves through performing others' words or music (actors, singers, pianists)? How does biography tell the story of such public roles, or penetrate to the secret selves of figures who are – as Henry James said of Theodore Roosevelt – 'pure act'?

Biographies of leaders or activists must set the central performance of their subjects in the context of the political conditions that produce them, the society in and on which they operate, their race, class, nationality, and gender, and the many other figures who surround them. Biographers have to be aware of changing views – including their own view – of their subject's profession. The life, say, of a 19th-century Christian missionary in Africa is likely to be approached differently now than it would have been a hundred and fifty years ago. Biographies of sports personalities, rock stars, or film actors have to deal not only with an individual personality and life-story, but also with the army of talent-spotters, promoters, managers, agents, producers, backers, publicists, photographers, directors, writers, and audiences who surround and often create the central performance. No Life of Elvis could afford to ignore Colonel Tom Parker; no group biography of the Beatles would miss out Brian Epstein. Any life that is acted out through a profession, whether that of a judge or a gardener, a conductor or a cook, requires the biographer to grasp the network of forces and the social assumptions which surround that profession at that time and in that place, to look at how attitudes to the subject, and their profession, may have shifted through time, and to work out the relationship between public performance and identity.

And any public life will have its secrets, its peculiarities, and its contradictions, which it is the biographer's job first to discover and then to understand. There is no more humorous or touching commentary on this than W. H. Auden's 1930s sonnet, 'Who's Who', on the unaccountable private life of a heroic public man:

> A shilling life will give you all the facts:
> How Father beat him, how he ran away,
> What were the struggles of his youth, what acts
> Made him the greatest figure of his day:
> Of how he fought, fished, hunted, worked all night,
> Though giddy, climbed new mountains; named a sea:
> Some of the last researchers even write
> Love made him weep his pints like you and me.
>
> With all his honours on, he sighed for one
> Who, say astonished critics, lived at home;
> Did little jobs about the house with skill
> And nothing else; could whistle; would sit still
> Or potter round the garden; answered some
> Of his long marvellous letters but kept none.

The poem is at once a love-story, a satire on the limits of biography, and a meditation on life's choices – where the second figure stands as the first figure's alternative life, his 'road not taken'. And it suggests that some other kind of life-writing – quite different from the standard, cliché'd 'shilling life' – is needed for the second figure, the obscure beloved, living quietly in the everyday, not caring about fame or immortality.

One mighty example of the challenge to the biographer of a public life is the American financier and art collector J. P. Morgan, 'the most powerful banker in the world', whose ambitions, force, and control invite comparisons with his favourite childhood hero, Napoleon. Jean Strouse, Morgan's biographer, who started her work on him about seventy years after his death, had to master not only the enormous (and largely untapped) archive in the Pierpont Morgan Library, but also, for this quintessentially American story, big business, banking, the stock market, the press and politics at the end of the 19th century, the history of the American railroads, the steel industry, international shipping, museums, collecting, house decoration, and Gilded Age society. Meanwhile she was dealing with a character notorious for his defensiveness and oddness, 'brusque, publicity shy, neither introspective nor articulate', magnetic, forceful, depressive, hypochondriacal, conservative, sexually susceptible and unfaithful, greedy, acquisitive, and philanthropic. Sometimes it must have been hard to get beyond the notorious nose.

And there was a further problem. Attitudes to Morgan had been largely fixed for a century: he was 'exalted by the right as a hero of economic progress and vilified by the left as an icon of capitalist greed'. As her years of work went on, Strouse found she was too wedded to her preconception of a 'cynical tycoon'. The evidence she was unearthing was altering the picture. Against the grain of her own assumptions, she painstakingly recast her narrative to give a more truthful and complex picture.

Such revisionary work, and rethinking of myths, is likely to form part of any serious Life of a public figure. Secular hagiography does continue to be written. Idealized, exemplary Lives often serve, still, as elegies for representatives of victimized minorities, revolutionary leaders, political prisoners, or spokespersons for the oppressed. There is a huge political and cultural investment for certain groups in maintaining an inviolable biographical image of figures such as Gandhi, Steve Biko, Mother Theresa, Martin Luther King, Rosa Luxembourg, Che Guevara, or, above all, Nelson Mandela. A recent analysis by Elleke Boehmer of the 'heroic symbolization' of Mandela as 'secular saint and architect of democracy', a global and national 'icon' who has been 'over-represented to the point of being rendered banal, excavated for meaning till all sense of the human being behind the public face disappears', argues that it is impossible for biographers in South Africa, or elsewhere, to write about him except in terms of his 'national symbolic significance'. Biographical representation is always entangled here with oral testimony, journalism, biopics, documentary film, and 'iconic' photographs, like emblematic images of Che Guevara in his beret (on every Western Marxist student's wall or T-shirt in the 1960s), or lying like Mantegna's dead Christ, bullet-ridden in the hospital in Bolivia. Sanctification, in most cases, then produces backlash, which veers to the other extreme of vilification. So Mother Theresa's self-serving, right-wing politics, Luther King's sexual exploits, or Guevara's thuggish killings in the Havana jails and his treatment of homosexuals are aired in myth-debunkings which, in turn, serve their own political and cultural purpose.

The politics of biography come sharply into focus when the subject stands for, or inspires, a debate about national myths and character, as with the emphasis on 'national biography' in the 19th century. Churchill, Thatcher, De Gaulle come to mind; so, especially, does Horatio Nelson, England's greatest naval hero. The *New DNB* entry on Nelson describes his afterlife as an 'apotheosis', beginning with paintings of him 'at the moment he was struck

14. Che Guevara: The making and unmaking of a legend

down in compositions closely modelled on the deposition of Christ from the cross'. A 2004 biography of Nelson by John Sugden, a naval historian, tackles at length the challenge of a much-mythologized public life. Sugden takes over 900 pages to get Nelson halfway through his career. His story starts with Nelson's death in 1805, and the erecting of more than 'thirty monuments to his memory'. 'Biographies of Nelson are also monuments', he notes, 'and equally reflect shifting opinion'. The early two-volume life by James Clarke and John McArthur, published in 1809, relied heavily on what Sugden calls Nelson's 'self-congratulatory fragment' of autobiography, which represented his own life as an exemplary story of perseverance, heroic deeds, and public duty. Nelson's long and scandalous relationship with Lady Emma Hamilton was well known, so the authors could not plead ignorance, but 'merely declared the subject off limits', and concentrated instead on his 'splendid public character'. Southey's heroic Life of 1813 'cemented the admiral's status as the authentic British hero'. (Though Southey, as he said himself, was no naval expert: 'I walk among sea terms as a cat goes in a china pantry, in bodily fear of doing mischief, & betraying myself.') A thorough, candid Life of 1849 by Thomas Pettigrew was 'hissed out of print' because it proved that Nelson's child was the product of his adultery. At the end of the 19th century, biographies of Nelson presented him as 'the ultimate exemplar of naval achievement'. The *DNB* notes that the Navy League was promoting 'the cult of Trafalgar day' in the years before the First World War, with Nelson as 'a symbol of imperial Britain and its overarching sea-power, and a talisman against anxiety... Nelson the man... had largely been forgotten in Nelson the hero.' His ardour, naivety, arrogance, energy, lack of diplomatic skills, emotional susceptibility, and egotism had all been smoothed away into a monument.

During the Second World War, Nelson's heroic image came in useful again. Sugden notes that 'a remarkably wooden Laurence Olivier... portrayed the admiral in a British film designed to win American hearts to a crusade against the European dictators.'

A well-researched 1946 biography by Carola Oman and the editing of Nelson's letters in 1958 deepened the picture. But in the 1960s, Sugden maintains, naval history became unfashionable, and Nelson's patriotic virtues seemed 'outmoded'. Attention focused increasingly on his sexual rather than his naval conquests, culminating in a 'bravely irreverent' but at times 'vindictive'

15. Nelson: The national hero and his memorabilia

biography by Terry Coleman in 2001. Sugden promises his readers to set aside 'idolatry' and 'denigration' in favour of 'dispassionate judgment'. Yet, though he brings out Nelson's mixed qualities, his rhetoric is not quite free of heroic cadences: 'Nelson always identified his cause with that of the nation. Whether acting rightly or wrongly, he represented his struggle as one for the good of the realm. His honour was his country's honour, and his triumphs the country's triumphs.' Old biographical traditions die hard.

Nelson was loved and venerated; tyrants and mass murderers raise different problems for biographers. A tendency towards sycophancy in some political biographers, which has led Michael Holroyd to call them 'history's butlers', is not the problem if the subject is Hitler, Stalin, Nero, Idi Amin, Pol Pot, or Robert Mugabe. Baleful, destructive public lives require biographical steadiness and clarity, especially when the myth has outgrown reality, or when, like Napoleon or Alexander the Great, the subjects have been romanticized as much as vilified.

Psychoanalytical treatments of notorious public figures – Hitler as the product of childhood trauma – have had a lasting currency. Intriguing examples are Rebecca West's 1947 account of the Irish Nazi propagandist William Joyce, 'Lord Haw Haw', as a study of an inferiority complex, or Nicholas Mosley's painful memoir of his father Oswald Mosley, which is all about control: 'He felt he could order the world as he ordered words.' Less theory-driven accounts of appalling public figures, like Alan Bullock's double biography of Hitler and Stalin, concentrate on facts and context, though even this thoughtful approach can allow itself to express outrage:

> The indelible impression left by [*Mein Kampf's*] seven hundred pages is the vulgarity of Hitler's mind, cunning and brutal... intolerant and devoid of human feeling... But no less striking is the consistency and systematic character of his views, however crude. The struggle for existence is a law of Nature; hardness is the supreme virtue... power is the prerogative of a racial

elite; the masses are capable only of carrying out orders...force is the only means by which anything lasting is accomplished...Stalin would have found little to disagree with. Together they represent the twentieth century's most formidable examples of those *simplificateurs terribles'* whom the nineteenth-century historian, Jakob Burckhardt, foresaw as characteristic of the century to follow.

This measured tone contrasts sharply with a more recent, more populist version of Stalin. Simon Sebag Montefiore had the 21st-century advantage of gaining access to hitherto inaccessible archives and sources in Russia. His *Stalin: The Court of the Red Tzar* (2004) and *Young Stalin* (2007) pursued the staggering facts of Stalin's career with the boisterous drive of an adventure story or a thriller, avoiding psychoanalytical interpretations or historical moralizings, but every so often pausing to remind us that this rollicking yarn is the story of a psychopathic mass murderer. This is the roller-coaster version of tragic world history, biography not as sombre meditation but as action and event.

A regime such as Stalin's obliterated millions of lives, produced millions of unwritten biographies. Such phases in history, when so much human story is wiped out, and so much can only be reconstructed through oral testimony, silent photographs, or horrified guesswork, at once destabilize and intensify the value of life-writing. We want to find out everything we can about the life of, say, Anne Frank; at the same time, we are aware of the vast numbers of obliterated life-stories whose particularities we will never know.

Exceptional lives with strong public resonance emerging from such wastelands of history are likely to be especially contested. One of the most potent lives to have survived Stalinism was that of the composer Shostakovich, a tremendously complex subject for biography. Shostakovich's gigantically productive musical life (1906–75) spanned the Russian Revolution, the war, Stalin's murderous and repressive regime, with its mass purges and its silencing of artists, the straitjacket of 'socialist realism', Communism, the Cold War, and the cultural thaw. He received every kind of accolade and attack, from early fame to party threats, from criticisms of his 'compromised' musical manifestos to posthumous, post-Soviet-era revisionist claims for his irony and concealed subversiveness. Shostakovich's understandable refusal to speak out about his work except in 'sweeping platitudes' or enforced apologias, his holding back in secret of some works for many years, his complex, coded musical use of self-references and allusions, and the official titles often attached to his pieces, all make for biographical bafflement.

The huge changes in Russia during and after his lifetime produced dramatic shifts of attitudes towards him. Soviet obituaries and early biographies celebrated his assertion of 'the ideals of Soviet humanism and internationalism'. The reputation was startlingly altered by the publication in 1979 of the *Testimony* of Solomon Volkov, his devoted acolyte in later years, who claimed to be transcribing Shostakovich's private conversation – bitter, ironical, self-reproachful, subversive – and who described him as a '*yurodivy*', a 'holy fool'. But Volkov's reliability has been much questioned. As large numbers of first-hand descriptions and letters began to surface, and as Shostakovich's reputation as a great composer spread, biographers had to step clear of 'speculation and ideological tendentiousness'. Laurel Fay's meticulous, careful Life of 2000 picked its way through startlingly different versions of her subject. She comments:

> Writing about Shostakovich remains laced with political and moral subtexts. At its most extreme, it simply replaces one orthodoxy with another... The true-believing Communist citizen-composer is inverted into an equally unconvincing caricature of a lifelong closet dissident.... There is pressing need to sort... the man from the myths.

The difficulty that always arises in trying to read music directly back into the life of the composer is compounded by the long battle

16. The self-concealing composer: the life in the work

for survival which cloaked Shostakovich's motives and intentions. His best-known quartet, for example, the Eighth (written in 1960), an intensely and powerfully emotional piece, was written after a visit to Dresden and is said by some commentators to be a 'literal evocation of the Dresden bombings'. It was also, however, written soon after he had suffered what Laurel Fay calls an 'emotional breakdown' in response to being forced to become a member of the Communist Party, a recruitment which he had previously resisted. Volkov quoted him as saying that the quartet, though 'assigned to the department of "exposing fascism"', was 'autobiographical'. The quartet's allusions to earlier works, and his use of a repeated motif based on the initials of his own name, made this clear to anyone who was not 'blind'. A letter of 1960 corroborates Volkov: 'I've written this ideologically flawed quartet which nobody will be interested in... "Dedicated to the memory of the composer of this quartet", could be written on the title page.' In 2002, Shostakovich's daughter Galina remembered her father saying: 'I've just written a composition which I've dedicated to my own memory.' But after the quartet's success he was persuaded to change the dedication 'to the victims of fascism'. This dedication may have been forced upon him, but (as his son, Maxim Shostakovich, argued) it could, indeed, be read autobiographically. 'If you take "fascism" to mean "totalitarianism" the ambivalence disappears. Shostakovich was one of countless victims of a monstrous totalitarian regime.' Laurel Fay steps through these ambiguities by describing the quartet's powerful effect on its first listeners, who, though 'misdirected in their understanding of the... substance of the quartet... were stunned by its tragic depth'. They recognized that it was autobiographical 'in its essence', even if the quartet's many quotations from his own earlier scores and the insistent use of his 'motto' were thought to refer to his 'struggle against the dark forces of reaction'.

Those forces pressed especially hard on Shostakovich in the period from 1936 to 1937. After the popular success of his opera, *Lady Macbeth of the Mtsensk District,* he was threateningly denounced in a notorious article in *Pravda*, headed 'Muddle instead of Music'. Shostakovich was said to have contemplated suicide. He was writing his Fourth Symphony, with its two long, dark outer movements, its funeral march, and its slow fading away into *pianissimo* and silence. The symphony was finished in 1936, but was withdrawn from public performance, either because of external pressure, or his fear of reprisals. It was kept in a drawer for twenty-five years, and not performed until 1961. Instead, in 1937, he produced his Fifth Symphony, a more traditional work, with a hammering triumphal ending, greeted with huge public acclaim. It was given the subtitle 'A Soviet Artist's Practical Creative Reply to Just Criticism', a subtitle probably provided by a journalist, though Shostakovich gave it his tacit assent, perhaps 'as a subterfuge to assist in his rehabilitation'. After the Fifth Symphony's success, he said to the conductor Boris Khaikin (who did not then know about the Fourth Symphony): 'I finished the symphony *fortissimo* and in the major. Everyone is saying that it's an optimistic and life-affirming symphony. I wonder, what would they be saying if I had finished it *pianissimo* and in the minor?' In the 1970s, he told Volkov:

> I think that it is clear to everyone what happens in the Fifth. The rejoicing is forced, created under a threat... It's as if someone were beating you with a stick and saying, 'Your business is rejoicing, your business is rejoicing' and you rise, shakily, and go marching off muttering, 'Our business is rejoicing, our business is rejoicing.' What kind of apotheosis is that?

Shostakovich's life provides a major challenge for biographers, in matters such as reading the life from the work, trusting witnesses, understanding the historical context, deciding what to believe, trying to track the hidden agenda of a public life and – above all – explaining genius.

Other kinds of biographical challenges are presented by lives lived entirely through performance, celebrity lives that seem to make themselves completely available in the public domain. Commentary on such figures – especially if they are women – is profuse and relentless, much of it quick, ephemeral, invented, and intrusive. The scandals and tragedies of their lives seem part of their performances, produced by the conditions of fame. Their visual images fuel gigantic media sales, in some cases long after their deaths. Yet – or therefore – they may remain biographically puzzling or impenetrable, swallowed up by their own myth. The kind of celebrities who become sufficiently famous to be known by a single name – Garbo, Callas, Diana, Elvis, Piaf, Madonna, Dylan – require their biographers to sort out 'iconic' image from reality, myth from fact, surface from depth. And there is always a risk that there may be no depth after all, only appearance and performance.

The most alluring and insoluble of all such modern biographical subjects is, probably, still, 'Marilyn'. There are huge numbers of biographies of Marilyn Monroe, if the term is used loosely to include picture books, anthologies of images, clippings and quotations, showcases for 'the legacy of her legend', sensational thrillers about the mystery of her death ('the evidence points to premeditated homicide'), feminist interpretations, fictional versions of her story, and sociological analyses of the construction of the 'star' and the commodification of the female body through the Hollywood system.

All versions promise a deeper, truer, more authentic Marilyn. All – typically of 'star biographies' – promise to get 'under the public image to the true life below' and to write about her 'as a human being, as opposed to a celluloid invention' even while recycling the gossip and reproducing the most famous images. Many speak of a special sense of affinity for their subject: 'I felt immediately drawn to her.' Almost all use her first name – either her real one, Norma Jeane/Jean, or her Hollywood name. All versions talk about childhood abuse and neglect, madness, rape, sex, beauty, the image of the 'dumb blonde', magnetism, charisma, pornography, Hollywood and the movie industry, publicity, fame, power, marriage, divorce, miscarriage, abortion, drugs, alcohol, self-destruction, and death. There is no way of writing a Life of 'Marilyn' without dealing with these big topics, any more than without talking about Joe DiMaggio, Arthur Miller, or the Kennedy brothers. That is the attraction of the job: it is a big, symbolic American story.

All the biographies deal with her contradictions: natural and artificial, exhibitionistic and vulnerable, funny and tragic, dumb blonde and talented performer, desirable and frigid, sexually experienced and innocent-seeming, babyish and adult, mortal and immortal. An overview of such treatments, *The Many Lives of Marilyn Monroe* (2004), sees a shift over fifty years from 'sex symbol to symbol of mourning, from a promise of the liberation of sex to a cautionary tale about the dangers of loneliness'. The author, Sarah Churchwell, argues that the 'hidden' Marilyn is never to be found. The repeated dichotomies proposed by biography after biography – 'public/private, artifice/reality, fantasy/truth' – do not reveal a 'true' self: they reiterate a 'terminal either/or in which she is trapped'.

The most intensively interpretative versions, by three well-known American writers (Joyce Carol Oates, Norman Mailer, Gloria Steinem), all opt for the biographical theme of double identity. Norman Mailer read 'Marilyn', in his 1973 novel of that name, as both the ultimately desirable essence of Woman, described in lavish tumescent prose ('a cornucopia ... the angel of sex ... like a sweet peach bursting before one's eyes') and as a female Napoleon, an epic representative of archetypal human struggles. Joyce Carol Oates, in her fictional allegory of Eros and Thanatos, has 'Marilyn' as The Blonde who is pursued through her life by the Dark Prince and who is part smiling mask ('The Blonde Actress ... inhabiting her voluptuous body like a child crammed into a mannequin'), part abandoned 'unhappy little girl', always looking for her lost father.

The feminist writer Gloria Steinem's outraged lament for Monroe's tragic fate described her, in 1987, as split between the wretched, unloved Norma Jeane whom Marilyn spends her life trying to escape, and the public, artificially constructed Marilyn, who 'used her body as a gift to gain love and approval'. 'Whenever the public artifice failed and the private Norma Jeane seemed to be her only fate again...then depression and hopelessness took over...her body became her prison.' This protective elegy for Monroe as 'the emblematic female victim' may seem overly indulgent now, but its tone was in strong contrast to the locker-room ridicule and innuendo of many male treatments of the 'sex-goddess'. Anthony Summers's 1985 version was particularly snide: 'This need for a father figure seems to have become part of Marilyn's tapestry of fantasies'; 'One day Marilyn managed to break even her record for unpunctuality'; 'Marilyn now indulged her taste for intrigue and the ugly side of her temper'. The contrast in approaches points to more than differing treatments of one female superstar. It suggests biography's long-lasting tendency to treat exceptional and famous women differently from exceptional and famous men: not as 'role models' or admirable exemplars, but as freaks, warnings, objects of fear, desire, or ridicule, dangerous accidents, trouble-zones.

The two most famous and most reproduced images of 'Marilyn' are the publicity shot of her in the white dress blowing up over the subway vent (the huge entrancing smile, the amazing legs, the jokey sexiness, the mixture of natural life-force and urban sophistication, the exhibition for admiring onlookers) and the face as processed by another glamorous, short-lived media figure, Andy Warhol. Warhol's paintings of Marilyn, begun soon after her death in 1962, were part of his obsession with fame and violent early death, alongside Elvis with a gun and Jackie at the death of Kennedy. For *Marilyn Diptych* (1962), he used a cropped publicity photo which was enlarged and transferred to a silkscreen and became the basis for fifty identical images of Marilyn, laid out in ten regular blocks of five. On the left half of

17. Endless exposure: life flattened into myth

the diptych, the heads are coloured in lurid gold, pink, and blue. The right half is in black and white; some heads are heavily blotted with dark ink, some are fading out into nothingness. 'The row upon row of repeated heads call to mind postage stamps, bill board posters, but, perhaps, most of all... strips of film... both celebratory of a life and a mourning of a death.' Warhol's images of Monroe are the opposite of everything we want biography to be. They are flat, repetitive, banal, synthetic, journalistic, unrevealing. But they also offer a highly appropriate version of her life-story: endlessly exposed, instantly recognizable, unable to communicate anything except what has been constructed for public consumption. In that sense, they are the visual equivalent of a biography of a public life in the modern world, flattened irretrievably into myth.

Chapter 8
Telling the Story

'My God, how does one write a biography?' That was what Virginia Woolf asked herself in 1938, while she was trying to write a commissioned Life of her friend Roger Fry, and that was how I began my biography of her in 1996. It seemed a suggestive way in, since her life-story was already well known (so I didn't have to start 'Adeline Virginia Stephen was born on the 25th January 1882') and she herself was so interested in, and so articulate and sceptical about, biography and its conventions. I shaped her life-story not entirely chronologically but partly by themes, inspired by her own experimental novelistic strategies for accessing the interior lives of her characters and dealing with time, memory, and perspective. Any biographical narrative is an artificial construct, since it inevitably involves selection and shaping. No biographer is going to write down every single thing their subject did, said, and thought on every day of their life from birth to death, or the book would take longer than the life itself. Given my subject's own interest in how life-stories can be told, I decided to point up the artifice of the biographical narrative, and to concentrate on particular aspects of the life, on different 'selves'. Other contemporary biographers are similarly experimenting with form, building in an explicit commentary on their own relation to the subject, using fictional strategies, or playing with time and point of view.

There is an argument to be made against these sorts of experiments. Roy Foster, historian-biographer, faced with Yeats's mythologizing of his own life and its powerful after-effects on his biographers, wanted to 'restore the sense of a man involved in life, and in history: notably in the history of his country, at a time of exceptional flux and achievement'. '[Yeats's] *Autobiographies* dictates an arrangement for his life, and it is a thematic one... However, we do not, alas, live our lives in themes, but day by day; and WBY, giant though he was, is no exception.' Foster gets behind Yeats's commanding accounts of himself by use of steady chronological structure and massive investigative detail. But, in an admiring review of the biography, James Olney asks whether an undeviating chronological method, 'proceeding not by themes but day by day' is really possible. He cites Paul Valéry, wondering 'if anyone has ever tried to write a biography and attempted at each instant of it to know as little of the following moment as the hero of the work knew himself'. And he notes that Foster's biography 'commences in chronological record but then shades off into a fully interpretative and thematic narrative that is both retrospective and proleptic in its ordering'.

The examples of Woolf and Yeats suggest that different kinds of narrative may fit different kinds of biographical subjects. It would not have seemed helpful to experiment with form if I had been writing a Life of, say, Martin Luther King, or Ian Paisley, or Benazir Bhutto. In those cases, it would have been more useful to start with the history of American slavery and the Civil Rights movement, or with the tangled roots of·Protestant Unionism in Northern Ireland, or with the Indo-Pakistan wars and the rise of the Bhutto dynasty. For political or historical biography, the form of the narrative may have to be steady and unsurprising, solid scaffolding for the blocks of facts.

As this book began by saying, there are no rules for telling a life-story. But there *are* some inevitable conventions. Whatever the story is about, whatever race, nationality, sex, class, language, or history is involved, there will have to be time, place, character, and events. Most biography moves forward and onward, sets the main figure in its context, mixes the plot with accounts of the subject's work, of historical complexities or of subsidiary characters, and uses description and observation, documentary sources, witness testimony, peripheral materials, and first-hand knowledge to construct the story. Biographers may choose to concentrate on a particular part of the life. They may start with a death, or a telling anecdote, or the subject's posthumous reputation, rather than with a birth. They may allow gaps and puzzles into the narrative, or try to smooth these over. They may introduce moral judgements or personal opinions. But they all want to give as full, intelligible, and accurate a version of the subject's life as possible. And they all want to make the specific facts and details add up to some overall idea of the subject, so that their biography, for the moment, will give the truest answer to the question: What was she, or he, like?

But even that basic list raises many alternative possibilities. My hypothetical Lives of King, Paisley, and Bhutto could have started differently: with a shot and a fall on the balcony of the Lorraine motel in Memphis in 1968; with an account of Ballymena, County Antrim, in the 1930s; with a description of the holy shrine that Bhutto's tomb, in her family mausoleum in Sindh province, has now become. Beginnings want to catch the reader's interest, of course, but they also set up the biographer's tone. Here are some examples:

'There will always be Shelley lovers, but this book is not for them.' Richard Holmes tells us in his first sentence that he is not going to be idolatrous or romanticizing, that he is writing against received versions, that he is bold and clear about his reasons for doing this, and that he knows that *his* Shelley will be one more version, not a definitive account.

'The story of Rebecca West (who lived from 1892 to 1983) is the story of twentieth-century women.' Victoria Glendinning lets us know at once, and firmly, why her subject matters, how she feels about it, and and what her approach is likely to be.

'It was the best of times and it was the worst of times. In the London household of Alexander and Edith Pope, Edith was expecting her first child.' The Pope scholar Maynard Mack, setting out on his magisterial 1985 Life of the poet, starts with an echo of Dickens which suggests that this is going to be a big historical story with the rich thick density of a 19th-century novel.

'On 1 February 1984, an Englishman with a rucksack and walking boots strides into a bungalow in the Irene district of Pretoria. He is six feet tall, with fair hair swept over a huge forehead and staring blue eyes. He is only a step ahead of the illness that will kill him. He is 45, but he has the animation of a schoolboy.' The present-tense beginning of Nicholas Shakespeare's Life of Bruce Chatwin promises a gripping adventure and a racy, intimate piece of reportage about a remarkable person.

'Decades after the blazing hot afternoon in June 1933 when Ralph Ellison, on his first and last outing as a hobo, climbed fearfully and yet eagerly aboard a smoky freight train leaving Oklahoma City on a dangerous journey that he hoped would take him to college in Tuskegee, Alabama, his memories of growing up in Oklahoma continued both to haunt and to inspire him. For a long time he had suppressed those memories, then the time came when he began to crave them.' This long-winded opening to Arnold Rampersad's Life of Ralph Ellison sets up a complicated interplay between past and present, aspiration and recollection. It tells us we are setting out on an exhaustive biographical journey, with a biographer who is in full possession of his subject's inner and outer life.

In each of these cases – and in any example you care to pick – the opening moves set up the whole approach. And this will vary depending on the subject. The biography of an unknown figure who has never been written about before may have to justify its existence, but can be free of the claims for specialness and slapping down of previous versions that biographies of much-covered figures may find necessary. Tone and approach will usually reveal whether this is an unknown subject, a resuscitation, an act of iconoclasm, an interim report on a living person, or a revisionist return, with new materials or the key to long-kept secrets, aiming to change our whole view of a well-known story.

Biography has a different job to do if it is dealing with what Virginia Woolf called 'lives of the obscure', than if it is retelling the story of Shakespeare or Napoleon. As biography is always involved with the social and cultural politics of its time and place, so its assumptions change about what is major or minor, permitted or shocking, mainstream or alternative. One striking example of biography's shifting standards is the recent popularity of 'group' biography (an ancient genre, newly revived), arising from an interest in democratizing a form that has tended to focus on single, dominant figures, and from a desire, in Jenny Uglow's phrase, 'to uncover a past we might otherwise miss'.

Such biographies may be about royal families or political dynasties, but they may also involve a challenge to the 'dominant discourse'. A feminist biographer working in the 1990s on the life of a working-class, Communist woman migrant to Australia raised the question of authority for biographers who choose 'alternative' subjects:

> The biographer who prefers to construct a version of history that is not, say, Captain Cook single-handedly appropriating Australia for British imperialism but, rather, the version of one of the sailors, or of one of the Aboriginal people who resisted the invasion, is presented with a wide range of problems. One of the central ones is: Who will speak?

Biographies that speak for alternative or hidden lives, especially women's – Jean Strouse on Henry James's sister Alice (1980),

Brenda Maddox on Joyce's wife Nora Barnacle (1988), Claire Tomalin on Dickens's mistress Ellen Ternan (1990), Alison Light on Virginia Woolf's servants (2007) – grow out of a feminist interest in 'hidden histories'. In *A Room of One's Own* (1929), Woolf imagined the many untold stories of women's lives, 'these infinitely obscure lives that still remain to be recorded'. Woolf's idea of what an unrecorded life might be, or how it might be told, would look different a hundred years on. As with biographies of African-American subjects, or native peoples, or lives set in post-colonial and developing nations, or queer and lesbian life-stories, or working-class histories, feminist biography (which may of course overlap with any of those other categories) is a changing genre, not a fixed entity.

This genre went through a period of reaction against historical assumptions about 'separate spheres', domestic priorities, modest invisibility, or aberrant exceptions. But female biography no longer needs to ask, as Carolyn Heilbrun did in the 1980s, what the story of a woman's life 'should look like', or to argue that 'biographies of women, if they have been written at all, have been written under the constraints of acceptable discussion'. The phase of disinterring obscure lives and of claiming new status and significance for women's stories – a process of consciousness-raising that has been described as 'critical to the feminist project of transforming the public sphere' – can now be spoken about in the past tense, as by the historian Carolyn Steedman, in *Past Tenses*: 'A sense of that which is lost, never to be recovered completely, has been one of the most powerful rhetorical devices of modern women's history.' (And, she adds, of working-class history.)

The telling of women's stories has often been talked about in terms of difference. Any account of female biography notes that: 'In truth, writing the lives of men and women *is* different... What is acceptable, what is possible, what is imagined and attempted often differ.' 'If biographies of men are dominated by external events, most biographies of women are a blend of external and internal.' 'It

18. 'Pit Brow' girls: Group lives, women's lives, working lives

may be true that most women are still judged heavily by their private lives and men almost exclusively by their public.' If the subject is a writer, 'access to the privacy of the author seems more intensely desired when the author is a woman'. Women writers whose lives involved abuse, mental illness, self-harm, suicide, have often been treated, biographically, as victims or psychological case-histories first and as professional writers second. The agendas that surround such stories are acutely on view in biographies of Woolf or Plath, or, for instance, in Diane Wood Middlebrook's Life of the confessional American poet Anne Sexton, who killed herself, which made use of tapes of the subject talking to her analyst. Even if the various pitfalls in writing about women – personalizing, over-protectiveness, demonizing, punitiveness, condescension – have become much less common, the challenge remains of how best to tell the stories of the increasing numbers of women in the public sphere. 'It is still very difficult to account for women's influence and reputation in public arenas', writes one feminist critic, citing Steedman's biography of the early 20th-century socialist politician Margaret McMillan, which tried to find ways of lifting 'the dead weight of interiority that hangs about the neck of women's biography', and to tell the story of an entirely 'public life'.

A still lingering difference between biographies of men and of women is revealed by the matter of naming. Lives are no longer being written of 'Miss Austen', 'Mrs Woolf', or 'Mrs Gaskell'. But because biographies of women have for so long been more protective and intimate than those of great men, a biography of a famous English woman novelist might still refer throughout to Jane or Charlotte, while famous male English novelists are not usually called Charles or Anthony. Some biographers of women deal with this issue by switching from forename to surname, or from childhood nickname to married name, depending on whether early or later life, personal or professional matters, are being referred to. The *New Oxford DNB* has given this careful thought:

> Evans, Marian [pseud. George Eliot] (1819–80), novelist, was known under several names during her life: Mary Anne Evans (at birth), Mary Ann Evans (from 1837), Marian Evans (from 1851), Marian Evans Lewes (from 1854), and Mary Ann Cross (1880).

George Eliot can be found, in the online version of the DNB, under any one of these names.

Naming is just one signal of the biography's approach to its subject. The construction of that approach begins with the book's cover, title, and contents page. These paratextual elements may be partly the work of the publisher rather than the author, but they set up expectations for a certain kind of narrative.

Lives of Jane Austen tend to have similar covers, because there is only one known portrait of her, drawn by her sister Cassandra. But the biography's approach will be suggested by whether the original, rather grumpy-looking, unromantic image is used, or the prettified, genteel version which was touched up by the next generation.

Titles tell a story, too. A biography called *Shakespeare: The Biography* makes a different kind of claim from *Will in the World: How Shakespeare became Shakespeare*, or *1599: A Year in the Life of William Shakespeare*. Contents pages are also part of the narrative. A biography of Keats that is simply divided up by numbered sections (and so has no chapters listed on its contents page) has a less prescriptive or novelistic air – but is harder to navigate – than one whose contents page has chapter titles such as 'Mr Keats's Origins', 'Sparks of the Divine', or 'The Death Warrant'. Some biographers (mostly European) divide their chapter titles up into sections, like indexes. So Jean-Yves Tadié's 1996 Marcel Proust has headings like 'Contre Sainte Beuve: Pastiches 504, Living for Writing 507, Financial Speculations and Virtuous Habits 509', giving the impression that the Life has been sliced up with utmost precision. Some biographers imitate their subject's manner in their chapter titles, as though pretending to be novelists. So Adrian Frazier's Life of the ebullient, self-dramatizing Irish novelist George Moore has chapters called 'Don Juan Jr in the Age of the National Vigilance Association', or 'Jesus of Nazareth and the Sage of Ebury Street'.

All those sorts of choices – the fullness or scarcity of footnotes, whether the index includes topics and concepts as well as names,

19. Miss Austen; Jane Austen; Jane...

the range and number of illustrations – are part of how the story is told and what kind of readership is envisaged: general or specialist, trade or academic. Length, too, tells us about the approach. Why was this subject thought worthy of 900 pages?

Or, why has a big subject been dealt with in 150 pages? What has been left out?

Biography's narrative tactics – often barely noticed as the facts unroll and the story moves on – set the tone and create a point of view. Narratives that go in for thunderous climaxes ('This was a watershed event in her life'), or dramatic summings-up ('Henry James chose the path of safety. He remained celibate'), or suspenseful anticipations – *he would come to regret this decision bitterly, things would never be the same again, from this moment she never looked back* – are, in Leon Edel's phrase, trying to 'borrow some of the techniques of fiction without lapsing into fictional biography'. Some biographers make free more blithely than others with their 'must haves' and 'might haves', their 'perhaps' and 'probablys'. Some approach their subject with a predetermined theory about what shaped their lives – illness, a family relationship, some form of damage or abuse – and make the story fit the theory. Some biographers use a great deal of description and scene-setting, and some make empathetic rather than factual portraits of their characters. This is a risky strategy, but can work well if the biographer is also a fiction writer, as in V. S. Pritchett's fine short Life of Turgenev:

> [Turgenev's mother] Varvara Petrovna's command of the passions, in all their manifestations, was inexhaustible. She was a round-shouldered woman with large, glaring black eyes under heavy brows, her forehead was wide and low, the skin of her face was coarse and pocked, her mouth large, sensual and cruel, her manner arrogant and capricious. She was as self-willed as a child, though like many ugly women she could be fascinating and charm her friends, and was very witty. Her history is pitiable.

The tone of voice used about the subject is a vital part of how the biographical story is told. Biographers sometimes ask themselves whether they think of their subject as younger or older than they are, in need of sympathetic protection or a daunting object of respect. Modern biographers often speak in a humorous, ironic, unshockable voice, making it clear that nothing human disgusts them. John Haffenden embarks on his mighty, and mightily peculiar, Life of William Empson with a reminiscence of having heard him read, inaudibly, at Trinity College Dublin in the 1960s:

> A woman cried out with exasperation from the back of the hall, 'Speak out, you silly old fool!' Whole rows of necks shrank into their shoulders with the embarrassment of it all, though later I was tipped off that the outspoken woman had been Empson's wife – so that was all right.

This cool comical tone is quite often used when sexuality is being described. Andrew Motion, detailing Larkin's interest in pornography, tells this story:

> Once, hesitating outside a shop in a funk, Larkin was approached by the owner who discreetly asked, 'Was it bondage, sir?'

Fiona MacCarthy, establishing her attitude to Eric Gill's sexual acts with (his) children and animals, writes bravely:

> Even his... practical experiments with bestiality, though they may strike one as bizarre, are not in themselves especially horrifying or amazing. Stranger things have been recorded.

More solemn biographical approaches turn their subjects' stories into archetypal tragedies, as in the conclusion to Michael Reynolds's epic biography of Hemingway:

> His is a classic American story: the young man who transforms himself following his ambition, succeeds beyond his dreams, and finally burns out trying to be true to the person he has become... It is an old story, older than written words, a story the ancient Greeks would have recognized.

Less sympathetic biographers use their subject as target-practice, and try to bring them down:

> Writers who posed a threat to Bellow's hegemony got the cold shoulder; writers who occupied a place safely below his own on the literary ladder were seen as comrades in the 'travail business', as Bellow liked to refer to his profession.

> Bellow... inveighed against the unregulated sex of the permissive sixties while passing up no opportunity to indulge in it himself... It was as if he hoped that his persistent moralizing could somehow neutralize his own libertine impulses – the ineffectual superego chastising the guilty id.

Biography is bound to incorporate the relationship of the writer and their subject, even if only subliminally. There is no such thing as an entirely neutral biographical narrative. Not everyone will agree with André Maurois that the main subject of any biography is 'the medium of the biographer's own feelings'. Not all biographers choose to say 'I'. Not all would want to identify their life with their subject's quite as closely as this psycho-biographer of Thoreau:

> In the past few years, my 'marriage' to Thoreau has evolved in new, unexpected directions... Working... on 'dialogues' between myself and Thoreau... has revealed much to me about these directions in our relationship... When I first worked on the dialogues, I had a sense, inspired by the possibility that my wife and I might be pregnant, that I was on the verge of a new period of my life. With the confirmation that we were indeed going to have a child, I have unquestionably entered a new phase... I wonder now whether, or how, my relationship to Thoreau will be modified as I become involved in parenting... I am hopeful that I can maintain and nurture an enduring I-Thou relationship with Thoreau.

Biography may, indeed, be a kind of marriage. If the biographer knows or has met their subject, their own feelings about them will colour the picture in some way. Selina Hastings's difficult friendship with Rosamond Lehmann, who became demanding and impatient with her biographer, shadowed her view of her. Samuel Beckett's characteristic response to his biographer Deirdre Bair – 'he would not help me, he said, but he would not hinder me, either' – left her free, but dogged by the feeling that 'he did not want this book to be written and would have been grateful if I had abandoned it'. Even when the biographer has not met their subject, they may find them resistant or obstructive, as Judith Thurman found Colette: 'She actively disdains all forms of empathy and resists being known.'

All biography is an attempt to take possession of the subject (A. S. Byatt's novels *Possession* and *The Biographer's Tale* deal passionately with this idea), but some biographers are more possessed – or possessive – than others. Some try to crawl right inside their skin, sleep in their beds, give their whole lives up to the pursuit. Norman Sherry, who tracked Graham Greene over many decades and volumes, put himself everywhere into the story, including illustrations of himself 'on the trail' of 'Our Man', to the point where Sherry seems to have become 'the virtual subject of the biography with Greene serving more as a vehicle for Sherry's self-portrayal than anything else'. Some biographers wrestle for years with rivals who believe that the subject belongs to them. Some take such masterful possession that they become forever associated with their subject; so we speak of Boswell's Johnson, Edel's James, Ellmann's Joyce. But biographers should beware, says Robert Graves:

> To bring the dead to life
> Is no great magic...
> Subdue your pen to his handwriting
> Until it prove as natural
> To sign his name as yours.
> Limp as he limped,
> Swear by the oaths he swore;

If he wore black, affect the same;
If he had gouty fingers,
Be yours gouty too.
Assemble tokens intimate of him –
A ring, a hood, a desk:
Around these elements then build
A home familiar to
The greedy revenant.
So grant him life, but reckon
That the grave which housed him
May not be empty now:
You in his spotted garments
Shall yourself lie wrapped.

Biographers who are totally in possession, who know everything there is to know, have different kinds of narrative problems from biographers who know too little. Shakespeare is the obvious example. His many biographers differ widely – or wildly – in their lines of approach, between romantic guesswork, dogged sleuthing, historical contextualizing, postmodernist indeterminacy. Two 21st-century examples illustrate the range of possibilities. Charles Nicholl quests like a detective, through the record of a 1612 court case at which Shakespeare gave evidence, into the time he spent living in a house in Cripplegate, where he was known as 'merely the lodger, the gent in an upstairs chamber: a certain Mr Shakespeare'. Tracking Shakespeare down to Silver Street involves the close reading of a few scattered clues, guesswork, and invention: the result is the opening of 'an unexpected little window into Shakespeare's life'. By contrast, Jonathan Bate takes a broad, sweeping, inclusive approach in *Soul of the Age*, a masterly intellectual biography of Shakespeare, constructed not strictly chronologically, but on the basis of the 'seven ages of man', to reveal what he refers to as Shakespeare's cultural DNA.

James Shapiro, in his 'micro-biography' of a year in Shakespeare's life, argues that to read back from the works into Shakespeare's feelings, as if the plays were a 'two-way mirror', ends in 'circularity and arbitrariness'. But there is a great temptation for Shakespeare's biographers to make as much as they can of the little they know. Take one of the many baffling and obscure facts of Shakespeare's life, the death of his son Hamnet at the age of 11 in 1596, about which Shakespeare made no recorded utterance. The closeness of the names Hamnet and Hamlet, and the fact that Shakespeare played the Ghost of Hamlet's father, has led to a wealth of quasi-fictional speculations, from Stephen Dedalus's theories of fatherhood in Joyce's *Ulysses* to Anthony Burgess's blithe claim, in a popular 1970 picture book on the Bard, that 'Shakespeare transmuted his own son into a mad Danish prince'. In Shapiro's biography, Hamnet's death is treated as follows. He works out exactly where Shakespeare would have been (on tour) when he heard the news in August 1596; he tells us which Stratford carrier would have brought him the news, and what that carrier's knowledge of Shakespeare was. He establishes that Shakespeare would not have had time to get home for the funeral, and he tells us how little Shakespeare knew his son and how rarely he saw him. 'Which is not to say', Shapiro adds, 'that he did not feel his loss deeply. It may even have accounted for his diminished output in the year or so that followed. We just don't know.' When he discusses *Hamlet*, he deals minutely with the play's textual versions, ethics, cultural references, production, performance, and reception, but says nothing about the play's possible relation to Shakespeare's dead son.

Other biographers take different tones. Park Honan's 1998 Life methodically tracks all the known facts and received opinions back to their sources, and describes itself as 'dispassionate', yet still allows itself a little emotional guesswork. From the evidence of Shakespeare's work after 1596, Honan supposes that the death of Hamnet 'changed him', that 'he seems never to have recovered from the loss', and that it 'deepened him as an artist and thinker'. Honan's speculations are mild, though, compared with Stephen Greenblatt's in his bold, popular *Will in the World: How*

Shakespeare became Shakespeare (2004). Greenblatt jumps from saying that 'there is, at the very least, no reason to think that Shakespeare simply buried his son and moved on unscathed', to a full-blown hypothesis about the 'deep wound reopening', leading to 'a crisis of mourning and memory', 'a psychic disturbance that may help to explain the explosive power and inwardness of *Hamlet*'. Not for Greenblatt the words 'we just don't know'. Peter Ackroyd's 2005 biography does more hedging of bets:

> So Shakespeare had lost his only son... It is of course impossible to gauge the effect upon the dramatist. He may, or may not, have become inconsolable. He may have sought refuge, as so many others have done, in hard and relentless work. The plays of this period have nevertheless been interpreted in the light of this dead son... Indeed it cannot be wholly coincidental that Shakespeare was drawn at a later date to the tragedy of Hamlet.

All biographers have at times to suppose and infer. If their research is good and their sense of the subject is strong, then their guesses will be worth listening to. Purists would argue, though, that there are things that biography ought to leave to fiction, or to biopics like *Shakespeare In Love* or *Becoming Jane*: imaginary conversations, invented dreams and fantasies, emotional crises for which there is no evidence, unproven psychic traumas. For all biography's efforts to place the fish in the stream, to provide detailed material texture, cultural contextualizing, and social particularity, to go as far as it can in the interpretation of character, there will always, also, be areas of obscurity and absence. Biographers may – and probably ought to – end their work still feeling that there were many things they never discovered.

There is often a wistful note on the last page of biographies, as though the end of the task is also the end of a relationship. Biographers find it hard to narrate the deaths of their subjects without any emotion, as simply the next and final event in the

20. William Shakespeare?

story. Most biographers feel the need to make some gesture of farewell. The final stage of writing a biography is separation and letting go, and the recognition that the version that has been constructed is bound to be partial and temporary. At the end of all the labour of reconstruction and representation, the biographer is left looking at the receding view of the person they have been obsessed with, moving away from them into the silence of the past.

References

Chapter 1: The Biography Channel

P. 2

Henry James to Harry James (1915), *Henry James: Letters*, ed. Leon Edel (Harvard University Press), Vol. IV, p. 806, quoted in Ian Hamilton (1992), p. 220. Shakespeare's epitaph: 'Good Frend For Jesus Sake Forbeare,/To Digg The Dust Encloased Heare!/Blest Be Ye Man Yt Spares Thes Stones,/And Curst be He Yt Moves My Bones.'

P. 3

For Hazlitt on portraits, see Wendorf (1990), p. 7. For Plutarch, see 'Life of Alexander', in *Greek Lives*, tr. R. Waterfield (Oxford University Press, 1998), p. 312. For Boswell on portraits, see Wendorf (1990), p. 260, and Redford (2002), pp. 57-64.

Keats, *Letter to George and Georgiana Keats*, 19 March 1819, *The Letters of John Keats*, ed. H. E. Rollins (Harvard University Press, 1958), Vol. II, p. 80.

'Light gleams': Carlyle, Review of Croker's edition of Boswell's *Life of Johnson*, April 1832, in Clifford (1962), pp. 82, 83.

P. 4

'Biographical subjects...': Wendorf (1990), p. 13.

P. 5

For definitions of 'biography', see the *New Oxford Thesaurus of English* (2000), the OED of 1971 and the New OED of 2001.

For postmortems, see Stefan Timmermans, *Postmortem; How Medical Examiners Explain Suspicious Deaths* (University of Chicago Press, 2006).

P. 6
Jenny Uglow, *The Lunar Men* (Faber, 2002); Megan Marshall, *The Peabody Sisters: Three Women Who Ignited American Romanticism* (Houghton Mifflin, 2006).

P. 7
John Updike, *New York Review of Books*, 4 February 1999, quoted in France and St Clair (2002), p. 8.

P. 8
Alethea Hayter, *A Sultry Month: Scenes of London Literary Life in 1846* (Faber, 1965); David Edmonds and John Eidinow, *Wittgenstein's Poker* (Faber, 2001); James Shapiro, *1599: A Year in the Life of William Shakespeare* (Faber, 2005), p. xx.

P. 9
For 'public sphere', see Jürgen Habermas, *The Structural Transformation of the Public Sphere*, tr. T. Burger and F. Lawrence (Polity Press, 1989).

'Saints' Lives': Jocelyn Wogan-Browne and Glyn Burgess (eds.), *Virgin Lives and Holy Deaths* (Everyman, 1996), p. xvi.

'Social Intercourse': Boswell, *Life*, 31 March 1772, cited in Clifford (1962), p. 47.

'Autobiography': E.g. Maurois (1929), p. 112, on biography as 'disguised autobiography'; Phyllis Rose, in Rhiel and Suchoff (1996), p. 131, on biography as a form of autobiography.

'Broken bridge': Holmes (1985, 1995), p. 27.

John Donne, 'Meditation XVII', in *Devotions Upon Emergent Occasions* (1624), *John Donne: Complete Poetry and Selected Prose* (Nonesuch Library, 1955), p. 538.

Thomas Carlyle, review of Lockhart's *Life of Scott*, *The London and Westminster Review*, January 1838, in Clifford (1962), pp. 84–5.

Virginia Woolf, 'Sketch of the Past', *Moments of Being* (1985; Pimlico, 2002), p. 90.

'Status quo': Holroyd, in Homberger and Charmley (1988), p. 98.

P. 10
J.-P. Sartre, *L'Idiot de la Famille: Gustave Flaubert de 1821 à 1857* (Paris, 1988); John Gibson Lockhart, *Memoirs of the Life of Sir Walter Scott* (Edinburgh, 1837); Leon Edel, *Henry James: A Life* (Harper & Row, 1985).

'Unauthorized': E.g. Carole Klein, 'There are a great many others who would only speak to me on promise of anonymity'. 'Acknowledgements', *Doris Lessing: A Biography* (Duckworth, 2000), p. vii.

'Secrecy': E.g. Victoria Glendinning, *Elizabeth Bowen: Portrait of a Writer* (Weidenfeld & Nicolson, 1977), cites love-letters between Bowen and Humphry House, given to the biographer by Humphry House's widow on condition that he should not be named. The paperback (Penguin, 1985), published after Madeline House's death, identifies him.

P. 11
Johnson, *The Rambler*, 60, 13 October 1750, in Clifford (1962), pp. 40–3.

Chapter 2: Exemplary Lives

P. 19
Moses: 'The Book of Deuteronomy', *Old Testament*, Authorized Version, Ch. 34, verses 4–8.

Socrates: Plato, *Phaedo*, tr. David Gallop (Oxford University Press, 1993, 1999), p. 77.

Alexander: Plutarch, 'Life of Alexander', in *Greek Lives*, tr. R. Waterfield (Oxford University Press, 1998), p. 323.

P. 20
Jesus: 'The Gospel according to St Matthew', *New Testament*, Authorized Version, Ch. 26, verses 38–41.

Caligula: Suetonius, 'Caligula', *Lives of the Caesars*, tr. Catharine Edwards (Oxford University Press, 2000), p. 165.

Jerome: 'St Jerome and the Lion', Yale University MS Beinecke 317, reprinted in Gordon Whatley, Anne Thompson, and Robert Upchurch (eds.), *Saints' Lives in Early Middle English Collections*, Middle English Text Series (2004), p. 147.

PP. 20–1
Old Testament narrative: see Erich Auerbarch, *Mimesis*, tr. Willard Trask (1953; Doubleday, 1957), Ch. 1, 'Odysseus's Scar'.

P. 22
Gilgamesh and Egyptians: see Nigel Hamilton (2007), pp. 13-17; Parke (2002), pp. 1-2.

P. 23
Plutarch, 'Life of Pericles', 'Life of Alcibiades', 'Life of Alexander', in *Greek Lives*, pp. 145, 242, 312. For Plutarch as moralist and biographer, see Christopher Pelling, *Plutarch and History* (Duckworth, 2002), esp. Ch. 10, ' The Moralism of Plutarch's Lives'; Pelling (ed.), *Characterisation and Individuality in Greek Literature* (Oxford University Press, 1990); Timothy Duff, *Plutarch's Lives* (Oxford University Press, 1999), and Reed Whittemore, *Pure Lives: The Early Biographers* (Johns Hopkins, 1983), pp. 4-26.

'Lasting influence': see J. W. Smeed, *The Theophrastian 'Character': The History of a Literary Genre* (Clarendon Press, 1985); Judith Mossman, 'Plutarch and English Biography', *Hermathena* (2007), No. 183: 71-96.

P. 24
Dryden: Preface to the *Lives of Plutarch*, 1683.
'Hagiography': Gordon Whatley, *op. cit.*, p. 2.
'Prototypical virtues': see Sergei Averintsev, 'From Biography to Hagiography', in France and St Clair (2002), pp. 19-36.
'Hagiography... dominant': Sherry L. Reames, *Middle English Legends of Women Saints* (Kalamazoo, 2003), p. 1.

PP. 24-5
Later hagiographies: Mrs John Sandford, *Lives of English Female Worthies* (Longmans, 1883); Gamaliel Bradford, *Saints and Sinners* (Kennikut Press, 1931); Evelyn Waugh, *Edmund Campion* (Longmans, 1935); Kathryn Spink, *Mother Theresa: An Authorised Biography* (HarperCollins, 1997); Jose Luis Gonzalez-Balado, *Mother Theresa: Her Life, Her Work, Her Message* (Hodder & Stoughton, 1997); Anne Sebba, *Mother Theresa: Beyond the Image* (Weidenfeld & Nicolson, 1997); David Lewis, *Martin Luther King: A Critical Biography* (Allen Lane, 1970); Valerie Schloredt, *Martin Luther King: America's Great Non-Violent Leader* (Exley, 1988); David J. Garrow, *Bearing the Cross: Martin Luther King and the Southern Christian Leadership Conference* (William Morrow, 1986).

P. 26

St Catherine: Sherry L. Reames, *op. cit.*; Jocelyn Wogan-Browne, *Virgin Lives and Holy Deaths* (Everyman, 1996), pp. 3–42; Karen Winstead, 'Saintly Exemplarity', in *Middle English: Oxford 21st Century Approaches to Literature*, ed. Paul Strohm (Oxford University Press, 2007), pp. 335–46.

Saints' Lives: Winstead, *op. cit.*, pp. 338, 346; Wogan-Browne, *op. cit.*, p. xiii. See also Anne Thompson, *Everyday Saints and the Art of Narrative in the South England Legendary* (Ashgate, 2005), and Thomas J. Heffernan, *Sacred Biography* (Oxford University Press, 1988).

P. 28

Worthies: Thomas Fuller, *Worthies of England* (1662; ed. J. Nichols, London, 1811).

Edmund Gosse: 'Biography', *Encylopaedia Britannica*, 11th edition (1910–11), pp. 952–3.

Attacks on hagiography: Kendall (1965), pp. 41, 59; Parke (2002), p. 7; Nigel Hamilton (2007), p. 57. Reames, *op. cit.*, p. 2.

P. 29

Lydgate: Stauffer (1930), pp. 28–9; *The Mirour for Magistrates*, ed. Lily B. Campbell (Cambridge University Press, 1938).

Alexander: Richard Stoneman (ed.), *Legends of Alexander the Great* (Everyman, 1994).

P. 30

'Rhetorical performances': Debora Shuger, 'Life-Writing in Seventeenth-Century England', in Coleman, *op. cit.*, p. 73.

Francis Bacon: *The Advancement of Learning*, in *The Major Works*, ed. Brian Vickers (Oxford University Press, 2002), pp. 180–2. Cited in Altick (1965), p. 8; Parke (2002), p. 13, and many other books on biography.

'Dangerous': see Shelston (1977), pp. 18–19; Nigel Hamilton (2007), pp. 70–4.

Cavendish: see Stauffer (1930), pp. 123–9; Anderson (1984), Ch. 3.

Sir Thomas More, *History of Richard III* (1557; Hesperus, 2005), p. 55. See Anderson (1984), pp. 78–92.

Walpole: cited in Pat Rogers, 'Introduction', Boswell's *Life of Johnson* (Oxford University Press, World's Classics, 1980) [hereafter *Life*], p. xxiv.

Macaulay: Review of 'Croker's Edition of Boswell's *Life of Johnson*', *Edinburgh Review*, 54 (September 1831): 1–38.
For Boswell's writing of the *Life*, see Sisman (2000), and Redford (2002). For Boswell's works, see *The Yale Editions of the Private Papers of James Boswell*. For Johnson separated from Boswell, see Donald Greene (ed.), *Samuel Johnson* (Oxford University Press, 1984); Norma Clarke, *Dr Johnson's Women* (Hambledon & London, 2000); Holmes (1993). Roger Lonsdale (ed.), *Johnson's The Lives of the Poets*, 4 vols (Oxford University Press, 2006).
'Pickling': *Life*, pp. 862, 297.
French 'ana': Jefferson (2007), pp. 36 ff.
Margaret, Duchess of Newcastle, *The Life of William Cavendish, Duke of Newcastle* (1667; ed. C. H. Firth, Routledge, 1907). Pepys on Cavendish, 18 March 1668, in *The Diary of Samuel Pepys: A New and Complete Transciption*, ed. Roberth Latham and William Matthews, vol. 9 (1668–9; G. Bell & Sons Ltd, 1976), p. 123.
Lucy Hutchinson, *Memoir of Colonel Hutchinson* (1664; Longmans, 1810). Margaret Oliphant, *Blackwood's Edinburgh Magazine*, July 1882, quoted in Marcus (1994), p. 46.

P. 31
William Roper, *The Life of Sir Thomas More* (Early English Text Society, Oxford University Press, 1935), pp. 83, 102.
17th-century French biography: see Jefferson (2007), pp. 31–9, and Peter France, 'The French Academic *Eloge*', in France and St Clair (2002), Ch. 5.
Italian biography: see Martin McLaughlin, 'Biography and Autobiography in the Italian Renaissance', in France and St Clair (2002), Ch. 3.
'Memoirs, diaries...': Shuger, *op. cit.*, p. 63.

PP. 34–5
Johnson's *Lives*, ed. Lonsdale: panegyric, 'Cowley', vol. I, p. 191; actions, 'Cowley', vol. I, p. 198; 'Milton', vol. I, p. 276. On Johnson's irony, Lonsdale, 'Introduction', p. 98.

PP. 34–6
Walton: see Jessica Martin, *Walton's Lives* (Oxford University Press, 2001), pp. 132, 169, 311, 315, and *passim*; Wendorf (1990), Ch. 2; Anderson (1984); David Novarr, *The Making of Walton's Lives* (Ithaca, 1958; Epstein, 1987), Ch. 2.

P. 36
Johnson's talk: *Life*, pp. 444, 1285, 343. 'Very uncivil', *Life*, p. 864.

'Newborn child': *Life*, p. 421. Leslie Stephen, *Samuel Johnson* (Macmillan, 1878), p. 90.

PP. 36-8

'Skediasmata': Anthony Powell, *John Aubrey and His Friends* (Eyre & Spottiswoode, 1948), p. 127.

John Aubrey to Anthony Wood, 15 June 1680, in *Aubrey's Brief Lives*, ed. Oliver Lawson Dick (Secker & Warburg, 1949), p. cxiii.

Chapter 3: Warts and All

P. 39

'We danced...': Boswell, *Journal of a Tour to the Hebrides*, [hereafter *Tour*], 1785, 'Sunday 2 October 1773'.

P. 42

'Assiduous enquiry': *Tour*, 'Thursday 14 October 1773'.

P. 46

Boswell in trouble: see Sisman (2000), Ch. 6.

'Wens and warts': Elizabeth Montagu to Hester Thrale [Piozzi], quoted Clifford, 'How Much Should a Biographer Tell?', in Daghlian (1968), p. 87.

PP. 46-7

'Conversation': *Life*, p. 23. 'Authenticity': quoted Sisman (2000), p. 114. 'Minute particulars': *Life*, p. 25.

P. 47

Roger North: see Clifford (1962), pp. xii, 27-37, and Wendorf (1990), pp. 152-4.

Johnson's essays, in Clifford (1962), pp. 40-3. First OED citation of 'autobiography', Robert Southey (1809).

PP. 47-8

Savage: Holmes (1993).

'Instructive detachment': Roger Lonsdale, 'Introduction', Johnson's *The Lives of the Poets*, vol. I (Oxford University Press, 2006), p. 85.

P. 48

Addison: *The Freeholder*, No. 35, 20 April 1716, in Clifford (1962), p. 25.

PP. 48-9

Curll: see Paul Baines and Pat Rogers, *Edmund Curll: Bookseller* (Oxford University Press, 2007). Arbuthnot's remark, often misquoted as 'he adds a new terror to Death', is made in 1733 in a letter to Swift about Curll's forthcoming life of Gay.

P. 49

'Flemish picture': Boswell, *Journal*, 1775, from *Boswell: The Ominous Years, 1774–1776*, ed. C. Ryskamp and F. A. Pottle (Heinemann, 1963), p. 103, cited Wendorf (1990), p. 266, in a full account of Boswell's use of portraiture. 'Act of looking', Redford (2002), p. 15.
Johnson's appearance: *Life*, pp. 280, 105, 330, 342, 1212.

PP. 50–1

'Jack Wilkes': *Life*, pp. 764–76. See Redford (2002), pp. 104–9. Jack Ketch was a famous hangman.

P. 50

Johnson's sayings: *Life*, pp. 299, 1023, 435, 777, 400, 1217.

P. 51

Johnson's heroism: *Life*, pp. 416, 427.
Johnson's sentiment: *Life*, pp. 359, 1210.
Johnson's stoicism: *Life*, pp. 328, 240.

P. 53

'He disappeared': *Life*, p. 334.

Chapter 4: National Biography

P. 54

'Self-fashioning': Lucy Newlyn, *Coleridge, Wordsworth and the Language of Allusion* (1986), Preface to the Second Edition (Oxford University Press, 2000), p. xv, citing Stephen Greenblatt.
Herder: see Park Honan (1990), p. 28, on the importance of Herder's *On the Origin of Language* (1772) for the development of life-writing.

P. 55

'Boswell Redivivus': Hazlitt, *Conversations of James Northcote*, 1826–7, in *The Collected Works of William Hazlitt* (Dent, 1903), vol. VI, Notes, p. 505.
'Minutiae': Coleridge, *The Friend* (1850), II, p. 225, in Altick (1965), p. 193.
James Field Stansfield: *An Essay on the Study and Composition of Biography* (Sunderland, 1813), pp. 14, 21, 26.

PP. 55-6
Coleridge: Hazlitt, 'Mr Coleridge', in *The Spirit of the Age*, 1824-5; compare with 'My First Acquaintance with Poets', 1823. See also on Coleridge's conversation, Virginia Woolf, 'The Man at the Gate', 1940, *Collected Essays*, ed. Leonard Woolf (Chatto & Windus, 1966-7), vol. IV, pp. 117-21, and Seamus Perry, 'The Talker', *Cambridge Companion to Coleridge* (2002), pp. 103-25. Carlyle, *The Life of John Sterling* (Chapman & Hall, 1851), pp. 69-71.
'Human soul': Carlyle, *op. cit.*, p. 8.

P. 57
'Open loving heart': Carlyle, Review of Croker's edition of Boswell's *Life*, *Fraser's Magazine*, April 1832, in Clifford (1962), pp. 78-83.
'Damocles' sword': Carlyle, Review of Lockhart's *Life of Scott*, *The London and Westminster Review*, January 1838, in Clifford (1962), pp. 85-6.
'Outcry': John Gibson Lockhart, *Life of Robert Burns* (Edinburgh, 1828), p. 227, in Cockshut (1974), p. 27. Ian Hamilton (1992), p. 117. Altick (1965), p. 238. Richard Holmes, *Shelley: The Pursuit* (Weidenfeld & Nicolson, 1974; Quartet Books, 1976), pp. x-xi.

P. 58
'Johnson's brother': F. W. Maitland, *The Life and Letters of Leslie Stephen* (Duckworth & Co., London, 1906), pp. 419-20.

P. 59
Gaskell's Brontë: Elizabeth Gaskell, *The Life of Charlotte Brontë* (1857; Everyman, ed. J. Uglow, 1992), p. 245. Jenny Uglow, *Elizabeth Gaskell: A Habit of Stories* (Faber, 1993), p. 406.

PP. 61-2
On Gaskell's Brontë: Heilbrun (1988), p. 22. Heather Glen, *Charlotte Brontë: The Imagination in History* (Oxford University Press, 2002), pp. 274-6. Margaret Oliphant, quoted in Jenny Uglow, *Elizabeth Gaskell*, pp. 391, 407. Christopher Ricks, 'E. C. Gaskell's Charlotte Brontë', *Essays in Appreciation* (Oxford University Press, 1996), p. 145.

P. 62
Eccentrics: see James Gregory, 'Eccentric Biography and the Victorians', *Biography*, 30.3 (2007): 342-76. In France, Gérard de Nerval specialized in biographies of eccentrics; see Jefferson (2007), Ch. 9. For oddities in the DNB, see Keith Thomas on eccentrics, *Changing Conceptions of National Biography*

(Oxford University Press, 2004), pp. 22–4. For English eccentricity, see also Virginia Woolf, 'The Eccentrics', 1919, *Collected Essays*, vol. III, p. 29.

P. 63

'Reticence': Gladstone on Cross, in Kathryn Hughes, *George Eliot: The Last Victorian* (Fourth Estate, 1998), p. 485.

Death-beds: John Morley, *Life of Gladstone* (Macmillan, 1903), p. 528. John Wolffe, *Good Deaths* (Oxford University Press, 2000), p. 158. Lee (2005, 2008), p. 202.

Nelson: Robert Southey, *Life of Nelson* (John Murray, [1813], 1832), p. 296.

P. 64

Biographical dictionaries: Nadel (1984), p. 47. Jefferson (2007), pp. 83–5. Keith Thomas, *op. cit.* (2005), p. 15. G. F. Watts (1887), cited in Peter Funnell, *Victorian Portraits in the National Portrait Gallery Collection* (NPG Publications, 1996), p. 4. Parke (2002), Ch. 5.

P. 65

'The lives of women': Mrs John Sandford, *Lives of English Female Worthies* (Longmans, 1883), vol. I, pp. ix–x.

Samuel Smiles: *Self-Help* (1859; Oxford University Press, 2002), pp. 20, 29.

P. 66

'Saints' legends': Richard Altick, *The English Common Reader* (1957; Ohio State University Press, 1998), p. 242.

'Polemical agenda': David Amigoni, *Victorian Biography* (Harvester, 1993).

DNB: Leslie Stephen, 'A New *Biographia Britannica*', *Athenaeum*, 23 December 1882, in Novarr (1986), pp. 1–2. See Ian Donaldson, 'National Biography', in France and St Clair (2002), pp. 78–80. Sidney Lee, 'The Leslie Stephen Lecture', May 1911, published as *Principles of Biography*, 1911; Leslie Stephen to Norman Moore, 1884, both quoted in Nadel (1984), pp. 54–6. Leslie Stephen, 'National Biography', March 1896, *Studies of a Biographer* (Duckworth, 1898), vol. 1, pp. 21–2. Keith Thomas, *op. cit.* (2005), pp. 23, 45. Gillian Fenwick, *Women and the DNB* (Aldershot, 1994), calculated that of the 28,201 entries in the DNB and its 31,901 supplements, 998 were on women. The Oxford DNB (2004) raised the proportion to 10%.

P. 67
'Missing persons': C. S. Nicholls, 'Preface', *Missing Persons Supplement to the DNB* (Oxford University Press, 1993), pp. vi–vii. See also Robert Faber and Brian Harrison, 'The DNB: A Publishing History', *Lives in Print*, eds. Robin Myers, Michael Harris, and Giles Mandelbrote (Oak Knoll Press and British Library, 2002), pp. 171–92.

PP. 67–8
'Oblivion': Leslie Stephen, 'Forgotten Benefactors', 1895, in *Social Rights and Duties: Addresses to Ethical Societies*, 2 vols (Macmillan, 1896), II, p. 225. George Eliot, *Middlemarch* (1871–2), Finale.

P. 68
'Squalor': Jefferson (2007), Ch. 4.

PP. 68–9
On exposure: Browning, 'House', 1876. Tennyson, 'After Reading a Life and Letters' [of Keats], *The Examiner*, 24 March 1849. Ian Hamilton (1992), p. 181. George Eliot, Letter to Mrs Thomas Trollope, 19 December 1879, *The George Eliot Letters*, ed. Gordon Haight, vol. 7 (Oxford University Press and Yale University Press, 1956), p. 230. Thackeray, in Henrietta Garnett, *Anny: A Life of Anne Thackeray Ritchie* (Chatto, 2004), p. 265.

P. 69
James: Henry James to Edith Wharton, 13 March 1912, p. 215, in Hermione Lee, *Edith Wharton* (Chatto & Windus, 2007), p. 227. Henry James to Edmund Gosse, 8 April 1895, in Philip Horne (ed.), *Henry James: A Life in Letters* (Allen Lane, 1999), p. 279. Henry James, Review of William Ellery Channing's correspondence (1875), in Richard Salmon, 'The Right to Privacy/The Will to Knowledge', in Gould and Staley (1998), pp. 135–49, and Salmon, *Henry James: the Culture of Publicity* (Cambridge University Press, 1997). Ian Hamilton (1992), pp. 207–8.
'Ethics': Margaret Oliphant, 'The Ethics of Biography', *Contemporary Review*, July 1883, XLIV: 76–93, in Clifford (1962), pp. 97–102.

P. 70
Froude/Carlyle: J. A. Froude, *My Relations with Carlyle* (J. Lane, 1903). Sir James Crichton-Browne, *British Medical Journal* 27 June 1903: 1498, in Broughton, (1999), p. 140. See Elinor Shaffer, 'Shaping Victorian Biography', in France and St Clair (2002), pp. 115–33, and Altick (1965), Ch. 7.

P. 71
'The world has no business': Carlyle, *Journal*, 10 October 1843, in Origo (1984), p. 1.

Chapter 5: Fallen Idols

P. 72
Shaw: in Holroyd (2002), p. 25.
'Clumsy and laborious': Virginia Woolf, 'The New Biography', *Collected Essays* (Chatto & Windus, 1966–7), vol. 4. For 'Victorians', see also Strachey (1918, 2003), 'Preface'; Nicolson (1928); Kendall (1965), p. 105; Holroyd, in Homberger and Charmley (1988), p. 98; Nigel Hamilton (2007), Ch. 4.
'Marionette': Evelyn Waugh, *Rossetti: His Life and Works* (Duckworth, 1928), p. 12.

PP. 73–5
'Fish in the stream': Virginia Woolf, 'Sketch of the Past', *Moments of Being* (Pimlico, 2003), p. 92.

P. 75
Gosse: Edmund Gosse, 'Preface', *Father and Son: A Study of Two Temperaments* (Heinemann, 1907). Evan Charteris, *The Life and Letters of Sir Edmund* Gosse (Heinemann, 1931), p. 305. See Lee (2005, 2008), pp. 100–11, and Ann Thwaite's biographies of Edmund Gosse (1984) and Philip Gosse (2002).

PP. 75–6
Strachey: John Sutherland, 'Introduction', *Eminent Victorians* (Oxford University Press World's Classics, 2003), p. x. Strachey (1918, 2003), 'Preface', pp. 5–6, 162, 98, 201.

P. 77
'Condescension': Origo (1984), p. 21.

P. 78
Gosse: Edmund Gosse, 'Biography' (1911), pp. 952–3; Gosse (1925), pp. 8, 14.
Schwob: see Jefferson (2007), pp. 206–9.
New biography: Nicolson (1928). See Edel (1959, 1973), pp. 6–7; Marcus, in France and St Clair (2002), pp. 199–200; Hoberman (1987), Ch. 3.

P. 79
Maurois (1929). See Jefferson (2007), pp. 221, 224–5; Marcus, *op. cit.*, pp. 200–1.
Ludwig: see Marcus (1994), p. 131, and Altick (1965), p. 289.
Gamaliel Bradford: 'Confessions of a Biographer', in *Wives* (Harper & Bros, 1925), p. 12, and *A Naturalist of Souls* (Houghton Mifflin, 1926), pp. 5–8, quoted Marcus, in France and St Clair (2002), p. 207.

PP. 80–1
Woolf: 'The New Biography' (1927), 'The Art of Biography' (1939) in *Collected Essays* (Chatto & Windus, vol. 4). See also her 'An Unwritten Novel', 'The Genius of Boswell', 'A Talk about Memoirs', 'Walter Sickert', and see Hermione Lee, *Virginia Woolf* (Chatto & Windus, 1996), Ch. 1, 'Biography'. *Orlando* (1928; Penguin, 1993), p. 213.

P. 82
Zélide: Richard Holmes (ed.), *Scott on Zélide* (Harper Perennial Classic Biographies, 2004).
Corvo: A. J. A. Symons, *The Quest for Corvo: An Experiment in Biography* (Cassell, 1934, 1955), p. 219. See Marcus in France and St Clair (2002), pp. 211–14; Epstein (1987), pp. 170–1.

PP. 84–6
Freud: Freud to Strachey, 1928, Marcus, in France and St Clair (2002), p. 216. Adam Phillips, 'The Death of Freud', *Darwin's Worms* (Faber, 1999), pp. 85, 88, 93, 107. *Leonardo Da Vinci and a Memory of Childhood* (1910), pp. 50–3, 99, in *The New Penguin Freud*, ed. Adam Phillips; *The Uncanny*, tr. David McLintock (Penguin, 2003), Hugh Haughton, 'Introduction', pp. xxix, xxxvii. Freud followed a German mistranslation, 'vulture', for the Italian word 'nibio', 'kite', leading him to an interpretation of Leonardo's memory of 'a vulture putting its tail into his baby mouth' as 'a coded homosexual fantasy of oral sex'. See also Malcolm Bowie, 'Freud and the Art of Biography', in France and St Clair (2002), pp. 187–8.

P. 86
Freud's influence: Anthony Storr, *Freud* (Oxford University Press Past Masters, 1989), p. 73. Backscheider (1999), p. 114.

P. 87
Sartre: Jean-Paul Sartre, *The Family Idiot: Gustave Flaubert* [*L'Idiot de la Famille*, 1971], tr. Carol Cosman (University of Chicago,

1981-7), Preface, pp. x, I, 29, 46. Ellis (2000), pp. 145, 149. France and St Clair, p. 282. Barnes (1984, 1985), p. 86.

P. 88

Erik Erikson: *Young Man Luther* (Knopf, 1958); David Ellis (2000), p. 84. Ellmann, (1973), p. 4.

'Put on the couch': see 'The Historical Growth of Psychobiography' in Dan P. McAdams and R. L. Ochberg, *Psychobiography and Life Narratives* (Duke University Press, 1988), pp. 296-9.

Opposition: Bernard De Voto, 'The Sceptical Biographer', *Harper's Magazine*, January 1933, in Clifford (1962), p. 146.

'Overcome a wound' : Edel (1959, 1973), pp. 91-122.

'Manipulate': Ellmann (1973), pp. 9, 13.

'Different aims': see Nadel (1984), pp. 188 ff; Ellis (2000), Ch. 4; David A. Jopling, 'At the Limits of Biographical Knowledge: Sartre and Levinas', in Donaldson (1992), pp. 78-81.

PP. 88-9

Edel: Leon Edel, *The Life of Henry James* (Penguin Books, 1977), vol. I, pp. 49, 53. This was a two-volume revised and shortened version of his five-volume *Life*, published between 1953 and 1971, later re-revised as *Henry James: A Life* (Harper & Row, 1985).

P. 89

Proust: Ellis (2000), p. 60. George Painter, *Marcel Proust: A Biography* (Chatto & Windus, 2 vols, 1959, 1966-7), vol. I, pp. xiii, 115. See John Halperin, 'The Biographer's Revenge', in Salwak (1996), p. 160.

P. 90

Joyce: Richard Ellmann, *James Joyce* (1959; Oxford University Press, 1966), pp. 525, 692, 559, 452, 390, 756.

P. 91

'Notorious exceptions': see Lawrance Thompson's *Robert Frost* (1964, 1977; Holt Rinehart and Winston, 1981); Henri Troyat's *Tolstoi: A Biography* (Doubleday, 1967); and James Atlas's *Bellow: A Biography* (Random House, 2000).

Chapter 6: Against Biography

P. 93

Baudelaire: see Jefferson (2007), p. 162.

'Bundle of accidents': W. B. Yeats, *Essays and Introductions* (Macmillan, 1961), p. 509.
'perfect artist': T. S. Eliot, 'Tradition and the Individual Talent', 1919, *Selected Essays* (Faber & Faber, 1951), p. 18.
'Biografiend', 'Beogrefright': James Joyce, *Finnegans Wake* (1939), 1.3, 3.12. James Joyce, *A Portrait of the Artist as a Young Man* (Penguin, 1960), pp. 214–15.

PP. 93–4

Modernism and biography: Max Saunders, 'Ford, Eliot, Joyce and the Problems of Literary Biography', in Gould and Staley (1998), p. 151. Jefferson (2007), pp. 258, 359, on the *nouveau roman* and biography. Roland Barthes, 'Death of the Author', *Image, Music, Text*, tr. Stephen Heath (Hill & Wang, 1977), pp. 142–8; Michel Foucault, 'What is an Author?', *Language, Counter-Memory, Practice: Selected Essays and Interviews*, ed. D. F. Bouchard (Cornell University Press, 1977), pp. 113–38. Parke, pp. 30, 142. For discussions of literary theory v. biography, see Parke (1996), p. 30; Edel (1959, 1973), Ch. 3; Nigel Hamilton (2007), Ch. 8.

P. 94

Untheorized: see Ian MacKillop, 'Vignettes: Leavis, Biography and the Body', in Gould and Staley (1998), p. 297; Rhiel and Suchoff (1996), p. 1.

P. 95

'Peeping through the keyhole': Malcolm (1993), p. 8.

P. 96

'Bloodsport': Michiko Kakutani, 'Biography as a Blood Sport', *New York Times*, May 1994, cited in Eakin (1999), p. 170; Louis Menand, 'Lives of Others: The Biography Business', *New Yorker*, 8 August 2007.
'Titillation and shock': Justin Kaplan, 'A Culture of Biography'; Martin Stannard, 'The Necrophiliac Art?'; and Natasha Spender, 'Private and Public Lives', in Salwak (1996), pp. 1–6, 36, 101–6.
'Back fire': Ian Hamilton (1988). Ronald Suresh Roberts, *No Cold Kitchen: A Biography of Nadine Gordimer* (STE Publishers, Johannesburg, 2005); Rachel Donadio, 'Nadine Gordimer and the Hazards of Biography', *New York Times Book Review*, 31 December 2006; Rory Carroll, 'Nobel writer Gordimer... accused of censorship', *Guardian*, 7 August 2004.

P. 98
'Self-defence': Doris Lessing, *Under My Skin* (HarperCollins, 1994; Flamingo, 1995), pp. 11, 14.
'Monsters': Philip Larkin, 'Posterity', 1967, in *High Windows* (Faber, 1974); Carol Ann Duffy, 'The Biographer', *Mean Time*, 1993, in *Selected Poems* (Penguin, 1994), p. 123.

P. 99
Fictional biographers: see Holroyd (2002), p. 16; Jon Stallworthy in Batchelor (1995), pp. 29 ff.; Martin Stannard in Gould and Staley (1998), p. 7.
Zuckerman: Philip Roth, *Exit Ghost* (Cape, 2007), pp. 273, 182, 275.
'net': Barnes (1984, 1985), p. 38.

P. 100
'Owns the facts': Ted Hughes, letter to the *Independent*, 20 April 1989.

Chapter 7: Public Roles

P. 101
'social self': Ellmann (1973), p. 2.
'great man': Maurois (1929), pp. 47–8.
'defensive practices': Erving Goffman, *The Presentation of the Self in Everyday Life* (1959; Pelican Books, 1971), pp. 25, 63.

P. 102
Sartre: Goffman, *op. cit.*, p. 42, citing *Being and Nothingness* (1957).
Browning: Henry James to Alice James, 8 April 1877, and 'The Private Life' (1892), both cited in Philip Horne, *Henry James: A Life in Letters* (Allen Lane, 1999), p. 86.

PP. 102–03
Philosophy and biography: 'two schools', James Conant, 'Philosophy and Biography', in James C. Klagge (ed.), *Wittgenstein: Biography and Philosophy* (Cambridge University Press, 2001), p. 17. 'His work is his life', *op. cit.*, p. 19.

P. 103
Wittgenstein's life: James C. Klagge, 'Introduction', *op. cit.*, pp. ix, xiii. David Wiggins, 'Wittgenstein on Ethics and the Riddle of Life', *Philosophy* 79 (2004): 375. Conant, *op. cit.*, pp. 26, 27, summing up Ray Monk, *Ludwig Wittgenstein: The Duty of Genius* (New York, Free Press, 1990; Penguin, 1991).

PP. 103-04
Ray Monk: 'Philosophical Biography: The Very Idea', in Klagge, *op. cit.*,
p. 5; 'Life without Theory: Biography as an Exemplar of
Philosophical Understanding', *Poetics Today*, Vol. 28 No. 3 (Fall
2007), p. 528.

P. 104
'enacted narratives': Stephen Mulhall, 'The Enigma of Individuality:
Identity, Narrative and Truth in Biography, Autobiography and
Fiction', unpublished paper, 2003, citing Alasdair MacIntyre, *After
Virtue* (Duckworth, 1981), A. S. Byatt, *The Biographer's Tale*
(Chatto & Windus, 2001), and Peter Conradi on writing the
biography of Iris Murdoch.
'pure act': Henry James, quoted in Jean Strouse, *Morgan: American
Financier* (Random House, 1999), p. xiii.

P. 105
'A shilling life': W. H. Auden, 'Who's Who', 1934, *Collected Shorter
Poems*, 1927-1957 (Faber & Faber, 1966), p. 78.

P. 106
Morgan: Jean Strouse, *op. cit.*, pp. ix, xiii.

P. 107
Elleke Boehmer, *Nelson Mandela: A Very Short Introduction* (Oxford
University Press, 2008), pp. 3-7.
For modern saints' lives, see reference to 'later hagiographies' in Ch. II.
On the 40th anniversary of Che Guevara's death, see Jay Ambrose,
The Washington Examiner, cited in *The Week*, 20 October 2007,
p. 14.

PP. 107-111
Nelson: N. A. M. Roger, 'Nelson, Horatio, Viscount Nelson', *Oxford
DNB*, Vol. 40. John Sugden, *Nelson: A Dream of Glory* (Cape,
2004), pp. 1-13, 787.

P. 111
'history's butlers': Holroyd (2002), p. 5.
Lord Haw-Haw: Rebecca West, *The Meaning of Treason* (Viking, 1947).
Mosley: Nicholas Mosley, *Oswald Mosley: Rules of the Game* and
Beyond the Pale (Secker & Warburg, 2 vols, 1982, 1983), pp. I, 178.

PP. 111-12
Stalin: Alan Bullock, *Hitler and Stalin, Parallel Lives* (HarperCollins,
1991), p. 801. Simon Sebag Montefiore, *Stalin: The Court of the Red*

Tzar (Weidenfeld & Nicolson, 2004), *Young Stalin* (Weidenfeld & Nicolson, 2008).

P. 113
Shostakovich: 'sweeping platitudes': Laurel E. Fay, *Shostakovich: A Life* (Oxford University Press, 2000), p. 104. 'Soviet humanism': 'Shostakovich', Grove's *Dictionary of Music and Musicians* (Oxford University Press, 2001), pp. 290–300. 'Volkov's reliability': *A Shostakovich Casebook*, ed. M. H. Brown (Indiana University Press, 2005), pp. 19, 81, 315, 370. 'Speculation': Elizabeth Wilson, *Shostakovich: A Life Remembered* (Faber, 1994), p. xi. 'The man from the myths': Fay, p. 2.

P. 115
'Dresden bombings': Christopher Norris, 'Shostakovich: Politics and Musical Language', in *Shostakovich: The Man and His Music*, ed. Christopher Norris (Lawrence and Wishart, 1982), p. 179. 'Emotional breakdown': Fay, p. 216. 'Autobiographical' quartet: Solomon Volkov, *Testimony: The Memoirs of Dmitri Shostakovich*, tr. A. W. Buis (Hamish Hamilton, 1979), p. 118. Galina and Maxim: interviewed in Michael Ardov (ed.), *Memories of Shostakovich*, tr. R. Kelly and M. Meylac (Short Books, 2004), p. 158. 'Dark forces': Fay, p. 219.

P. 116
'Subterfuge': Grove's, p. 290, Elizabeth Wilson, p. 126. 'Pianissimo': Fay, p. 103. 'Our business': Volkov, p. 140.

P. 117
Marilyn: 'legacy': Mike Evans, *Marilyn Handbook* (MQ Publications, 2004), jacket-copy. 'Homicide': Donald H. Wolfe, *The Assassination of Marilyn Monroe* (Sphere, 1998), p. 575.

PP. 117–21
'Star biographies': Richard Dyer, *Heavenly Bodies: Film Stars and Society* (Macmillan, 1986), p. 11. 'Drawn to her': Michelle Morgan, *Marilyn Monroe: Private and Undisclosed* (Constable, 2007), p. 9. 'Either/or': Sarah Churchwell, *The Many Lives of Marilyn Monroe* (Granta, 2004), pp. 8, 194. 'Cornucopia': Norman Mailer, *Marilyn* (Hodder & Stoughton, 1973). 'Mannequin': Joyce Carol Oates, *Blonde* (HarperCollins, 2000). 'Her prison': Gloria Steinem, *Marilyn* (Gollancz, 1987), p. 154. 'Emblematic': Julian Barnes, 'Requiem for a Goddess', *Observer*, 22 February 1987. 'Ugly side': Anthony Summers, *Goddess: The Secret Lives of Marilyn Monroe*

(Gollancz, 1985), pp. 83, 221, 394. 'Freaks': see Backscheider (1999), Ch. 5. 'Strips of film': Keith Hartley, *Warhol: A Celebration of Life ... And Death*, National Galleries of Scotland, 2007, Catalogue 31.

Chapter 8: Telling the Story

P. 122

Hermione Lee, *Virginia Woolf* (Chatto & Windus, 1996; Vintage, 1997), p. 3.

P. 123

Argument against: see Mark Kinkead-Weekes, 'Writing Lives Forward', in France and St Clair (2002), pp. 238, 253. R. F. Foster, *W. B. Yeats: A Life, I: The Apprentice Mage 1865–1914* (Oxford University Press, 1997), p. xxvi. James Olney, 'The Taking of a Life: Some Versions of Biography', *The Cincinnati Review*, Spring 2005: 73–4.

PP. 124–5

Beginnings: Richard Holmes, *Shelley: The Pursuit* (Weidenfeld and Nicolson, 1974; Quartet, 1976). Victoria Glendinning, *Rebecca West: A Life* (Weidenfeld and Nicolson, 1987), p. 1. Maynard Mack, *Alexander Pope: A Life* (Yale University Press, 1985), p. 3. Nicholas Shakespeare, *Bruce Chatwin* (Vintage, 2000), p. 1. Arnold Rampersad, *Ralph Ellison: A Biography* (Knopf, 2007), p. 3.

P. 126

'Lives of the obscure': Virginia Woolf, 'Lives of the Obscure', *The Essays of Virginia Woolf*, ed. Andrew McNeillie (Hogarth Press, 1986–), vol. 4.

'Uncover a past': Jenny Uglow, 'Friends Reunited', *Guardian*, 30 April 2005, pp. 34–5.

'Who will speak?': Carole Ferrier, 'Resisting Authority', in Donaldson (1992), p. 104.

PP. 126–7

'Hidden histories': Jean Strouse, *Alice James: A Biography* (Houghton Mifflin, 1980); Claire Tomalin, *The Invisible Woman* (Viking, 1990); Brenda Maddox, *Nora: The Real Life of Molly Bloom* (Houghton Mifflin, 1988); Alison Light, *Mrs Woolf and the Servants* (Penguin Fig Tree, 2007). Virginia Woolf, *A Room of One's Own* (1929; Penguin, 1993), p. 88.

P. 127
'Constraints': Heilbrun (1989), pp. 28, 30.
'Feminist project': Kay Ferres, 'Gender, Biography and the Public Sphere', in France and St Clair (2002), p. 307, citing Maria Pia Lara, *Feminist Narratives in the Public Sphere* (Cambridge University Press, 1998).
'Past tenses': Steedman (1992), pp. 160-4.
'Women's stories': Backscheider (1999), pp. 132, 11, 147.

P. 128
'Access to privacy': Alison Booth, 'Biographical Criticism and the "Great Woman of Letters"' in *Contesting the Subject*, ed. William Epstein (Purdue University Press, 1986), p. 89. See also Alison Booth, *How to Make It as a Woman* (University of Chicago, 2004).

P. 129
Sexton: Diane Wood Middlebrook, *Anne Sexton* (Houghton Mifflin, 1990).
'Public life': Kay Ferres, p. 303, and James Walter, 'The Solace of Doubt? Biographical Methodology after the Short Twentieth Century', in France and St Clair (2002), pp. 330-1, both citing Steedman (1992), pp. 164-6.
Lives of Jane Austen: see Kathryn Sutherland, *Jane Austen's Textual Lives* (Oxford University Press, 2005); Claire Harman, *Jane's Fame: How Jane Austen Conquered the World*, Canongate, 2009.

P. 130
Shakespeare titles: Peter Ackroyd (Chatto & Windus, 2005); Stephen Greenblatt (Cape, 2004); James Shapiro (Faber, 2005).
Lives of Keats: Andrew Motion, *Keats* (Faber, 1997); Robert Gittings, *John Keats* (Heinemann, 1968).
Contents pages:
Jean Yves Tadié, *Marcel Proust*, tr. Euan Cameron (1996; Viking, 2000), p. ix. Adrian Frazier, *George Moore* (Yale University Press, 2000), p. v.

P. 132
'Watershed': John Halperin, *The Life of Jane Austen* (Harvester, 1984), p. 124. 'Celibate': Leon Edel, *Henry James: A Life* (Harper & Row, 1985), p. 16. 'Techniques of fiction': Edel (1959, 1973), p. 151.
On illness and biography: Ellis (2000), Ch. 5.
Turgenev: V. S. Pritchett, *The Gentle Barbarian: The Life and Work of Turgenev* (Chatto & Windus, 1977), p. 9.

P. 133

Empson: John Haffenden, *William Empson: Among the Mandarins* (Oxford University Press, 2005), vol. I, p. 9.

Larkin: Andrew Motion, *Philip Larkin: A Writer's Life* (Faber, 1993), p. 266.

Gill: Fiona MacCarthy, *Eric Gill* (Faber, 1989), p. viii.

Hemingway: Michael Reynolds, *Hemingway: The Final Years* (Norton, 1999), p. 360.

P. 134

Bellow: James Atlas, *Saul Bellow* (Random House, 2000), pp. 284, 372.

'Autobiography': Maurois (1929), p. 112.

Thoreau: Richard Lebeaux, 'Thoreau's Lives, Lebeaux's Lives' (Baron and Pletsch, 1985), p. 247.

P. 135

Lehmann: Selina Hastings, *Rosamond Lehmann: A Life* (Chatto & Windus, 2002); see Lee (2005, 2008), pp. 145–8.

Beckett: Deirdre Bair, *Samuel Beckett: A Biography* (Cape, 1978), p. 10.

Colette: Judith Thurman, *Secrets of the Flesh: A Life of Colette* (Knopf, 1999), p. xiii.

On Sherry and Greene, see James Olney, 'The Taking of a Life: Some Versions of Biography', *The Cincinnati Review*, Spring 2005, pp. 73–4.

On wrestling, see Holroyd's tragi-comic account of his battle over Shaw with the scholar Dan Lawrence (2002), pp. 169–83.

'To Bring the Dead to Life': Robert Graves, 1936, in *Collected Poems* (Cassell, 1938).

PP. 136–7

'Micro-biography': James Shapiro, *1599: A Year in the Life of William Shakespeare* (Faber, 2005), pp. xvii, xix.

P. 137

'The little they know': see Ellis (2000), pp. 120, 185, note 6, on Samuel Schoenbaum's account of the many versions of Shakespeare's life.

PP. 137–8

VIII, p. 93 Death of Hamnet: 'Mad Danish prince': Anthony Burgess, *Shakespeare* (Cape, 1970; Penguin, 1971), p. 65. 21st-century versions: Charles Nicholl, *The Lodger: Shakespeare on Silver Street* (Allen Lane, 2007; Penguin, 2008), pp. 6, 15; Jonathan Bate, *Soul of the Age: The Life, Mind and World of William Shakespeare* (Viking, 2008). 'We just don't know': Shapiro, *op. cit.*, pp. 14–15, 260–1, 309–58. 'Dispassionate': Park Honan, *Shakespeare: A Life* (Oxford University Press, 1998), pp. 235, 236. 'Deep wound': Stephen Greenblatt, *Will in the World: How Shakespeare became Shakespeare* (Cape, 2004), pp. 290, 311, 318. 'He may, or may not': Peter Ackroyd, *Shakespeare: The Biography* (Chatto & Windus, 2005), pp. 270–1. See Lois Potter, 'Having Our Will: Imagination in Recent Shakespearian Biographies', *Shakespeare Survey* 58 (Cambridge University Press, 2005), pp. 1–8, for a comparative account of Honan, Greenblatt, and others.

PP. 138–40
Narrating the deaths: see Lee, 'How to End it All', (2005, 2008), pp. 200–18.

Bibliography

Main titles referred to are given here in full, and in abbreviated form in the Chapter References.

Aaron, Daniel (ed.), *Studies in Biography* (Harvard University Press, 1978)

Altick, Richard, *Lives and Letters: A History of Literary Biography in England and America* (Knopf, 1965)

Anderson, Judith, *Biographical Truth: The Representation of Historical Persons in Tudor-Stuart Writing* (Yale University Press, 1984)

Backscheider, Paula, *Reflections on Biography* (Oxford University Press, 1999)

Barnes, Julian, *Flaubert's Parrot* (Cape, 1984; Picador 1985)

Baron, Samuel H., and Pletsch, Carl (eds.), *Introspection in Biography* (The Analytic Press, University of North Carolina, 1985)

Batchelor, John (ed.), *The Art of Literary Biography* (The Clarendon Press, 1995)

Bell, Susan G., and Yalom, M. (eds.), *Revealing Lives: Autobiography, Biography and Gender* (New York State University Press, 1990)

Bertaux, Daniel (ed.), *Biography and Society: The Life History Approach in the Social Sciences* (Sage, 1981)

Boswell, James, 'Advertisements' and 'Preface' to *The Life of Samuel Johnson* (London, 1791; a new edition corrected by J. W. Fleeman, ed. R. W. Chapman, Oxford University Press, 1953; *The Life of Johnson*, 1791, Oxford University Press, World's Classics)

Bromwich, David, 'The Uses of Biography', *Yale Review*, 73 (Winter 1984): 161–75

Broughton, Trev Lynn, *Men of Letters, Writing Lives* (Routledge, 1999)
Carlyle, Thomas, Review of Croker's edition of Boswell's *The Life of Samuel Johnson*; Review of Lockhart's *The Life of Scott*, see Clifford, James
Clifford, James, *Biography as an Art: Selected Criticism, 1590–1960* (Oxford University Press, 1962)
Cockshut, A. O. J., *Truth to Life: The Art of Biography in the Nineteenth Century* (Collins, 1974)
Daghlian, Philip (ed.), *Essays in 18th Century Biography* (Indiana University Press, 1988)
Donaldson, Ian, Read, Peter, and Walter, James (eds.), *Shaping Lives: Reflections on Biography* (Humanities Research Centre, Canberra, 1992)
Eakin, Paul J., *How Our Lives Become Stories* (Cornell University Press, 1999); *The Ethics of Life Writing* (Cornell University Press, 2004)
Edel, Leon, *Literary Biography* (Indiana University Press, 1959, 1973); *Writing Lives: Principia Biographia* (Norton, 1984)
Ellis, David, *Literary Lives: Biography and the Search for Understanding* (Oxford University Press, 2000)
Ellmann, Richard, *Golden Codgers: Biographical Speculations* (Oxford University Press, 1973)
Empson, William, *Using Biography* (Chatto & Windus, 1984)
Epstein, William H., *Recognizing Biography* (Pennsylvania University Press, 1987)
France, Peter, and St Clair, William (eds.), *Mapping Lives: The Uses of Biography* (British Academy and Oxford University Press, 2002)
Gaskell, Elizabeth, *The Life of Charlotte Brontë* (1857; ed. Jenny Uglow, Everyman, 1992)
Gosse, Edmund, 'Biography', *Encylopaedia Britannica*, 11th edition (1910–11), pp. 952–3; *Father and Son* (Heinemann, 1907); *Tallemant des Réaux, or the Art of Miniature Biography* (Oxford University Press, 1925)
Gould, Warwick, and Staley, Thomas (eds.), *Writing the Lives of Writers* (Macmillan, 1998)
Hamilton, Ian, *In Search of J. D. Salinger* (Heinemann, 1988); *Keepers of the Flame: Literary Estates and the Rise of Biography* (Hutchinson, 1992; Pimlico, 1993)
Hamilton, Nigel, *Biography: A Brief History* (Harvard University Press, 2007)
Heilbrun, Carolyn, *Writing a Woman's Life* (Norton, 1988; Ballantyne Books, 1989)

Hoberman, Ruth, *Modernizing Lives: Experiments in English Biography 1918-1939* (Southern Illinois University Press, 1987)
Holmes, Richard, *Footsteps: Adventures of a Romantic Biographer* (Hodder & Stoughton, 1985; Flamingo, 1995); *Dr Johnson & Mr Savage* (Hodder & Stoughton, 1993)
Holroyd, Michael, *Works on Paper* (Little, Brown, 2002)
Homberger, Eric, and Charmley, John (eds.), *The Troubled Face of Biography* (St Martin's Press, 1988)
Honan, Park, *Authors' Lives* (St Martin's Press, 1990)
James, Henry, *The Aspern Papers*, 1888 (Everyman, 1994)
Jefferson, Ann, *Biography and the Question of Literature in France* (Oxford University Press, 2007)
Johnson, Samuel, 'On Biography', *The Rambler*, 13 October 1750, No. 60; *The Idler*, 24 November 1759, No. 84, in Clifford, James. Roger Lonsdale (ed.), *Johnson's Lives of the Poets* (Oxford University Press, 2006)
Jolly, Margaretta (ed.), *Encylopaedia of Life Writing* (Fitzroy Dearborn, 2 vols, 2001)
Kendall, Paul Murray, *The Art of Biography* (Allen & Unwin, 1965; Norton, 1985)
Lee, Hermione, *Body Parts: Essays on Life-Writing* (Chatto & Windus, 2005; Pimlico, 2008)
Lee, Sidney, *Principles of Biography* (Cambridge University Press, 1911); *The Perspective of Biography* (Cambridge University Press, 1918)
Malcolm, Janet, *The Silent Woman: Sylvia Plath and Ted Hughes* (Picador, 1993)
Marcus, Laura, *Auto/Biographical Discourses: Theory, Criticism, Practice* (Manchester University Press, 1994)
Maurois, André, *Aspects of Biography* (1928; tr. S. C. Roberts, Cambridge University Press, 1929)
Meyers, Jeffrey (ed.), *The Craft of Literary Biography* (Macmillan, 1985)
Miller, Lucasta, *The Brontë Myth* (Cape, 2001, 2005)
Nadel, Ira Bruce, *Biography: Fiction, Fact and Form* (Macmillan, 1984)
Nicolson, Harold, *The Development of English Biography* (Hogarth Press, 1928)
Novarr, David, *The Lines of Life: Theories of Biography, 1880-1970* (Purdue University Press, 1986)
O'Connor, Ulick, *Biographers and the Art of Biography* (Quartet Books, 1991)

Oliphant, Margaret, 'The Ethics of Biography', *Contemporary Review*, XLIV (July 1883)
Origo, Iris, *A Need to Testify* (Harcourt Brace, 1984)
Parke, Catherine N., *Biography: Writing Lives* (Twayne, 1996; Routledge, 2002)
Redford, Bruce, *Designing the Life of Johnson* (Oxford University Press, 2002)
Rhiel, Mary, and Suchoff, David (eds.), *The Seductions of Biography* (Routledge, 1996)
Salwak, Dale (ed.), *The Literary Biography: Problems and Solutions* (Iowa University Press, 1996)
Shelston, Alan, *Biography* (Methuen, 1977)
Sisman, Adam, *Boswell's Presumptuous Task* (Hamish Hamilton, 2000)
Stauffer, Donald, *English Biography before 1700* (Harvard University Press, 1930); *The Art of Biography in 18th-Century England* (Princeton University Press, 1941)
Steedman, Carolyn, *Past Tenses: Essays on Writing Autobiography and History* (Rivers Oram Press, 1992)
Stephen, Leslie, 'National Biography', in *Studies of a Biographer*, vol. 1 (Duckworth, 1898)
Strachey, Lytton, *Eminent Victorians* (Chatto & Windus, 1918; Oxford University Press World's Classics, 2003)
Symons, Arthur, *The Quest for Corvo: An Experiment in Biography* (Cassell, 1934, 1955)
Tomalin, Claire, *The Invisible Woman: The Story of Nelly Ternan and Charles Dickens* (Penguin, 1991)
Wagner-Martin, Linda, *Telling Women's Lives: The New Biography* (Rutgers University Press, 1994)
Wendorf, Richard, *The Elements of Life: Biography and Portrait Painting in Stuart and Georgian England* (Oxford University Press, 1990)
Whittemore, Reed, *Pure Lives: The Early Biographers* (Johns Hopkins University Press, 1983); *Whole Lives: Shapers of Modern Biography* (Johns Hopkins University Press, 1989)
Woolf, Virginia, 'The New Biography' (1927), 'The Art of Biography' (1939); *Collected Essays*, ed. L. Woolf (London, Chatto & Windus, 1966–7)

Publisher's Acknowledgements

'Biography' taken from *The Collected Poems of Ian Hamilton* © The Estate of Ian Hamilton and reproduced by permission of Faber and Faber Ltd. *Keepers of the Flame: Literary Estates and the Rise of Biography*, permission granted by Aitken Alexander. © Ian Hamilton Estate. 'The Silent Woman' by Janet Malcolm, permission granted by Pan Macmillan, London. Copyright © Janet Malcolm, 1994. 'Posterity' by Philip Larkin, from *High Windows*, 1974, permission granted by Faber and Faber Ltd/ © The Estate (UK rights) and Farrar, Straus, and Giroux, LLC (US rights). 'The Biographer' by Carol Ann Duffy, from *Mean Time*, 1993, published by Anvil Press Poetry, 1993, new edition 1998. 'Flaubert's Parrot' by Julian Barnes, copyright © Julian Barnes, 1984, permission granted by United Agents on behalf of Julian Barnes. 'A Shilling Life Will Give You All The Facts', by W.H. Auden, from *Selected Poems, Expanded Edition* by W.H. Auden, edited by Edward Mendelson, copyright © Edward Mendelson, William Meredith and Monroe K. Spears, Executors of the Estate of W. H. Auden, 1979, 2007. Used by permission of Faber and Faber Ltd (UK rights) and Vintage Books, a division of Random House, Inc (US rights). 'To Bring the Dead to Life' by Robert Graves, copyright © Robert Graves, from *Complete Poems in One Volume*, Carcanet Press Limited.

The publisher and the author apologize for any errors or omissions in the above list. If contacted they will be happy to rectify these at the earliest opportunity.

"牛津通识读本"已出书目

古典哲学的趣味	福柯	地球
人生的意义	缤纷的语言学	记忆
文学理论入门	达达和超现实主义	法律
大众经济学	佛学概论	中国文学
历史之源	维特根斯坦与哲学	托克维尔
设计，无处不在	科学哲学	休谟
生活中的心理学	印度哲学祛魅	分子
政治的历史与边界	克尔凯郭尔	法国大革命
哲学的思与惑	科学革命	民族主义
资本主义	广告	科幻作品
美国总统制	数学	罗素
海德格尔	叔本华	美国政党与选举
我们时代的伦理学	笛卡尔	美国最高法院
卡夫卡是谁	基督教神学	纪录片
考古学的过去与未来	犹太人与犹太教	大萧条与罗斯福新政
天文学简史	现代日本	领导力
社会学的意识	罗兰·巴特	无神论
康德	马基雅维里	罗马共和国
尼采	全球经济史	美国国会
亚里士多德的世界	进化	民主
西方艺术新论	性存在	英格兰文学
全球化面面观	量子理论	现代主义
简明逻辑学	牛顿新传	网络
法哲学：价值与事实	国际移民	自闭症
政治哲学与幸福根基	哈贝马斯	德里达
选择理论	医学伦理	浪漫主义
后殖民主义与世界格局	黑格尔	批判理论

德国文学	儿童心理学	电影
戏剧	时装	俄罗斯文学
腐败	现代拉丁美洲文学	古典文学
医事法	卢梭	大数据
癌症	隐私	洛克
植物	电影音乐	幸福
法语文学	抑郁症	免疫系统
微观经济学	传染病	银行学
湖泊	希腊化时代	景观设计学
拜占庭	知识	神圣罗马帝国
司法心理学	环境伦理学	大流行病
发展	美国革命	亚历山大大帝
农业	元素周期表	气候
特洛伊战争	人口学	第二次世界大战
巴比伦尼亚	社会心理学	中世纪
河流	动物	工业革命
战争与技术	项目管理	传记